CREATIVITY IN EXILE

Rodopi Perspectives on Modern Literature

29

Edited by
David Bevan

CREATIVITY IN EXILE

Edited by
Michael Hanne

Amsterdam - New York, NY 2004

The paper on which this book is printed meets the requirements of "ISO 9706: 1994, Information and documentation - Paper for documents - Requirements for permanence".

ISBN: 90-420-1833-X (DVD in PAL) (Bound)
ISBN: 90-420-1843-7 (DVD in NTSC) (Bound)
©Editions Rodopi B.V., Amsterdam - New York, NY 2004
Printed in The Netherlands

CONTENTS

Creativity and Exile: An Introduction
Michael Hanne

Michael Hanne was born and grew up in Britain. Following studies in
French and Italian at the Universities of Oxford and Glasgow, with
periods of research in Paris and Rome, he migrated to New Zealand to
teach Italian language and literature at the University of Auckland. In
1996 he founded the university's programme in Comparative
Literature. Over the years he has had the opportunity of travelling, for
extended periods of research and teaching, to many parts of the world,
including Australia, Canada, the USA, Italy, India, Indonesia, Japan,
Sweden, Croatia and the Republic of Georgia. He is in no sense an
exile, well aware that his extensive journeying has been undertaken by
choice and from a position of privilege. He edited a previous volume
for Rodopi, *Literature and Travel* (1993) and wrote *The Power of the
Story: Fiction and Political Change* (Berghahn, 1996). In July 2003,
he co-ordinated the conference *The Poetics of Exile* from which the
present project grew.

In this introduction he draws attention to the distinctive features of the
project: the great ethnic and cultural diversity of its contributors, many
with intense personal experience of geographical and cultural
dislocation; the acknowledgement it offers of the wide range of
circumstances and experiences now covered by the umbrella-term
'exile'; its concern with the part played historically by colonization
and currently by globalization in bringing about massive
displacements of human beings around the world; its recognition of
the rich variety of means, from poetry, to film, to music, to painting
and sculpture, to cooking and the creation of gardens, with which
people in exile have expressed their creativity; its use of the DVD
format, alongside the printed volume, for the presentation of studio
interviews, readings, and creative materials in many media.

In 1956 the International PEN Club Centre for Writers in Exile, based
in London, published an impressive volume of essays, poetry, and
short stories entitled *The Pen in Exile*. In her Foreword to the
collection, British historian C.V. Wedgwood referred to the "fortitude
and integrity" of the contributors, as "writers who have been
compelled by harsh circumstance to leave their homes" (Tabori 1956:
3). Hungarian-born Paul Tabori, in his Editor's Preface, described the

"almost impossible task" faced by writers who, having fled the threat of imprisonment or death in their homeland, sought to communicate something of their experiences to readers who had had no such experience. On the one hand, he wrote, readers often found their accounts "melodramatic, unreal, lacking credibility" (1956: 5). A powerful poem, 'Indictment', by Estonian writer Maria Under, included in that collection, may well have evoked just such a response in some readers. It begins:

> I cry with all my people's lungs and lips:
> A terrible, unbearable disease
> Has struck our land – a blight of gallows-trees,
> A plague of deadly fear that sears and grips.
>
> (Tabori 1956: 100)

Other writers, said Tabori, found themselves accused of "nostalgia, of turning to the past, refusing to face the realities of the present", though "what else could the exile be except nostalgic and homesick?" (1956: 6). Wedgwood, while acknowledging that it would be no great consolation to them for the "evils and sorrows" they had endured, noted that they were following in the footsteps of some of the greatest writers of all time, including Dante Alighieri, who composed his *Divina Commedia* in exile from the Florentine city-state (1956: 3).

Despite the quality and emotional force of much of the work included, and the continuing validity of these comments by Wedgwood and Tabori, readers of *The Pen in Exile* today will be immediately struck by the narrow basis for selection of the writers, in terms not only of their geographical and ethnic origins, but of the contexts from which they had fled. While Wedgwood referred to the volume as representing "a cross-section of modern writing" by writers in exile, the reader in the twenty-first century will note that, of the forty-three contributors, all except two were survivors of Nazi German rule and/or had emigrated from the Soviet bloc – indeed, thirty-four of them were born in Estonia, Latvia, Poland, or Hungary. The only non-European contributor was Tung Shih-tsin, who had fled Communist China in 1949. For the purposes of that volume, published in deepest Cold War Britain, the category 'exiles' was deemed to consist entirely of writers who had fled fascism or communism (mostly in Central and Eastern Europe) to take up residence in Western Europe, the United States or Israel. Most had been intellectuals in their country of origin, who subsequently joined or formed communities of intellectuals in the countries where they sought exile.

Just how much has changed over the years in our conception and depiction of 'writers in exile' is evident from the merest glance at the work of International PEN today, which offers a model of global inclusiveness and activism. The Eurocentric bias of fifty years ago has gone. The organisation is now represented in around one hundred countries and its Writers in Exile Committee assists refugee and émigré writers from every continent, as well as working with human rights advocates, diplomats, and NGOs to protect writers facing extreme risk in their homelands. PEN Canada is at the forefront of this activism, working in particular to establish placement opportunities for exiled, immigrant, and refugee writers from many countries at Canadian universities, colleges, and learning centres. Their Writers in Exile Network lists writers from eighteen countries, ranging from Afghanistan to Bosnia to Eritrea to Peru to Sri Lanka. Other organisations, such as Exiled Writers Ink! (UK), offer opportunities to writers originating in every continent, to meet and publish their work on-line. (See their beautifully produced website at: www.exiledwriters.co.uk, which presents not only written texts of work in translation, but also haunting samples of work read by authors in, for instance, the original Arabic.) Other on-line publications which welcome the work of exiled writers include: *Words Without Borders: The Online Magazine for International Literature* at www.wordswithoutborders.org/.

The present project, *Creativity in Exile*, displays and examines the extraordinary creative endeavours in a wide range of media of men and women originating in almost every part of the world, who, for a host of different reasons, have experienced displacement from their homelands. It brings together papers by academics, many of whom have experienced exile themselves, on a vast array of topics associated with artistic production in exile, which are interspersed with poems by contemporary writers in exile. The accompanying DVD comprises: studio interviews with notable exiled writers, extracts from two films relating to exile, live readings of poetry by their authors, an audio and sculptural installation, and a performance by a group of musicians in exile. It aims to illustrate just how productive, on the human, the aesthetic, and the intellectual level, a broadly inclusive conception of 'artists in exile' can be.

Even the terminology associated with the field has altered over the last half century. In the 1950s, the designation of someone as an 'exile' was widely used, as it had been through the twenties and thirties, alternately with 'émigré'. For both words, as Christine

Brooke-Rose has written, "the clanging connotations are of suffering in banishment, but also of springing forth into a new life, beyond the boundaries of the familiar" (Brooke-Rose 1998: 9). The implied emphasis of both terms was on the individuality of the person who had fled an intolerable political situation. For those who had not personally experienced such a trauma, there was even a certain glamour attached to the figure of 'the exiled writer'. Since then, with the sheer growth in numbers of those fleeing international and intercommunal conflict, repression, and religious or ethnic persecution, those forced to live away from the country of their birth have come to be referred to less and less as 'exiles', and much more frequently as 'refugees', 'displaced persons', and 'asylum-seekers', of whom only quite a small number will be writers or artists. While each term has its own particular weighting, their use, in the words of Rudolphus Teeuwen in the final paper for this book, represents "a shift in perspective away from individual distress and escape toward international crowd control".

The concept of exile has been further complicated, in the context of globalization, by ever-more-massive population movements motivated, in contributing countries, by the desire for economic improvement and, in the host countries, by a demand for labour, at both the skilled end of the spectrum and at the low-skilled, and low-paid, end. Depending on their skill-level, and on their desirability in the eyes of governmental authorities and employers in the host countries, they are variously categorised along a continuum that runs from 'expatriates' and 'economic migrants' to 'guest workers' and 'illegal aliens' and live their lives at points on an economic and social scale that extends from extreme luxury to abject poverty. While all live at a distance from their place of birth and most express a sense of loss in relation to 'home', such diversity of human experience cannot readily be conveyed by a single term, such as 'exiles'. Russian-born poet Joseph Brodsky opened his address to a conference on writing in exile held in Vienna in 1987 with these salutary words:

> As we gather here, in this attractive and well-lit room, on this cold December evening, to discuss the plight of the writer in exile, let us pause for a minute and imagine some of those who, quite naturally, didn't make it to this room. Let us imagine, for instance, Turkish *Gastarbeiter* prowling the streets of West Germany, uncomprehending or envious of the surrounding reality. Or let us imagine Vietnamese boat people bobbing on high seas or already settled somewhere in the Australian outback. Let us imagine Mexican wetbacks crawling the ravines of Southern California, past the border patrols into the territory of the United States. Or let us imagine shiploads of Pakistanis

> disembarking somewhere in Kuwait or Saudi Arabia, hungry for
> menial jobs the oil-rich locals won't do... Whatever the proper name
> for these people, whatever their motives, origins, and destinations,
> whatever their impact on the societies which they abandon and to
> which they come may amount to – one thing is absolutely clear: they
> make it very difficult to talk about the plight of the writer in exile with
> a straight face. (Brodsky 1994: 3)

If the designation 'exile' has almost disappeared from popular use as referring to individuals, it has nevertheless been appropriated as an abstract term by some intellectuals and given an at least partially metaphorical turn. As a paper by Farhang Erfani and John Whitmire points out, twentieth-century philosophers, from Heidegger to Sartre and beyond, came to identify being exiled as a primary human condition: in an existential sense we are all 'not at home'. Moreover, as the paper by Rudolphus Teeuwen, already mentioned, suggests, thinkers in the post-modern period have tended to embrace the intellectual stance of the metaphorical exile, to glorify the mental travelling, the double vision, as both insider and outsider, that such a posture makes possible. This has had the effect of devaluing the reality of the terror and the loss experienced by those who have fled for their lives from war or famine, witnessed barbarities, seen family members killed, and ended up as refugees in countries which have often been less than wholly welcoming. In Teeuwen's words: "Once the designation of a horrible fate, 'exile' today is a term so eagerly embraced that a deep forgetting of what it means to be an exile must be at the root of it". One of the first aims of the present project is to counter such a tendency, by including work by Ethiopian Yilma Tafere Tasew, Nigerian-born Chris Abani, and Iranian Shahin Yazdani, whose personal experience of dislocation from their homelands has been appallingly non-metaphorical.

Alongside these very necessary reality checks come several others. While, to the publishers of the 1956 volume, the division between the countries forcing writers and others into exile and the countries receiving them seemed clear-cut – Paul Tabori wrote of aiming to "build a few bridges between the readers of the free world and the exiled writers" (Tabori 1956: 5) – the current project highlights the part played historically by the countries of that so-called 'free world', not only in directly bringing about enforced displacement of vast numbers of peoples through their imperial ventures, but of establishing the political, economic, and social conditions that are, to this day, contributing to further large-scale displacements. In the words of Kirsty Reid, one of the contributors to this volume, exile is not just an occasional or incidental effect of colonization, but one of the 'marks of empire'. So, for instance, Saddik Gohar's paper alludes to the exile to which African slaves traded to the Americas were subjected. Isabel Moutinho's paper reminds us of the many forms of deportation practised by successive governments in the name of the Portuguese Empire, ranging from the forcible transportation of two hundred Jewish children from Portugal to the island of São Tomé off the west coast of Africa in the 1490s, to the movement of indentured workers from its African colonies to Timor in more recent times. Kirsty Reid examines the practice within the British Empire in the nineteenth century of transporting convicts to colonies as diverse as Australia, Bermuda, and Gibraltar. The artwork of Dolleen Manning and the paper of Hsinya Huang treat the land usurpations, enforced resettlements, and, indeed, near eradication of indigenous peoples in the processes by which Europeans colonised the Americas.

Other contributions focus on kinds of displacement which have occurred following the supposed decolonization of certain territories, in particular as a consequence of partition and other decisions relating to boundaries. So, in her paper, Urbashi Barat explores the human effects of the partition of Bengal between India and (initially) East Pakistan, whereas the poetry of Nora Nadjarian (which she reads in the interview on the DVD) relates to the nearly thirty-year partition of Cyprus into a Turkish northern sector and a Greek southern sector. Others again concern the double or multiple nature of many of the processes of human displacement seen in recent times. Both Saddik Gohar's and Nir Yehudai's papers treat the displacement of millions of Palestinians by Jewish refugees, who themselves fled from persecution in Europe and elsewhere. Nora Nadjarian refers to the fact that her family, of Armenian origin, having first sought refuge in Cyprus from Asia Minor, experienced a second exile with the partition of that island.

In our conception of the present project, it seemed important also not to limit the focus just to *writing* in exile, but rather to communicate something of the rich diversity of media in which displaced persons express their creativity. While many of the papers do deal with poetry and narrative fiction – from Africa, from Europe, the Middle East, India, South East Asia, and the Americas – others treat such topics as: the way in which refugees and migrants use cooking to maintain links with their homelands (Hilary Funnell); the creation of a vast and beautiful garden by an exiled Chinese official in the seventeenth century (Duncan Campbell); the anonymous personal testimonies of ordinary people separated from their homes by the partition of Bengal (Urbashi Barat); the expression of protest at the mass displacements of communities in Colombia through paintings and visual installations (Marta Jimena Cabrera); the production and display of traditional weaving, embroidery, dresses, and other domestic artefacts by Palestinians living in the USA (Nir Yehudai). By considering creative work in media other than the written word, we were able to draw into the project – and, to a striking degree, into the conference from which these publications derive – a much wider constituency of creative people in exile than would otherwise have been possible.

The availability of the DVD format greatly facilitated the plan to include work in a range of media. So, the reader/viewer/listener will find: a musical performance (drumming by a group of refugees from Burundi now living in New Zealand); a complete short film (by Iranian Shahin Yazdani); a multi-layered sound recording in Ojibwe and English by First Nations Canadian Dolleen Manning with accompanying images; a live performance by Iraqi poet Emad Jabbar in Arabic, with English-sub-titles; and an extract from a documentary film by Shuchi Kothari and Sarina Pearson, *A Taste of Place: Stories of Food and Longing*, showing an Ethiopian refugee preparing food from her homeland.

Whereas Paul Tabori, back in the 1950s, saw writers in exile as too often trapped in the binary modes of, on the one hand, outrage at the circumstances which had made flight necessary and, on the other, nostalgia for their lost homeland, this collection displays an almost infinite range of emotions, thoughts, insights, and creative responses demonstrated by people of different personal make-up and different cultures, whose concrete experiences of displacement and alienation, and whose linguistic, family, and educational situations, vary greatly. I can only offer the merest hint of that range here.

Many of the works reproduced or discussed here focus directly on the devastating sense of loss felt by those who have been cast out of their homeland. The range of psychological states experienced – anger, mourning, nostalgia, anxiety, loss of identity – and the imagery employed to express them are almost infinite. So, in his paper, Saddik Gohar quotes Mahmud Darwish, who has written of Palestinian refugees as being both uprooted and shattered:

> we are what's left of us in exile
> we are the plants of broken vase
> we are what we are but who are we?

The anguish is all the more acute when loved ones have been left behind and news of them is hard to get. Yilma Tafere Tasew, a refugee from Ethiopia, in the poem which appears next in this volume, asks:

> Can you tell me?
> How my Mum is doing? Is Mum hungry?
> Thirsty? Sick? In agony? Naked?

For some writers and creative artists, forced to live away from their place of birth, the first priority is to maintain their original national and cultural identity as fully as possible, to construct a home-away-from-home. Their subject matter, their audience, and, in the case of writers, their language, are almost exclusively linked to the place, and, frequently the time, they have been cut off from. Alexander Solzhenitsyn, living in exile in a forested part of Vermont, was a famous example of such a writer, who, many would argue, nevertheless became increasingly cut off from the realities of his beloved Russia. To the extent that the work of such writers records their experience of an adoptive country, it shows the absence of real engagement with the people and the culture they encounter, and in some cases the perceived hostility of the local population. (In the words of a Pakistani taxi-driver in New Zealand, quoted in Kothari and Pearson's film: "They like our food more than they like us.") Others, however, interact vigorously with their new environment, and some go so far as to forge some kind of new, hybrid identity for themselves. Several papers and creative pieces describe the very different forms of hybridity which individuals may arrive at. Xenia Srebrianski Harwell examines the work of a Russian woman émigré writer whose young émigré characters adopt a range of identities as they grow up in France. In general, of course, the capacity to adapt is determined by the age at which the person migrates, but Fiona Doloughan's paper takes up the remarkable case of Milan Kundera who fled Czechoslovakia for France in his mid-forties, and has not only written increasingly of characters living outside his and their country of origin but shifted to actually writing in French.

There are other facets to the question of language for the creative person in exile. Indigenous peoples, who have, through colonization, war, theft and/or legislative manipulation been dispossessed of their land, frequently find themselves exiled also from their language. Hsinya Huang's paper and Dolleen Manning's audio installation on the DVD both deal with the attempts of First Nations peoples in North America to resist linguistic theft. Trudy Agar's paper explores the complex situation of an Algerian woman writer Assia Djebar whose French education has, to a large extent, cut her off from the language and world of the women she grew up with. At the same time, Djebar concedes the uncomfortable truth that her ability to write in French, the language of 'yesterday's enemy', has freed her from some of the most fundamental features of Algerian patriarchal control. Zawiah Yahya examines another dimension again of the 'language question' in the postcolonial situation: the dilemma of English-language writers in Malaysia after independence, as the authorities asserted the primacy of Malay in education, journalism, and literature.

Chris Abani, in his paper and his interview, introduces some of the many dilemmas faced by writers and, by implication, artists working in exile, which are then taken up by other commentators. To what extent should the fact of being in exile constitute his or her (sole) subject matter and focus? How is the person who has suffered torture, imprisonment, or the threat of execution in their country of origin to handle the special consideration offered, not only by members of the public, but even by government authorities, in the receiving country? Bulgarian-born Kapka Kassabova, who eschews the title of 'exile', declaring that she is simply an economic migrant, acknowledges in an interview that, for her, at least, there is a strange kind of comfort to be found in not being tied to a single location, and that being displaced serves as a clear motivating factor for much of her writing. Nevertheless, in the course of that interview, she reads poems in which she identifies with those, especially refugees, who do not have that luxury:

> We must remember – memory is hope.
> But quietly, for words can cut out gaps in us
> So wide we'd find
> Too many bodies lying there

Several contributors note a tendency among creative people in exile to transmute their own bitter experience into an affinity with others in distress. In Chris Abani's words, "the condition of exile allows us to explore an international/human identity", to develop a universal empathy. This is a topic explored in depth by Saddik Gohar in his study of Afro-American poets who have delved into their own experience of exile and alienation to find empathy with the sufferings of the Palestinians.

Gohar highlights another issue which, however, divides groups of displaced persons from each other: the question of return. For some, the belief, however much or little rationally based, that they, or at least their descendants, will be able to return to the homeland they have lost is fundamental. That, he asserts, is the conviction of the great majority of Palestinians. For other groups, all hope of a return has been abandoned – time has passed, borders have been redrawn, oppressive regimes have established an unshakeable grasp on power, ethnic or religious groups have seized all the land, or a political situation has been sanctioned by international authorities. Three papers in this volume explore more nuanced situations. Isabel Moutinho examines a novel set in Timor, during the Salazar regime, in which the central character, supposedly 'exiled' from Portugal, refuses not only to consider returning to the metropolis but to feel any nostalgia for the land of his birth. The Czech-born characters in Milan Kundera's *Ignorance*, discussed by Fiona Doloughan, achieve their long-held dream of returning to the country from which they have been exiled, only to discover that their lives in their adopted countries have more reality to them than what they have returned to find. The plot of Israeli writer S.Y. Agnon's *Only Yesterday* is shown by Arnold Band to lead to an equally counter-intuitive outcome when the idealistic hopes of the naive young Zionist settler from Galicia, who returns to 'the promised land', are dashed.

There were many possible principles according to which this publication – the book and the DVD – might have been organised. My initial assumption was that a thematic sequence would work best, but, as I hope this introductory essay has demonstrated, the thematic links between items constitute an intricate network rather than a straight line. Somewhat to my surprise, it seemed that a broadly geographical sequence would work better, starting, as we know all human movement did, in Africa, then proceeding to Europe, with a detour to North America, proceeding around the Mediterranean, across the Middle East, to India and South East Asia, with brief visits to China and Latin America. Given that the conference to which reference has several times been made took place in New Zealand, readers may be surprised that there is little reference to exile as it relates to the South Pacific, and especially to the many forms of dispossession – territorial, cultural and linguistic – which indigenous peoples have suffered in this region at the hands of European settlers. It is not a matter of our focusing on tragedies occurring at a distance, while failing to notice those which have taken place in our own backyard. It is rather that my colleagues Hilary Chung and Leonard Bell are planning a separate volume (publisher and title still unconfirmed), encompassing Pacific-related materials not only from this conference, but from two earlier conferences convened by Bell, and I invite readers of this project to look out for it.

It seems invidious to refer too much to the conference *The Poetics of Exile* (Auckland, July 2003), which most readers of this volume will not have had the opportunity to attend. Nevertheless I feel it is appropriate in concluding this essay to refer to the session with which that conference ended. The conference was remarkable, not only for the contributions by over 200 outstanding academics, writers, and artists from forty-seven countries, who travelled long distances to take part, but also for the participation of a large number of 'local' refugees and migrants – people from Afghanistan and Ethiopia, Iraq and former Yugoslavia, China, Vietnam and Argentina who have settled in New Zealand, and who are contributing their creativity in many different and often unexpected ways to this country. The final session of the conference was slated as an Open Forum. To the delight of the organisers, it was several of the local refugees, who had often sat quiet over the preceding days, but who now, without prompting, stood up one by one to recount their own personal stories and to explain the importance of having their experiences and creative contributions acknowledged. Several academics who had prepared brief contributions to round off the event held back from doing so, knowing that these were the voices which would echo in our memories of the event.

My thanks:
I offer gratitude in equal measure to those who travelled thousands of kilometres to participate in the conference and to the many 'local' refugees and migrants whose writings, music, visual art work, and moving personal testimonies ensured that the academic discussion remained anchored in human reality. My thanks go also to Auckland City Council and Waitakere City Council for assisting several recent refugees to attend with grants from the Creative New Zealand Communities Fund. Major financial assistance with the costs of production of the DVD was received from three community funding organisations: Pub Charity, the Scottwood Group, and the Southern Trust. Alison Steiner, at the University of Auckland, was instrumental in obtaining that funding. Mark Summerville and the team from

Zoomslide Media have done a wonderful job in production of the DVD. Monica Conlon, Richard von Sturmer, Hilary Chung, and the fifteen students who participated in the graduate course COMPLIT 702 Poetics of Exile, which ran alongside the conference, not only gave much practical assistance in the running of the conference but contributed greatly to the ongoing development of this project. Of these students, Laura Macfehin and Ruth Diver also provided valuable assistance with the editing and proofreading of the text. Hilary Funnell, whose fine paper on 'Food and the Exile' appears in the book, has performed the role of editorial assistant to the whole project with tremendous intelligence, practical skill, and good humour.

Bibliography

Brodsky, Joseph. 1994. 'The Condition We Call Exile: An Address' in Robinson, Marc (ed.) *Altogether Elsewhere: Writers on Exile*. San Diego, New York, London: Harcourt Brace: 3-11.
Brooke-Rose, Christine. 1998. 'Exsul', in Suleiman, Susan Rubin (ed.) *Exile and Creativity: Signposts, Travellers, Outsiders, Backward Glances*. Durham and London: Duke University Press: 9-24.
Tabori, Paul. 1956. *The Pen in Exile: A Second Anthology of Exiled Writers*. London: International P.E.N. Club Centre.

Poem: 'Can You Tell Me?'

Yilma Tafere Tasew

Yilma Tafere Tasew is from Ethiopia where he was a primary school teacher and published small newspapers. He has always been a writer. He was living in a small rural town in southern Ethiopia in May 1991 when rebels overthrew the Marxist Dergue regime. He heard shooting and, not knowing what would come next, decided to move to the town his parents were living in. With many roads blocked, he found himself, with thousands of others, crossing the border into Kenya. He never guessed it would be a one-way trip. The Kenyan government was not accepting refugees as permanent residents, and for the next eight years he lived in a series of refugee camps in arid northern Kenya. He says of that period:

> The first refugee camp where I stayed for more than two years, 125 kms from the border of Ethiopia, was a nightmare. Malaria, typhoid and hunger killed people every day. Unknown armed gangs in the bush often killed refugees. You heard guns firing every night and the sound of munitions exploding in the camp. You didn't know what would happen from one day to the next.

He became a community organiser in the transit camp at Walda, and was then transferred to the refugee-town of Kakuma, with its 47,000 residents from many countries. In September 1993, Yilma started a refugee-run newspaper *Kanebu* that published news articles, short stories, poems, artworks and interviews with UN officials about conditions in the camps. From 1997 he was employed by UNHCR in Nairobi as an assistant translator and transport officer. In 1999 he moved as a refugee to New Zealand where he now lives. He is an activist on behalf of refugees from all countries and his poetry is central to his activism. A collection of his poems *Agonising Wounds* was published in 2001 by the New Zealand Refugee and Migrant Service. He believes that his is the first book to be published by an African in New Zealand. He says of his own writing: 'Through my writings I have cried with my pain, I have shown my hunger, my thirst, my homesickness. I have shown my views and ideas to the world to say I am a human being who is part of the world.'

In the poem that follows, he asks the anguished questions which so many exiles utter when they have left family members back home.

Can You Tell Me?

The shining moon
Surrounded, guarded by twinkling stars
Can you tell me?
How my Mum is doing? Is Mum hungry?
Thirsty? Sick? In agony? Naked?

The shining moon
Surrounded, guarded by twinkling stars
Can you tell me?

Our small cottage
Is it strong like before, or tilting?
The shining moon
Surrounded, guarded by twinkling stars
Can you tell me?

Is my Mum's hair full of grey?
Her face wrinkled?
Strong enough to collect firewood?
Has she planted cabbage, pumpkins, potato like before?
The shining moon
Surrounded, guarded by twinkling stars
Can you tell me?

Is my brother alive
Who was forced to join the army 'National Service'?
Is my sister who eloped coming back to visit Mum?
The shining moon
Surrounded, guarded by twinkling stars
Can you tell me?

What's my Mother's income?
Is she brewing local liqueur, beer, 'Tela Arecki'?
The shining moon
Surrounded, guarded by twinkling stars
Can you tell me?

Our neighbours
Emama Fatuma, Ababa Tolcha
Emama Aselefech, Ababa Zerayie
The rest, are they alive or dead?
The shining moon
Surrounded, guarded by twinkling stars
Can you tell me?

The green fertile field where I grew up
Playing, looking after cattle
Shaded by acacia trees
Does it exist?
The shining moon
Surrounded, guarded by twinkling stars
Can you tell me?

The attractive rivers of the village
Springs: Tegona, Tercha, Dekisa, Melebo
Are they really flowing like before?
Across the village, towards uneasy distance
The shining moon
Surrounded, guarded by twinkling stars
Can you tell me?

Is Alamirew still there with his 'Washint'[1]
Entertaining the village
Or deceased, like my uncle?
And the other strong, sentimental people of the village?
The shining moon
Surrounded, guarded by twinkling stars
Can you tell me?

Are there social gatherings?
Evening campfires?
Coffee ceremonies? Story telling?
That harmony – is it there?
The shining moon
Surrounded, guarded by twinkling stars
Can you tell me?

---

[1] 'Washint' – local flute

The folklore, the riddles, the games I played
With friends of childhood
Are they in existence?
Or are they replaced by new 'Play Games'?
By federalism, democracy, tribalism
Being imposed on the villagers to be played
The shining moon
Surrounded, guarded by twinkling stars
Can you tell me?

Are people punished who don't play this 'new game'?
Like before, like the time of 'fashion play'?
'Socialism – Communism'
Are they arrested, killed?
The shining moon
Surrounded, guarded by twinkling stars
Can you tell me?

Do you know if Mum is alive or dead?
Joined my Father?
The shining moon
Surrounded, guarded by twinkling stars
Can you tell me?

Do you know Mum's feeling about me?
Her flesh, blood, elder son
Her hope, support when she 'retired'
Whose name is changed in time
'REFUGEE'
Who expects charity of twelve beans?
Two weeks rationing
Who is pushed to the edge of this planet?
Who is buried alive under the sandy desert?
The shining moon
Surrounded, guarded by twinkling stars
Can you tell me?

Whatever happened to Mum?
Sadness or joy? Tell me!
Let me know, I am dying to know

But no energy for grief, no drop of energy
Good to know, to burn to ash
Knowing, burning! Burning, knowing!
For 'normal' life
Knowing is a choice for refugees
To throw away
Dry leaf. Dry stream of draining life
Tear one chapter of hope
Destroy every time
To cool down the desert heat
Save haemoglobin
Of last breath
No shock! No surprise!
All feelings drained away
By the scorching sun
Been long
Since I drained
The shining moon
Surrounded, guarded by twinkling stars
Can you tell me?

CAN YOU TELL ME!
CAN YOU TELL ME!
CAN YOU TELL ME!

22 January 1999, Nairobi, Kenya

Burundi Drummers: Performance

This group of drummers, led by Sylvestre Gahungu, is made up of refugees from the small central African nation of Burundi. They came to New Zealand following the political and ethnic violence of the 1990s. On the accompanying DVD they perform live at the "Poetics of Exile" conference, in Auckland, New Zealand in July 2003. They all work at other jobs, but undertake public performances whenever they have the opportunity. They explain that they play for New Zealand audiences "to entertain and to make ourselves known. Drumming is part of our history and our life. We drum to express ourselves, proud of who we are."

See DVD

Resisting the Anomie: Exile and the Romantic Self

Chris Abani

Chris Abani is from Nigeria and wrote his first novel at the age of 16 for which he suffered severe political persecution including imprisonment. He has lived in exile in England and the United States since 1991. He continues to write novels, plays and poetry, as well as teaching at several universities. His novels are *GraceLand* (Farrar, Straus and Giroux, 2004) and *Masters of the Board* (Delta, 1985). His poetry collections include *Dog Woman* (Red Hen, Fall 2004), *Daphne's Lot* (Red Hen, 2003), and *Kalakuta Republic* (Saqi, 2001). He teaches in the MFA Program at Antioch University, Los Angeles and is a Visiting Assistant Professor at the University of California, Riverside. A Middleton Fellow at the University of Southern California, he is the recipient of the 2001 PEN USA Freedom-to-Write Award, the 2001 Prince Claus Award and a 2003 Lannan Literary Fellowship.

In the following paper, which was the opening presentation at the conference "The Poetics of Exile" in July 2003, he explores the uneasy dialectic which dominates the discourse of exile. On the one hand are those who view exile as redemptive, seeing it as encouraging a form of double-mindedness that offers great creative potential. On the other hand are those who emphasise the sense of loss and injury experienced by people who have suffered exile. He reflects on the difficulty which political exiles, such as himself, have in navigating the confused and confusing responses of those they encounter.

"What does exile mean to you?"

The question hung in the air for a few very long moments. We all stared uncomfortably into the opaque blackness of our coffee. Some of us stirred the half empty cups earnestly. Someone coughed. I glanced at my watch. It was eleven a.m. and through the window, the Pacific was a lazy stretch of blue. There were twelve of us sitting in the corner of a coffee shop in Santa Monica, occupying three tables pushed together. We were here for the second session of the PEN Writers' Café, which was created to serve as a meeting place for intellectuals and writers in exile or interested in the theme of exile.

Our enthusiastic host, a Los Angeles based poet, had asked the uneasy question that hung between us.

Nearly seventy people had attended the first meeting of the PEN Writers' Café. It was held in the Culver Hotel in Culver City, and we were fêted by the new owners who explained that the hotel was famous because the Munchkins from the *Wizard of Oz* had stayed here all those years ago. The bulk of the crowd were screenwriters and television producers who had come to find the latest best plot or story line to develop into a made-for-television movie. Business cards changed hands quickly and there were promises to call or do lunch.

"As a poet I feel exiled from my community, my family, even from the themes of my work," our enthusiastic host said. "Come on people, don't be shy, let's talk about what exile means to each of us."

Next to me, my friend E., an Ethiopian journalist in exile, put down his coffee cup and cleared his throat.

"I listened to my mother die over the telephone," he said. "That's what exile means to me."

                                        *

The condition of exile and its discourse speak to an uneasy dialectic between at least two dominant binaries, and a multiplicity of other concerns. On the one hand are those who celebrate exile as redemptive. Homi Bhabha and Arjun Appadurai speak to the possibilities that displacement and exile offer. Salman Rushdie, C.L.R. James, and George Lamming believe exile to be a vital condition for writing, a form of alienation that produces a useful double-mindedness. Yet this double-consciousness, common among all ex-colonials and people of any marginalized group, requires no physical displacement to develop. If anything, it requires a more mental, and in many ways, more egregious breach with the self. This of course brings us to questions about the actual nature of what constitutes exile, and even, when exile?

Proponents on this positive, even optimistic, side of the debate typically celebrate and even romanticize the position of the exile, elevating the exilian to noble standing. (*Exilian* being a word Wole Soyinka jokingly coined to refer to one living in a state of exile, as though it were it a real country with real citizenship). The exilian's position is often difficult to reconcile with the difficult, continuous, and ever-shifting business of remaining human, as exiled writers like Salman Rushdie have discovered.

In "Reflections on Exile," Edward Said contends, "exile is strangely compelling to think about, but terrible to experience" (Said 1994: 137). He describes exile as a "crippling and unhealable rift forced between a human being and a native place." And yet Said goes on to point out a romantic benefit of this condition. "If true exile is a condition of terminal loss," he argues, "why has it been transformed so easily into a potent, even enriching motif of modern culture? …Modern Western culture is in large part the work of exiles."

The negative position often has tragic examples, as in the case of Arthur Nortje, a South African poet exiled by the then-apartheid regime who committed suicide.

Global culture – dominated by America and the myth of white supremacy – permeates even the remote mountain ranges of the Himalayas and is not only present but is in fact an overpowering obstacle to self-rule in post-colonial contexts. Exceptions to this seem to occur where the post-colonials are themselves white settlers, as in America, Australia and possibly even New Zealand. Frantz Fanon has made the case for the fractured and often schizophrenic self produced as a legacy of this global whiteness in his books *The Wretched of the Earth* and *Black Skins, White Masks*. So one need not leave one's home, in forced or voluntary exile, in order to experience this double-mindedness; one need only be an ex-colonial or a descendant of people bound over to slavery.

*

I was twenty when my father disowned me publicly for my actions as an anti-government activist. That term itself still bothers me. I wasn't necessarily anti-government as much as anti-human rights violation or anti-poverty and such policies of the Nigerian government that were intended to achieve a fascist and oppressive result.

It is often difficult to define the psychological and emotional damage something like that can have on the psyche of an Igbo, and by extension, a Nigerian and African: in a culture where people, on meeting you, don't ask you your name but your father's name, and by implication, the clan you belong to. This is still part of modern practice and is a way of deciding whether to continue interacting with you, or how to interact with you.

To be disowned publicly is to be cut off from this, to be placed in a limbo of homelessness, clanlessness, to become nothing. A ghost. This is another form of exile, one even more damaging because you are in the home of your birth and yet treated like a pariah. The question becomes – what atrocity had you committed that your own father, your lineage would disown you? Or as my grandfather said to me, "You have become a bat: a creature that is neither bird nor animal. Creatures like that are feared and despised."

*

Sociologists point out that one's experience of exile depends very much on one's cultural and material capital. The exile of certain individuals or even whole cultural groups places them higher or lower on an imaginary yet paradoxically "real" hierarchy of value.

There is exile caused by war or ideological difference. There is even self-exile as a form of protest. But there is also the exile of the former political prisoner. The cultural, humanitarian and even intellectual cachet of this position probably ranks highest. How do the exiles in this situation navigate the romantic ideals placed on them and still maintain a degree of integrity? How does one keep being human while labouring under this imposed nobility? Is there a way to live that faces up to the horrors and displacement felt daily, yet resists the anomie of romance?

This romantic value is placed on exile by all cultural institutions and everyday people. One can argue that this fascination goes back to pre-biblical days and probably for very good reason. In a world that wants to control and classify its relationships with all individuals and groups, the exile is possibly the most frightening, because he or she occupies that liminal space that defies any category. This ideal "where" of exile, a physical, mental and imaginative place, as liminal as it is, has a concreteness to it, and I think all exiles would agree that one knows when one arrives there. This *terra firma* is however given its dimensions and shape by those not in exile. This liminal space can be a wasteland often difficult to conceive – not only for the outsider, but for natives too – and so the process of rationalization begins: the construction of a consolation.

*

Sitting in the poets' lounge of Rotterdam's Poetry International Festival in June 2003, I was approached by an Iranian poet now living in London. Over tea we talked about our memories of London, where I used to live, and about being ex-political prisoners and being tortured.

"Do you remember how you could get extra money for healthcare if you had been tortured?" he asked me.

I remembered only too well. I also remembered the humiliation of having to prove your torture, and also my shame at getting more money from the state than regular exiles, who needed it just as much, simply because I had been tortured. My new Iranian friend laughed at this, calling it VAT.

"Value added tax?" I asked, confused.

"No, value added torture," he replied.

*

The value placed on exile is immense and grows in proportion to the cause of said exile. No national allegory or national mythology is complete without reference to colonies of exiles, outposts of the real state, the romantic state and the self. These colonies are usually made up of writers, painters and other artists. From the self-exile of writers like James Baldwin from the cultural state of America that limited his imagination and the right to express it, to the immigration to America of Germans and Jews between the two world wars. These intellectuals are revered because they refused to compromise and rejected all states of oppression. The value of the exilian grows when the process or factors of exile are not self-chosen but imposed punitively by the community the exile originates from, including those displaced by war and unable to return. One question this begs is that of creative/intellectual output, the second is the question of identity (as in: "Am I a writer because I am in exile, or, a writer in exile?").

In the first instance, there is the assumption that exile can, might, or even should interrupt or enhance the creative flow. There is also the assumption that one's product must necessarily reflect the themes and locale prior to exile, or else, dwell on endlessly unravelling the nature and being of exile. This is not an imaginary predicament, but a real constrictive aspect of the liminal limbo of exile. Publishers and other art producers or facilitators demand this material, which can be fed to a waiting audience desperately in need of heroes of any kind, indulging in ambulance chasing. This of course raises the question of whether we really value the suffering of others as some morality tale or whether we just enjoy the suffering of others. Are we slowly developing safe blood sports? Even an inability to produce work can be work in itself and can sometimes gain more popularity and cachet than actual work as one laments endlessly being unable to produce, because we all love the myth of the tortured artist, and here we have one who has actually been physically tortured to spice up the serving. Am I unduly cynical? I think not.

I am always asked – "Can you still write? What will you write about now that you are cut off from your subject?" Always by people who have never read my work, nor care to really. Why bother when you can get your fix this way? Or I get the reverse – you are so noble, after listening to what you've gone through, I feel ashamed to worry about the mortgage. One day I'm going to pluck up enough courage to say: "You'd better worry about your mortgage or else you'll be homeless." *I* certainly do. But in this role as confessor, I realize that the statement comes from a deeper place than even they are aware of. It is not just a flippant, easy way to mitigate something, which Victor Burgin refers to as "the melancholy tension of separation from all our origins" (Burgin 1991: 29).

This melancholy tension is the wound the true self carries. It is the thing that alerts us to our real predicament as humans: to make sense of the state of being, whatever it is. Consider even that it is comparable to the condition of our relationship to the grotesque, as an aesthetic, a device even, to mediate death, as argued by Bakhtin. The loss of that aesthetic in our literature and culture forces us to seek it out: in the pain and suffering of others and in the subsequent ennoblement of the sufferer. This condition of exile, perhaps more easily identified in recent exiles, is the thing we all wrestle with – outsiders and natives alike. An interesting binary that exacerbates the condition rather than solving it.

And what of identity? What is it? How does one construct it and resolve its many contradictions and then what to do with it subsequently? While trying to steer clear of Foucault and Freud, among others, the argument can be made that we do for the most part construct our identity, and at an even deeper more ineffable level, the self, from our interaction with our environment. It can even be argued that identity is not a 'thing' or 'place' we construct or arrive at, but simply a constant flux created by the tensions between the promptings of our internal voice and the external forces of experience. For most of us this is not too difficult because we are surrounded by the familiar with regard to the external and its tensions, and so we know our place. Any movements within this field are small and still mostly manageable. We first begin to understand the confusion facing the exile with regards to identity when we lose someone in our lives to death. This is further complicated by the addition of an unresolved tension or by the fact that we have often based our ideas of who we are in conflict or in opposition to the one lost.

So, for instance, a mother who loses a child faces a real crisis of identity. Who is she now? Is she still a mother? Does she have enough of the self prior to motherhood left over to reconstitute a new one? And what of the relationship to her husband and the broader society? Has she failed because she couldn't sustain the life we believe was entrusted to her? Sad and tragic as all this is (and touching on the sexist as this analogy is), it is still occurring within familiar territory, within the context of a clear physical sense of belonging or entitlement to belonging.

So while the exile is not alone in the struggle to find, negotiate, or even construct a self, an identity, there is still something unique to that experience. Analogies are notoriously inadequate and even simplistic, such as likening the exile to the adoptee who has lost its primal family and yet can never really find acceptance or possibly even certain depths of emotional syntax. This is probably alleviated for exiles because they at least possess memory, of the longed-for object/subject, a memory that allows them to begin to construct new depths of emotional syntax. Yet this very relief, this very memory, is the source of the pain, the insatiable hunger. In *The Satanic Verses* Salman Rushdie talks about exile as the dream of glorious return. He later uses this line as the title of an essay for the *New Yorker* in which he writes about his return to India after the Iranian government had lifted the fatwa. In that essay, Rushdie also demonstrates the disappointment of that return. There is no glory, more like a whimper. And so the romantic desire, the dream that has made exile bearable, finally collapses in the reality of the return to the object of desire.

As an exile, one butts up against the tensions of an unfamiliar world. The one role that feels real is that of displacement, of not being able to reconcile one's internal landscape – intellectual, emotional and mental – with the external. And if there are natives of this land in which the bubble of the exile exists that celebrate the bubble and the individual therein contained? And if they say, "What a thing you are! Here, stay in this bubble so that we can be reminded of the nobility that is possible for all of us." Can the exile resist it? Say, "No! I am a vile and loathsome creature at times, and I like sugar and hey, I am not a disappointment because I eat meat, and yes, I curse and traffic does bother me despite the fact that I have been beaten to unconsciousness before and yes, I hate deadlines and being broke and God give me some love please!?" And what is the cost if one does?

There are exiles who treat their condition as freeing and in fact a necessary precondition to working. Writers like James Baldwin and Ben Okri come to mind. Other writers, perhaps myself included, find that the condition of exile allows us to explore an international/human identity both as a state of being and a focus for our work, freed from the limiting arguments of place and its responsibility. Some exiles are not so well adjusted and treat their host locales with an irresponsible exploitation, an almost angry retaliation, not always directed in the right place. Whatever the case - be it Socrates who chose death over exile or Ovid who thought it spelt life - identity and the negotiation of it are complex.

There are real costs to this sort of complexity, not least of which is the withdrawal of funding that depends on an often-narrow benevolence. But the costs also extend to the loss of sympathy that is often necessary to achieve real changes not just in the condition of the exile, but the very cause of it. As with any kind of human suffering (and sufferers), an industry has grown around exiles. There are grants to organizations that offer to treat victims of torture, re-house exiles and refugees, and individual grants to exiles and those like them, to assist in resettlement, research and/or publication in that field among others. Despite a long list of criteria, there is an unwritten, unspoken one that is applied in judging all funding applications: namely, is the applicant enough of a victim? In this world, there is no room for grey categories. What do I mean? In my collection of prison poetry, I make it clear that there is an ego that walks hand-in-hand with the altruistic impulse. That there can be some other payoffs for the activist or intellectual who has been exiled other than the satisfaction of a job well done. This nuance of the exile's character is problematic because its richness and diversity confound easy categories like nobility, because the line between helpless victim and evil perpetrator is blurred, because it defeats the mystification of sacrifice and confronts us all with the inescapable guilt that we have not acted because we are less special or because we lack courage, but simply because we haven't.

This goes straight to the heart of the questions about identity, and how to resist the anomie of noble categories that attempt to erase any complications of character. As one caught in this net, I have no easy answers. And so we come back to the circle, the self-defeating logic that cannot say, "This is not truth", because that would be arguing that this thesis is true.

*

I could tell you no end of anecdotes about exile and its misunderstood protagonists, like the one about my arrival in Heathrow from Nigeria, fresh from prison and its risks. Still bleeding from unhealed anal trauma caused by repeated rape with foreign objects, I was wearing a small sanitary pad to staunch the flow. A suspicious customs officer pulled me aside and inspecting my passport, asked: "What is your country of origin?"

And in that moment, I was truly confused. Was I a Nigerian? A national of a country that has tried to kill me and to which I couldn't freely return to – at least not to my thinking? What was I? Mistaking my hesitation for guilt, the customs officer opted for a full body search. Finding my bloody pad, in a place where no pad was designed to be, he smiled happily thinking he had caught one of the famed Nigerian drug mules. I was X-rayed, questioned, humiliated. Nobody believed my story about rape and prison and exile, until a doctor confirmed that the findings of his physical exam were consistent with the rape story. Then followed the anger from the male customs officers, the pity from the female and the whole unsavoury business about how best to get rid of me quickly, yet tactfully in that oh-so-British way.

Instead I want to tell you a story about the last poem in my prison book, *Kalakuta Republic*. The poem talks about a new friend taking me out to his garden in London and showing me the spot where his cat, Tiddles, was buried and telling me, "See, I know your loss." After a reading in Ireland, a woman came up to me and smiled.

"I loved your last poem especially," she said. "Because it speaks to me. You see I love cats, too."

*

Lacan has an interesting view on desire. He maintains that the intensity of the desire is proportionate to the distance between the desire and the object of desire. Once the object of desire is attained, not only does desire cease, but there is also a loss of satisfaction with the object. It would seem then that the point is to never attain the object of desire, and that this condition of insatiable longing is what makes life interesting. Perhaps this is what drives the impulse to create heroes, to romanticize those we think have stepped beyond the measure of the ordinary.

This is good: that all our responses – inadequate, confused, limiting and otherwise – are driven by an insatiable melancholy and maybe even some deeper human syntax we can only guess at – that we value the lives of others precisely because we know the limits of our own.

Bibliography

Appadurai, Arjun. 1996. *Modernity at Large: Cultural Dimensions of Globalization.* Minneapolis: University of Minnesota Press.

Bhabha, Homi. K. 1994. *The Location of Culture.* London, New York: Routledge.

Burgin, Victor. 1991. "Paranoiac Space" in *Visual Anthropology Review* 7(2): 22-30.

Fanon, Frantz. 1967. *The Wretched of the Earth.* With preface by Jean-Paul Sartre (tr. Constance Farrington). Harmondsworth: Penguin.

- - - . 1968. *Black Skin, White Masks* (tr. Charles Lam Markmann). London: Macgibbon & Kee.

James, C.L.R. 1992. *The C.L.R. James Reader* (ed. and introduction by Anna Grimshaw). Oxford; Cambridge, Mass.: Blackwell.

Lamming, George. 1991. *In the Castle of My Skin.* Foreword by Sandra Pouchet Paquet. Ann Arbor: University of Michigan Press.

Rushdie, Salman. 1989. *The Satanic Verses.* New York, NY: Viking.

Said, Edward. 1994. "Reflections on Exile" (1984) in Robinson, Marc (ed.) *Altogether Elswhere: Writers on Exile.* Boston and London: Faber and Faber: 137-49.

Interview and Poems:
'Ode to Joy', '1971', 'People Like Us'

Chris Abani

In the 20-minute interview presented on the accompanying DVD, Chris Abani refers to his early writing and political activism in Nigeria, the response of the Nigerian regime, his three periods of incarceration, and the decision by his father, a senior government official, to publicly disclaim any connection with him, thereby sending him into internal exile before he was actually forced to leave his homeland. He talks about his personal experience of exile as being deprived of "the primal connection you have to the planet" and of the means he has found to build a new sense of home: of belonging to a wider, even global, humanity. He finishes by reading and talking about three poems. 'Ode to Joy', from his collection *Kalakuta Republic* (2001), is addressed to his fourteen-year-old cell-mate, who was tortured to death simply for being the son of an escaped political activist. '1971' is a segment from a recently published 80-page poem *Daphne's Lot* (2003), which sets his English mother's life against the background of war-ravaged Nigeria. Here he imagines his mother writing a diary entry about the kind of man, very different from her husband, that she would want. The last piece, 'People Like Us', comes from near the end of the same volume, and aims to show the extraordinary resilience of people who have lived through war and other forms of horror and who may achieve a kind of transfiguration through stitching together the most ordinary moments of everyday life.

See DVD

Ode to Joy

John James, 14
Refused to serve his conscience up
to indict an innocent man
handcuffed to a chair; they tacked his penis
to the table
with a six inch nail
and left him there
to drip
to death
3 days later

Risking death; an act insignificant
in the face of this child's courage
we sang:

Oje wai wai,
Moje oje wai, wai.

Incensed
they went
on a
killing rampage

guns
knives
truncheons

even canisters of tear-gas,
fired close up or
directly into mouths, will
take the back
of
your head off
and many men
died singing,
that night.

Notes caught,
surprised,

suspended
as blows bloodied mouths
clotting into silence.

1971

Daphne's diary spun a wish too precious to speak.
I want a man who smiles when he talks about me.

Smiles because he knows all of me and loves all
of me and does not want to change any of me.

I want a man like that. A man whose voice
is the pressure on my hips when he calls

my name. Whose shallow breathing traces
the arousal of my nipples as I cook him dinner.

Whose laugh dips between my legs, catching
me by surprise and rocking. Whose hands

are rough when he touches my face honestly.
Whose embrace is desperate as though

I were the only thing keeping him from drowning.
Whose lips are moist with desire when he kisses me

and whose eyes dance with a dangerous fire.
I want, I want, I want a man like that.

People Like Us

Standing at dawn in grandmother's kitchen
Hot tea mists the window as it warms me
Outside soft pre-dawn light drizzles over hens
scratching for truth beneath the stunted orange tree
The mauve dawn yawns in the slow approaching heat
exhaling dark shadows

As I sip, grandmother, arthritic, chops onions and
tomatoes ready for the sear of hot oil
Eggs crack like answers to unasked questions and I
realise that there is this stitching of life into
transfigurations.

6

Poem for Chris Abani: 'Parts of Speech'

Kapka Kassabova

Bulgarian-born Kapka Kassabova wrote this poem after meeting Chris Abani at the *Poetics of Exile* conference in Auckland in July 2003. For her biographical details see the introduction to the DVD interview with her at number 16 below.

Parts of Speech

for Chris Abani

There must be a verb
For when a country turns against you
Like a vengeful ex-lover

There must be an epitaph
For a human fed to crocodiles
For the sole reason of watching

There must be a sound for being
Unable to forget, yet humming
The perpetual melodies of being

I know someone
Who knows them
And translates them for the world

And when the world tires of listening
He wears them on his soul -
A talisman against silence

Film: *Three Riders of the Apocalypse*

Shahin Yazdani

Shahin Yazdani was born in Iran in 1958, into a large lower-middle class family. He spent his childhood and teenage years in Isfahan. His outstanding performance at school gained him free tuition at an elite private school. At the age of eight, with the help of his brother, he constructed a primitive projector out of a cardboard box, a magnifying glass, a series of discs made of card with movie frames at their circumference, and a lamp that was used as the light source. He used the tiny amounts of money he earned selling ice-lollies to buy single frames from famous American and Italian movies, from the local postcard shop. In the evenings, children from the neighbourhood came to watch the dance of shadow and light on the wall of the yard which his father had painted white. He taught himself to paint in water colours and oils at the age of thirteen and so impressed the owner of a photo and camera store in Isfahan that he lent him one of the new Super-8 movie cameras and helped him make his first short films: *Cry Under Water* and *Transcendence without Ascent*, which addressed social issues of the time.

In 1971-72, he led a protest in his high school against the oppressive policies of the Shah's regime and in support of the university students. He was only saved from SAVAK, the Shah's secret police, by the school's progressive deputy principal. A year later he moved to Tehran where he came into contact with a circle of university students who used theatre and creative undertakings to comment on social and political issues. He appeared in plays and wrote a screen adaptation of the novel *Ince Memed* (*Memed, My Hawk*) by Turkish writer Yashar Kemal, which was banned by the Shah's Ministry of Culture and Art as an attack on the Shah's policies towards peasants and workers. He enrolled in the College of Cinema and Television in Tehran, and became deeply involved in the democratic movement around the 1979 Iranian revolution. The establishment of the Islamic Regime and the subsequent closing down of the universities throughout the country by the regime for more than a year halted his studies and thwarted his hopes for a democratic political system.

Between 1979 and 1985 he was arrested three times by Revolutionary Guards of the Islamic Regime. On the first occasion, just a few months after the revolution, in a period of widespread popular protest and government repression, he was seized by Khomeini followers in the street and beaten up. He was then taken to a mosque, tied to a pole in the praying area and tortured by the guards

for some time before being transferred blindfolded to a military
barracks where he was put against a wall and threatened with
immediate execution if he didn't inform on opponents of the regime.
After days of physical and psychological torture, he was dragged out
of his cell by Revolutionary Guards, blindfolded, humiliated, and
driven out of Tehran. In an outlying area he was first interrogated
again and then forced to walk away from his captors across a
ploughed field. He was told to stop, "make his peace with God" and
be ready to be executed. The silence was broken by the sound of
bullets whistling past him. As Shahin recalls:

> It was as though, in that instant, the world contracted in my
> mind's eye and I experienced the slowest slow-motion
> moment of my life. It was only later, after being found by a
> few people who untied the blindfold, that I gradually came
> to grasp the depth of the trauma I had gone through. The
> close encounter with death in the form of a sham execution,
> which is indeed one of the most inhumane acts and by the
> same token one of the most horrifying experiences one can
> possibly undergo, changed my outlook on life permanently.

His second imprisonment was brief and relatively benign. His third
period of imprisonment, in Tehran's Evin Prison, was to last a horrific
three years. When he was not in a six-metre square cell with up to 100
other inmates, he was alone in a tiny cell in the torture block, or
undergoing torture himself. He says of that time:

> In those bleak nights I often wondered which was more
> unbearable; to be tortured or to be exposed to the seemingly
> perpetual agony of hearing, day in and day out, the piercing
> wailing of other inmates being tortured. This was a period
> when, more immediately than ever before in my life, I
> experienced the texture of calcified faith and blinkered
> views, witnessed the dark abyss of deception, went down
> the spiral of pain, baptised in the colour of blood, tasted the
> bitter flavour of humiliation, sensed the weakness of flesh
> as well as the might of spirit and the stature of will, saluted
> the magnificence of endurance, pitied the poverty of
> perception, the mirage of sterile beliefs, disgusted with the
> stench of ignobleness and Judas's loss of passion, longed
> passionately for the dance of letters and words on the stage
> of a book, inhaled the twinkle of freedom through the three
> slats of the window's metal blinds, celebrated the poetry of
> communality, welcomed the concurrent absurdity and
> beauty of life, and embraced the reinvigorating zephyr of
> love penetrating the cold walls of my prison cell.

After his release, he was able, with the help of friends, to get work in
the film industry. In the following seven years, he wrote, co-wrote,
and re-wrote film scripts, worked as unit director or was given the task
of co-directing in a number of feature films. Nevertheless, because of
his political track record, he was never given permission by the

Ministry of Culture and Islamic Guidance (MCIG) to direct his own work. What is more, although the few screenplays that he co-wrote were eventually made into feature films and, after some modification demanded by MCIG censorship committee, saw the light of day, all but one of his own scripts were rejected on ideological grounds.

In 1990 he travelled to Germany, where his wife and one-year old daughter were able, some months later, to join him. He attended German classes while working in a bar at night. He was then able to return to writing for movies, including the feature-length screenplays *Die Dämmerung* (1991), *Hinter der Nacht* (1992), and *Der Preis des Ungehorsams* (1992) as well as a treatment entitled *Suche nach dem Verlorenen* (1993). He was amazed and encouraged to obtain substantial funding for the last of these projects in competition with some very well-known film-makers. *Grief, Fear, Hope*, a fifty-three-minute docudrama which was showcased in October 1995 at the second *Festival for Iranian Films in Exile*, Gothenburg, Sweden, is another product of his time in Germany.

The rise of neo-fascism in reunified Germany, ongoing arson attacks on refugees' hostels and camps, and a frightening encounter his wife had with a couple of skinheads in an underground train station led them to migrate to New Zealand in late 1994. He completed his long-interrupted university studies in film at the University of Canterbury, in Christchurch, in 1999. On the creative front he has been involved in a number of film and video productions as writer, director, editor, director of photography, and sound designer since his arrival in New Zealand. In 1999 he was invited to join the staff of the Department of Theatre and Film Studies at the University of Canterbury to fill the position of Technical Director and Tutor for film. In addition to tutoring and teaching digital audio and video editing, he has lectured on Iranian Cinema in film studies courses.

In the seven-minute film, *Three Riders of the Apocalypse*, presented on the accompanying DVD, Shahin Yazdani offers a quasi-surrealistic meditation on the atrocities which war inflicts on the body of humanity. This film, made in 2000, was inspired by the work of Austrian writer Karl Klaus (1874-1936). His mammoth drama *Die Letzten Tage der Menschheit* (1918, *The Last Days of Mankind*) satirizes the hypocrisy of Austrian attitudes to the First World War. Yazdani's film constitutes a brief but sustained reflection on the relation between war and machine.

See DVD

8

Exile and the Philosophical Challenge to Citizenship

Farhang Erfani and John Whitmire

Farhang Erfani is the son of Iranian political refugees, who were exiled in 1982. By a circuitous route, the Erfani family arrived in France, where Farhang and his siblings went to high school. Farhang moved to the USA for his higher education and attended the University of the Pacific in Stockton, California, where he majored in philosophy and pursued his interest in philosophy and political thought. He obtained his PhD in philosophy at Villanova University, where he currently teaches in the Philosophy and Core Humanities programmes. His thesis, 'Left on the Road to Utopia: Social Imaginary in the Age of Democracy', focused on the hermeneutics of Paul Ricoeur and its compatibility with radical democracy, especially in the works of Claude Lefort, Chantal Mouffe, and Ernesto Laclau. His research is guided by a number of philosophical questions such as the importance of collective imagination and narratives – especially ideology and utopia – in the history of political philosophy, the question of exile and the challenges it poses to our philosophical understandings of identity and citizenship, and the history of French thought, from the Enlightenment to existentialism and post-structuralism.

John Whitmire is a native of North Carolina's Blue Ridge Mountains, in the USA. He studied philosophy and classics at Wake Forest University in Winston-Salem, NC, and Casa Artom, Venice, Italy, before moving to Philadelphia, Pennsylvania, to pursue a PhD in philosophy at Villanova University. His chief research interests are the theories of selfhood, subjectivity, and agency in the theoretical and literary works of nineteenth- and twentieth-century European continental philosophers. He is also interested in the socio-political ramifications of these theories and their relevance for national and institutional identity-construction. As a Rotary Foundation Ambassadorial Scholar, John worked in the Comparative Literature and Philosophy Departments at the University of Auckland in 2003. Although not an exile, his experiences as an American citizen studying in New Zealand during that year, as well as his time in Italy in 1996, gave him a measure of insight into the nature and importance of hospitality towards those who have – freely or under some form of constraint – left their own homes and native lands.

Their paper begins with the observation that, even though many philosophers, especially in the twentieth century, have had personal experience of exile, they rarely treat the topic of exile directly in their philosophical works. Existentialist thinkers such as Heidegger, it is true, have employed exile as a metaphor for the human condition, yet the concrete experience of political exile has been treated as somehow lacking the universality that canonical philosophy needs. This paper warns against the temptation to conflate the real situation of exile with a general condition of existential unbelongingness. It goes on to trace two major threads in the history of the philosophical treatment of citizenship, the one deriving from Plato and the other from Kant, and to explore their relevance to contemporary debate around the moral and legal status of those who seek refuge abroad from war, oppression, or other kinds of threat in their homeland. The Platonic tradition treats citizenship as deriving primarily from association with a land; it views foreigners as having the potential to contaminate the *polis* and any citizen who spends time away from the *polis* as likely to betray it. While many features of the Platonic position have not survived to the present, it is noteworthy that, for indigenous peoples in many parts of the world, attachment to the land remains of fundamental importance. At the same time, though migration of many kinds has become extremely common, some individuals and governments in the first world still demonstrate a visceral belief that refugees and immigrants to their country will somehow corrupt or contaminate it. The Kantian position, by contrast, treats citizenship as, ideally at least, cosmopolitan and global. It envisages nation states as moving towards "an enduring and gradually expanding federation likely to prevent war". Consequently, the stranger seeking refuge abroad from life-threatening persecution in his or her own country has what Kant refers to as a "right of resort" in another country. While Kant argues that we must therefore not show hostility to such people, our obligations to them do not extend to philanthropic hospitality. This assertion of a limited obligation to displaced persons forms the basis for much contemporary discussion around the rights of refugees and migrants. Globalization, of course, has not taken quite the form that Kant envisaged. While the United Nations asserts the universality of human rights, and certain clusters of countries, such as those in Western Europe, have moved towards federation and free internal movement of their citizens, so-called globalization has taken place primarily on the economic, rather than the political, level. The extreme international mobility of investment capital from first-world countries in search of cheap labour is not currently matched by an acceptance within such countries of the rights of third-world citizens to migrate to their shores in search of higher wages and improved living conditions. Finally, this paper offers a critique of both the Platonic and the Kantian positions and argues the need in the modern world for institutional arrangements which represent a variety of interests and struggles across national boundaries.

Why is it that philosophers rarely deal with exile? Social scientists, such as sociologists and psychologists, examine the empirical effects of the phenomenon, while others in the humanities focus on narratives of exile or their literary value. Some political theorists – here Judith Shklar comes to mind – look at exile from the point of view of the state and the question of obligation and loyalty. But it seems that even when philosophers do break the trend and take up the question of exile, they almost immediately feel the need to detach themselves from their own discipline in order to do so. In the preface to his recently published *On Immigration and Refugees*, British philosopher Michael Dummett notes that, whereas "I have a general belief that it is the duty of intellectuals to engage in any matter of social importance to which they see that they can contribute, [...] *philosophy* has not driven me in this respect" (Dummett 2001: xii, our emphasis).

So why is philosophy not interested in exile? After all, the twentieth century alone is teeming with philosophers who personally experienced exile, political banishment, or the trials of immigration. Marcuse, Adorno, Horkheimer, Levinas, Berlin, and Shklar all belong to an impressive list of philosophers, however, who have maintained Dummett's division between what happened to them personally and their philosophical works. What justifying credentials does exile, as a philosophical problem, lack? Alexis Philonenko recently wrote a short essay on the topic, which may provide us with a hint. He begins:

> I have personal ideas about exile. Of mixed blood, born from a Russian father and bi-racial mother (black-German), I have always had a hard time integrating within the French community, even though I speak and write in French. This essential distance is what I call exile-under-the-skin. I began writing a few pages on this topic, but I stopped: not only did it not have any academic value, the resemblance to a confession was all too strong. In a way, it is too bad: I had dealt with facts and not just ideas. I had approached an unusual dimension of existence, instead of imagining or dreaming about abstractions. But the law is the law: one must write and think as though one were another and appear integrated, even when it is not the case. (Philonenko 1999: 199, our translation)

Despite his "exile-under-the-skin", in order to be academically and professionally proper Philonenko knows that he must, *qua* philosopher, appear as another – he must adopt a tone of neutrality, of universality, that is unsuited for the experience of exile. One could argue, then, that the experience of exile lacks the universality that canonical philosophy needs.

Admittedly, some philosophers have tried to employ exile, metaphorically or structurally, as a universal human condition. Martin Heidegger is perhaps the most remarkable case here – though other existentialists such as Albert Camus have also dealt with exile in a similar fashion. Heidegger, in his magnum opus *Being and Time*, tells us that from an "existential-ontological point of view, the 'not-at-home' must be conceived as the more primordial phenomenon" (Heidegger 1962: 234).[1] For him, being exiled, 'not being at home', is a primary human condition. We believe, however, that we must resist the temptation to conflate the actual, concrete situation of exile with a more general condition of existential un-belongingness. According to this Heideggerian view, both the rich white American entrepreneur living in a Miami mansion and the destitute Cuban family in the dangerous neighbourhoods of 'Little Havana', fresh off a smuggler's boat, illegally living in the country with relatives, share the same existential situation of not-being-at-home. Obviously, in this case, the universalisation of exile blurs important distinctions. This is a dangerous trend. As Eva Hoffman correctly points out, there is now

> a vast body of commentary and theory that is rethinking and revising the concept of exile and the related contrapuntal concept of home. The basic revision has been to attach a positive sign to exile and the cluster of mental and emotional experiences associated with it. Exile used to be thought of as a difficult condition. It involves dislocation, disorientation, self-division. But today, at least within the framework of post-modern theory, we have come to value exactly those qualities of experience that exile demands – uncertainty, displacement, fragmented identity. Within this conceptual framework, exile becomes, well, sexy, glamorous, interesting. Nomadism and diasporism have become fashionable terms in intellectual discourse. (Hoffman 1999: 44)

So, when it comes to philosophy, there is a paradox. On the one hand, philosophy as a discipline tends to neglect exile. On the other, on the rare occasions that philosophy addresses the topic, the result seems to do injustice to the unfortunate fate of the exiled. We certainly have no definite answer in this essay regarding this larger paradox. But we would like to suggest that philosophy might look more closely at exile and learn something from it, without trying to appropriate it altogether as a universal medium of existence (thereby distorting its concrete existential character). In this essay, then, we look at one facet of exile: the philosophical challenge it poses to our understanding of citizenship. Without trying to appropriate exile, we hope to pay attention to the philosophical depth that is already present in the concept.

From its Western beginnings, exile as a form of political punishment implied a definite philosophical conception of citizenship: to be a citizen, to be a political agent, one had to be associated with a land. This relation between citizenship and the national land is still very much present in our juridical definitions of citizenship. Though there are undeniably other important facets to citizenship, it is essential that we recognize from the beginning this tight relationship of citizenship to a particular piece of the earth.

In the remainder of this essay, we briefly examine three different views of political agency and participation. The first two sections, in which we take Plato and Kant as exemplars, highlight the traditional philosophical emphasis on land as the ground for citizenship or political rights in the ancient and modern worlds. We suggest in the concluding segment that the notion of citizenship must be broadened in our current, post-modern condition. We certainly do not deny the importance of land, and perhaps more importantly the right to belong to a land; what we hope to challenge is the outdated notion that sharing a land means sharing the same political ideals or struggles.

*

With Plato, the question of the land – the uncontaminated land – is present in his two most important political works: the *Republic* and the *Laws*. For the purposes of this essay, we will focus on the *Laws*, as it is there that citizenship becomes fully associated with the land.[2]

The *Laws*, a trans-political and comparative dialogue, opens with an unidentified man, referred to only as the Athenian Stranger, asking Cleinias (a Cretan) and Megillus (a Lacedaemonian) about the origin and "authorship" of their laws (Plato 2000: 624). The discussion draws its initial focus from the fact that Cleinias is in charge of creating a new Cretan colony. Here is the dream of a philosopher: to create a city on the right philosophical foundation. Readers of the *Republic* will not be surprised to find out that the Athenian believes the only proper foundation for a city is virtue; a prosperous city is one where laws embody virtue, as only a virtuous city can – if necessary – legitimately require its citizens to defend it with their lives. Once the importance of virtue is posited, however, the Athenian turns his attention to a prerequisite to virtue. His first questions to Cleinias regarding the new colony are not about the education of the future citizens (as in the *Republic*); they concern, instead, the land.[3] In the ensuing discussion, the Stranger congratulates Cleinias for picking a somewhat fertile yet deserted site (with no neighbouring states), several miles from the sea, for this new city (Plato 2000: 704-705).[4] For in order to have virtuous citizens, he argues, one must have a city on land fertile enough to support its population without producing the surpluses that would encourage commerce (Morrow 1993: 96), and far enough away from the sea and other cities that even travel would become prohibitive. In the eyes of the Stranger, foreigners contaminate the *polis* with their trades, their culture, and their sheer presence; they make the *polis* 'unfaithful' to itself by turning the citizens' attention and devotion away from their political home.

To be a citizen, to be a political agent, for Plato, means being subject to a *polis*, belonging to a land. In this case, since there is no common history, language, or even religion to create a bond among citizens, the actual land becomes uniquely important. The very identity of the citizens is defined in their collective subjugation or subjection to this land. In other words, the condition *sine qua non* for a virtuous *polis* is an internal integrity entirely undisturbed by what lies beyond its boundaries. The Athenian had promised to legislate with nothing in view but virtue; and from the beginning virtue implies exclusion and, indeed, exclusion firmly rooted in the land: good citizenry is a matter of good land (Plato 2000: 705-709).

The Athenian proposes to develop this devotion much further through the internal organization of the imagined colony. The principles of self-sufficiency and equality in privilege necessitate that all citizens will be farmers. Their devotion to the land is thus heightened once more. To be a citizen is more than living on a land; it is to work *with* the land; only our citizens, not the (very few) foreigners who will be permitted to visit and work in the *polis*, will be allowed to do so. Further, this land is to be divided into an equal number of lots, which pass by inheritance but can neither be divided nor given away (Plato 2000: 855): in this way (and others) both wealth and poverty are kept in check.

Finally, a citizen may choose to travel outside of the city (against the legislators' preference), and, though this cannot be prevented (Plato 2000: 949), significant restrictions are placed on it in order to keep the citizens from importing a foreign culture. There is also a sort of public safety bureau that oversees the laws of the city and supervises its proper balance. This 'nocturnal council' may allow some foreigners to come and visit, but in general the council must approve anyone or anything that has to do with the 'outside', prior to entrances and exits. Now, given the importance of the land, it should come as no surprise that exile is the second harshest punishment, after the death penalty. Exile becomes a political punishment, then, because to be a citizen is to have a special rapport with the land. Accordingly, to be banned from the land means an end to one's political life.

Plato's position in the *Laws*, though perhaps exaggerated, represents a tradition to which we still very much belong. We still associate our capabilities and responsibilities as citizens with a particular land where we may participate in political life, a land we are always trying to keep pure and uncontaminated by foreign influences (metaphorically or more literally). All countries monitor the foreigners who are allowed to set foot on their soil (the American Patriot Act being only one of the more overt manifestations of this) through visa systems, and whatever foreigners wish to bring – from agricultural to cultural products – is rigorously controlled. Mad cow disease, tuberculosis, obscene materials, weapons, and so forth, are just a few of the many contaminants that contemporary nation-states may seek to exclude, even while nominally throwing open their borders to free trade. Our own bureaucratic versions of the nocturnal council also restrict the distribution of passports, and thereby travel, to those 'good' citizens whom we trust not to import a foreign culture inadvertently: felons and criminals forfeit not only their voting rights, but their right to travel freely, by violating the laws of their land. While we no longer (generally) exile our convicts – though we do deport citizens of other lands who break our laws – we still remove them from the land and significantly restrain their political agency by institutionalizing them in corrections facilities. As we can see, then, land and the rights and duties of citizenship continue to be intimately linked. This model, however, as we will see later on, is inappropriate for us today. Pure isolation, even as an ideal, is untenable.[5]

*

In the modern era, Kant has proposed a view of citizenship that is more global, yet also much 'thinner' than the ancient model, to make use of Geertz's famous categories. In two important texts, the 1795 essay 'Perpetual Peace' and the 1784 'Idea for a Universal History with a Cosmopolitan Purpose', Kant develops his notion of cosmopolitanism or world-citizenship. He argues – on a version of social contract theory extended to the national level – that just as individuals must leave the lawless state of nature in order to guarantee their own survival, so too must states eventually unite to deal with the problems of ungoverned antagonism. The broader argument is worked out in the 'Perpetual Peace'; the specific way that this will have to occur is found in the 'History' essay.

The argument runs as follows. We begin with a Hobbesian state of nature (or 'unrestricted freedom', a more Kantian term): each individual, outside civil society, is in a *de facto* state of war with all others. These battles are not in themselves bad, however; Kant emphasises that antagonism is nature's own way of developing heightened capacities in humankind. So political life does not end these battles; it only enforces certain restrictions within them that allow us to flower as human beings. Individuals unite into political bodies where justice can be administered in proportion to the "precise specification and preservation of the limits of freedom" (Kant 2000a: 45). Kant's teleological argument is that we are compelled by nature to discipline ourselves via the institution of this political body, as it is impossible for us to coexist in a state of "wild freedom" (Kant 1970a: 45-46).[6]

In the seventh proposition of the "History" essay, Kant reduplicates this same move on a larger scale. Concurrently with the administration of justice within the state, we must also solve the external problem of the relation of state to state, because though individuals within the various states are united in political bonds, these states themselves still effectively exist in a state of unrestricted freedom with regard to each other.

Eventually, after "wars, tense and unremitting military preparations [...] many devastations, upheavals and even complete inner exhaustion of their powers", individual states will, Kant argues, inevitably

> take the step which reason could have suggested to them even without so many sad experiences – that of abandoning a lawless state of savagery and entering a federation of peoples in which every state, even the smallest, could expect to derive its security and rights not from its own power or its own legal judgment, but solely from this great federation (*Foedus Amphictyonum*), from a united power and the law-governed decisions of a united will. (Kant 1970a: 47)

The ultimate goal of history, then, would be "a perfect civil union of mankind", a "universal *cosmopolitan existence* [...] as the matrix within which all the original capacities of the human race may develop" (Kant 1970a: 50). In 'Perpetual Peace', Kant repeats his claim that "just like individual men, [states] must renounce their savage and lawless freedom, adapt themselves to public and coercive laws, and thus form an *international state*", or, barring this, at least an "enduring and gradually expanding *federation* likely to prevent war" (Kant 1970b: 105). Kant is not, however, sanguine about the possibility of an international state, which would, in fact, demand either the dissolution of all individual states or the domination of all the nations by a single despotic state. The former of these "is not the will of the nations" (Kant 1970b: 105); the latter, though "the desire of every state", is luckily thwarted by the linguistic and religious differences among them (Kant 1970b: 113).

The most important point here, for our purposes, is that hand in hand with this gradual expansion of a peaceful federation goes the concept of cosmopolitan right, which extends to what Kant calls universal hospitality. By this he means that it is the right of every stranger, when in someone else's territory, not to be treated with hostility. The stranger "can indeed be turned away, if this can be done without causing his death, but he must not be treated with hostility, so long as he behaves in a peaceable manner in the place he happens to be in" (Kant 1970b: 106). Kant also refers to this as a "*right of resort*", which all human beings share by virtue of their original communal possession of the earth's surface. So, once again, we see a common land as the foundation of this right.

This argument opens up not only a right of resort, then, but a corresponding duty on the part of *political societies* – the duty of hospitality. This duty, however, marks the limits of cosmopolitan right – states and individuals are not required to go beyond it, and if they do, extending what Kant refers to as the "*right of a guest* to be entertained", they have entered the realm of philanthropy rather than right.[7] So while a dimension of existence as a cosmopolitan subject has been opened in the modern era by Kant, it is a rather thin one: so long as we do not have a universal, international state, real political participation remains effectively tied to a particular state, a particular piece of land, as it always has.

*

In sum, to rely once again on Geertz's model, we could say that whereas Plato championed a thick model of citizenship, heavily based on the purity of the land, Kant proposed a somewhat thinner model based on the universal, communal right of all humankind to the entirety of the earth's surface.[8] Both positions continue to exercise a strong sway over contemporary political discussions on immigration, refugees, and displaced persons: nation-states and international bodies tread the ground uneasily between hard parochial and cosmopolitan policies. In this concluding section, we make a few critical comments about our current 'post-modern' condition, and the inadequacies of the philosophical and political presuppositions of Plato and Kant, of the ancients and moderns. We briefly examine some of the problems with each model, and then propose an alternative solution. We do not offer a valorisation of the nomadic or exilic subjectivity that, as Hoffman has noted, is now very much in vogue within certain circles. What we have done, however, is to try to allow the real, factical experience of exile, of losing one's home and with it one's voice, one's political power or agency, to help us begin to formulate a kind of citizenship or political agency that is not solely based on the land. For us, this is the meaning of a poetics of exile lodged within the heart of philosophy.

From a philosophical perspective, Plato and Kant's paradigms are both grounded in essentialism, which has been largely discredited, especially by post-structuralist thought. In the case of Plato, the purity of the land is, of course, geographically untenable today. More importantly, his hope for creating a city that is essentially grounded in virtue is also irretrievable for us. Whose essences? Which virtues? The inextricable plurality of values in the modern nation-state simply does not lend itself to Platonic isolationism. In the case of Kant, nature as a political matrix is quite problematic, and cultural relativism represents a severe challenge to traditional human rights theories, customarily grounded in natural law and universal reason.[9]

Equally difficult to accept is another tradition that began with Plato and continued through Augustine, Kant, Hegel, and Marx: the ideal of full political reconciliation. Defenders of Kantian and other models of cosmopolitanism believe that it is possible to find a well-governed and peaceful reconciliation of all our differences, at least as a regulative ideal. David Held, a contemporary proponent of this idea, tells us that we need cosmopolitanism because of "the recognition by growing numbers of peoples of the increasing interconnectedness of political communities" and of the need to solve problems collectively (Held 2002: 12). We certainly agree that the political terrain is growing beyond the domains of traditional political thought; but we disagree with the chimerical view that hopes for the overcoming of all such conflicts in politics.[10] Even were it not for the theoretical challenges of post-structuralism, post-colonial studies alone have proven to us that 'reason' – even with the best of possible intentions –

can be oppressive, and, indeed, dangerous. In other words, from a philosophical point of view, the essentialism and rational universalism of the traditional cosmopolitan view make it inadequate for us.

From a political perspective, where instead of cosmopolitanism people speak of globalization, there are still other obstacles. Here, advocates of globalization such as Thomas Friedman and Francis Fukuyama defend the elimination of local boundaries in the name of a better and more global world. They see globalization as the work of integration (Friedman 2000: 8). In their view, the expansion of capitalism means the expansion of democracy. This conflation of democracy and market capitalism has had disastrous consequences: attacking capitalism – theoretically or otherwise – has meant attacking democracy. And democratization has come to mean opening one's boundaries to capitalism. Yet, at the same time, the World Bank and IMF projects in the Third World have failed at the staggering rate of sixty to seventy percent.

We must also take into account here the massive inconsistency in the argument of many advocates of globalization: whereas 'free trade' is heard often, 'open borders' is not.[11] 'Globalization' has tended to mean that capital may flow freely between nation-states, whereas labour remains largely restricted to those territorial boundaries. Poor workers are often forced to become illegal aliens in the search for better pay or working conditions. Consequently, as corporations have learned to move from one land to another, millions – in rich and poor countries – have lost their voices and political capacities *precisely by being restricted to their own land*. Decisions made by corporations nominally headquartered in the United States affect millions of people from China to Mexico, people who are either economically or legally prohibited from pursuing the consequences entailed by a consistent globalization. This is a kind of exile in reverse, in which ordinary people across the globe have not lost their land, but have lost their political powers.

Even this inconsistent globalization of 'free trade, closed borders', is often a ruse, however – a kind of parochialism in the guise of cosmopolitanism. 'Free trade', for First World nations, more often than not bears the qualification 'when it benefits us'. Subsidies for their own less-productive industries, and levies on correspondingly more-productive industries from poorer nations, are less an exception than a rule.

Against the failures and inconsistencies of globalization, some on the right, and many on the left, have retreated to a kind of parochialism. John Gray, an influential conservative, has come to criticize globalization and has proposed measures to protect nations – especially rich Christian nations – from savage capitalism. Many social democrats have also proposed using national politics to combat the evils of globalization, urging that economic control should happen at the state level in order to protect the workers' interests.[12] Whereas David Held and Thomas Friedman – though in different ways – are Kantians in today's world, these parochialists are our Platonists.

We have already seen the philosophical impossibility of a return to the ideal purity of the nation-state inherent in its essentially (and, we would add, productively) maculate collection of virtues and values. Another significant consequence implicit in this retreat to parochialism (whether tacit or open), however, is the rise of an ugly xenophobia in many of these richer nation-states. It has been seen rearing its head in more or less evident ways, but the most obvious of these is the increasing impermeability of borders to those who might otherwise have sought refuge on their far side. Those forced into exile for whatever reasons, and who might once have been welcomed as the tired, poor, huddled masses yearning to breathe free, thus become, to the 'receiving' citizens, the contaminating influences on the *polis* that Plato so feared. This fear of contamination (the residue of parochialism), coupled with the unwillingness simply to deny entry (the residue of cosmopolitanism) to all those fleeing from their homelands for political, socio-economic, racial, religious, or other reasons, gives rise to the horrifying modern phenomenon of the border camp.[13] There remains a further, dangerous corollary to the retreat to parochialism, however, and that is the spectre of an increased level of prejudice or hostility towards those fellow citizens who happen to share ethnic, religious, or national origins similar to those for whom the possibility of entry has been foreclosed.

Given that both globalization and parochialism have considerable failures, what are we to do? As we have seen, both operate on the model of political agency based on land: the parochials are trying to limit and protect the land for the sake of protecting their politics; the cosmopolitans are trying to expand the field of political action by making the entirety of the globe its proper terrain. But, to employ Benjamin Barber's categories, neither Jihad nor McWorld works for us.

In a fluid, post-modern world, which allows ideas, capital, and even some persons to move easily around the globe, and in which all of us are affected by others in unprecedented ways, we believe it is necessary to recognise that political participation is no longer (if it ever was) simply a local matter, contained within finite geographical boundaries. We can no longer afford the luxury of thinking and acting merely locally; indeed, the primacy of *locus*, or place, to political agency is what we have been chiefly interested in problematising here. We would argue that we must, instead, begin to think of citizenship in terms of strategic interest, in terms of what people have in common, and no longer solely in terms of land. Political participation must no longer be a local issue; it should be horizontal, across the globe, where similar political interests would be able to have a global and associated voice. The United Nations is certainly one such forum for discussion, but it is not, and should not be, the last word in political representation, inasmuch as it proceeds on the often-spurious presumption that states – and ultimately, as we have shown, all those who are tied to a given body of land – have something like a set of uniform political interests that override all other ties, whether these be economic, racial, gender, or otherwise.

We can only hint, in this context, at what that model might look like for us. Our central focus here has been economic, but we are not trying to claim the exclusive priority of economic considerations. We are simply arguing that the loss of political agency (if this ever existed) of oppressed groups – including, most fundamentally, exiles and displaced persons – must be addressed within the context of the economic issues we have already delineated. We are certainly not calling for a new Workers' International; rather, there will have to be a proliferation of sometimes conflicting, sometimes overlapping global organisations representing a variety of different struggles and movements. Economic issues are, in our view, a primary objection to the kind of cosmopolitanism-cum-globalization we have described, but there are other, equally legitimate struggles that must also be dealt with here. We must not lose sight of these struggles (e.g. over women's rights, racial discrimination, etc.), which have already called into doubt the legitimacy of the nation-state as the sole place where political agency may be exercised. We must empower and foster the growth of bodies such as the United Nations, Amnesty International, Greenpeace, Human Rights Watch, Doctors Without Borders, and other organisations that serve to articulate the concerns of voiceless interests – both broad and narrow, opposing and convergent – while at the same time insisting that they have sufficiently democratic structures and representation, with elected and accountable officials.

We would also hasten to add that by recasting political agency beyond its traditional, unique relationship to a land (or all land), we are not suggesting the abolition of national citizenships or of cosmopolitan right. Such citizenships retain many practical benefits, and in some cases our interests are tied more or less directly to the land.[14] But by expanding political agency, we would prevent the political death imposed on too many by exile. To utilise our earlier categories, we are proposing a thicker cosmopolitanism not restricted to the Kantian duty of hospitality towards the refugee, one built on the intercontextuality of conflicts and interests rather than on a universal hegemonic rationality.

We return, in concluding, to the question of exile. It used to be the case that banishment from one's own land meant the end of one's political life. Not to be there, on the land of one's nation, meant having no political voice. This is still the fate of too many people across the globe. But we are now presented with a different, more complicated situation in addition to this traditional quandary. The reverse exile and consequent loss of political capacities by millions around the globe, coupled with a 'cosmpolitanism' that is really an inconsistent globalization, necessitates a genuine re-opening of the question of political agency – that is, what we really mean when we say we are citizens of ---, with the powers that accrue thereto. We hope to have provided the beginnings of such a project here.

Notes

[1] For more on Heidegger and the impossibility of making exile a universal human condition, see Farhang Erfani. 2002. 'Being-There and Being-From-Elsewhere: An Existential-Analytic of Exile' in *Reconstruction* 2 (3): Online at www.reconstruction.ws/023/erfani.htm (consulted 25.04.2004).

[2] We certainly do not mean to say that the *Laws* is *the* foundational philosophical text on citizenship; it is, however, a very interesting text insofar as it represents an obsession that has defined the traditional views of political participation.

[3] We should notice the irony of three old men from three different lands attempting to create a new city in which the purity of the land will be the ultimate criterion of belongingness.

[4] Regarding this atypical concern in political philosophy, see Pangle 1980: 438-439.

[5] Even within Plato's own narrative this perfect isolation is contaminated. Despite his best efforts to keep foreigners out, teachers – a very important position in Plato's thought – have to be foreigners, since all citizens must be farmers.

[6] For more on the teleological views of Kant (anticipating the Hegelian dialectic of mastery and servitude in the *Phenomenology of Spirit*) in this respect, see Anderson-Gold, *Cosmopolitanism and Human Rights*, especially chapter 2, 'Kantian Cosmopolitanism'. She correctly points out that "Human capacities will not reach

their full development anywhere until a cosmopolitan condition exists" (Anderson-Gold 2001: 22).

[7] We must be certain not to conflate this notion of 'hospitality' with what Jacques Derrida, following Emmanuel Levinas, means by the term. In the work of Levinas and the later Derrida, 'hospitality' means something much more robust, far closer to what Kant calls 'philanthropy' or the 'right of a guest to be entertained' than the stricter notion of hospitality, *qua* 'right of resort', that Kant has in mind here. For Levinas and Derrida, 'hospitality' (or 'absolute hospitality') means throwing open the doors of one's home (or nation) in a completely unreserved manner. We must credit Kant for seeing the need for a transnational politics, even in face of his suspicion towards a transnational state. However, although he does insist on a very limited right of resort even within the current political situation, he never goes so far as to offer political agency – citizenship – to those exiles residing in another state.

[8] It must be noted that cosmopolitanism and globalization are not identical. Philosophers often speak of cosmopolitanism and its benefits. Globalization is a phenomenon that focuses more on economic expansion. There is, however, a theoretical connection: the champions of globalization believe that the global free-market will also contribute to the progress of human rights, peace efforts etc. which are cosmopolitan goals.

[9] See Anderson-Gold 2001 for a possible retrieval of the Kantian model.

[10] For more on this, see the works of contemporary thinkers of radical democracy such as Ernesto Laclau and Chantal Mouffe, who have argued that politics is, in fact, constituted by antagonism, e.g. their *Hegemony and Socialist Strategy: Towards a Radical Democratic Politics* (London: Verso, 1985). That any society, according to this view, regardless of its size, is constituted by difference is not a new idea. Hegel, most famously, defended it. But here the fragmentation of the *polis* is not seen as undesirable but as unavoidable, and the desire for a fully 'rational' society is critiqued as another mode of oppression. Even though contemporary cosmopolitan defenders are rhetorically less flamboyant than Hegel, David Held still believes that cosmopolitanism is based on reason's political capacities (Held 2002: 12-13).

[11] We owe our inclusion of this discussion to several conversations with Mike Hanne.

[12] See especially Paul Hirst and Grahame Thompson, *Globalization in Question* (Oxford: Polity Press, 1999). We must credit Michael Hardt's 'Globalization and Democracy', for pointing out the similarity between Gray and the social democrats. Hardt's essay is available on the *Institute on Globalization and the Human Condition*'s website. On line at: www.humanities.mcmaster.ca/%7Eglobal/wp hardtfinal.pdf (consulted 14.03. 2004).

[13] Our analysis thus differs from Giorgio Agamben's in suggesting that the phenomenon proceeds from the combination of parochial and cosmopolitan attitudes, rather than a consistently-applied Kantian right of resort.

[14] This could be construed in both a broad way – viz., the interest of humanity in the preservation of the planet as a whole – or more narrowly, as in the interest of small communities in local politics. We believe that the European Union is a good example of this kind of expansion of citizenship, while preserving the need for some local politics.

Bibliography

Anderson-Gold, Sharon. 2001. *Cosmopolitanism and Human Rights*. Wales: University of Wales Press.
Dummett, Michael. 2001. *On Immigration and Refugees*. London: Routledge.
Friedman, Thomas. 2000. *The Lexus and the Olive Tree*. New York: Anchor Books.
Fukuyama, Francis. 1992. *The End of History and the Last Man*. New York: Free Press.
Gray, John. 2000. *False Dawn: The Delusions of Global Capitalism*. New York: New Press.
Heidegger, Martin. 1962. *Being and Time* (tr. J. Macquarie and E. Robinson). New York: Harper and Row.
Held, David. 2002. 'National Culture, the Globalization of Communications and the Bounded Political Community' in *Logos: A Journal of Modern Society and Culture* 1(3): 1-17.
Hoffman, Eva. 1999. 'The New Nomads' in Aciman, André (ed.) *Letters of Transit: Reflections of Exile, Identity, Language, and Loss*. New York: The New York Press: 35-64.
Kant, Immanuel. 1970a. 'Idea for a Universal History with a Cosmopolitan Purpose' in Reiss, Hans (ed.) *Kant's Political Writings* (tr. H.B. Nisbet). Cambridge: Cambridge University Press: 41-53.
- - - . 1970b. 'Perpetual Peace: A Philosophical Sketch' in Reiss, Hans (ed.) *Kant's Political Writings* (tr. H.B. Nisbet). Cambridge: Cambridge University Press: 93-130.
Morrow, Glenn. 1993. *Plato's Cretan City: A Historical Interpretation of the Laws*. Princeton: Princeton University Press.
Pangle, Thomas, 1980. 'Interpretive Essay' in *The Laws of Plato* (tr. Thomas Pangle). Chicago: Chicago University Press: 375-511.
Philonenko, Alexis. 1990. 'Les Puissances de l'Exil' in Niderst, Alain (ed.) *L'Exil*. Paris: Klincksieck: 199-210.
Plato. 1985. *The Republic* (tr. Richard Sterling and William Scott). New York: Norton.
- - - . 2000. *Laws* (tr. Benjamin Jowett). New York: Prometheus Books.

9

Exile, Empire and the Convict Diaspora: The Return of Magwitch

Kirsty Reid

Kirsty Reid grew up in the Scottish Highlands but has lived at various periods in the US, Australia, and Zimbabwe. She is currently lecturer in Historical Studies at the University of Bristol, UK, where she teaches on the history of colonialism. She works on the British Empire and diasporic communities and her research to date has particularly focused on convict transportation to the British Australian penal colonies. She has published a number of articles on female convict transportation and is currently completing a book entitled *Gender, Crime and Empire: Convict Women and Colonial Australia* (Manchester University Press, forthcoming). She spends part of most years in Tasmania, Australia.

In this paper, she studies the nature of the exile imposed by nineteenth-century imperial British penal authorities on the convicts it transported to Australia and its other colonies. Banished from the 'old world' and abhorred in the 'new', convicts straddled the fault lines between metropolis and colony in precarious and unique ways. If empire depended upon rigid divisions between imperial and imperialised populations, convicts undermined such spatial and cultural boundaries. Although expunged from the 'mother country' and sentenced to a civic and social death, the figure of the convict repeatedly resurfaced. Through the published narratives and speaking tours of returned convicts such as Tolpuddle Martyr George Loveless and Chartists such as John Frost, exile informed contemporary cultures of radicalism and dissent. Exile also touched the everyday life of plebeian communities in manifold ways: from shared memories of those gone to personal letters read collectively, to prints, photographs, and ballads, convict shadows continued to cross metropolitan streets. The convict figure of Magwitch can be re-situated and Charles Dickens's *Great Expectations* can be re-read, not as canonical text, but as one strand within a wider cultural array. This paper asks what contributions convicts made to popular imaginings of empire and explores the ways in which the figure of the returned convict, in particular, threatened to unsettle and subvert hierarchies of metropolitan power and systems of imperial accumulation.

The return of Magwitch, the transported convict, who has haunted Pip since their first meeting in the opening passages of Charles Dickens's *Great Expectations*, is experienced as a great horror *and* as a moment of profoundly disturbing self-revelation. Pip learns through the reunion that it is Magwitch, not Miss Havisham, who has made him a 'gentleman'. He knows in this moment that he has turned his back on all that was good in his life and, in particular, on the 'simplicity and fidelity' of Biddy and Joe, his family, to pursue a corrupting and false dream in which he aspires to become a gentleman, in order to gain possession of Estella, his childhood love. Pip is lost, undone, exiled from his heart's desire: "O Estella, Estella!" he cries out (Dickens 1965: 338). Of the major characters, it will only be Magwitch who achieves a reconciliation of sorts by the end of the novel, dying in Pip's arms he has not only escaped the hangman but also achieved a return to his family. Pip, by contrast, is left to wander the world.

The returned convict was a recurring theme within Victorian fiction appearing, in Dickens's works alone, in *Great Expectations*, *Pickwick Papers* and *Dombey and Sons* as well as in the novels of numerous other nineteenth-century writers. As literary motif, the returned convict was thus a frequent expression of social and cultural unease.[1] In *Great Expectations*, Dickens presents Magwitch, the convict, in two key but contradictory ways. Firstly, as an alien other, a character who, regardless of his return to metropolitan space, is condemned to a permanent existence beyond the pale of the body politic and whose illegal act of self-repatriation must be punished by death. "The power of casting out dangerous members from its bosom is inseparable", the *Times* claimed in 1850, in an article on convict transportation, expressing broadly similar ideas about convict otherness, "from the notion of civil society" (1850). But in *Great Expectations*, Magwitch also functions simultaneously as Everyman, as a symbol of the universality of humanity, or at least, given Dickens's attachment to notions of race, the universality of Britons.

Magwitch's difference is undoubtedly and repeatedly racially inscribed. When Pip attempts to disguise Magwitch, for example, he discovers:

> Whatever he put on, became him less [...] than what he had worn before. [...] there was something in him that made it hopeless to attempt to disguise him. The more I dressed him and the better I dressed him, the more he looked like the slouching fugitive on the marshes. [...] from head to foot there was Convict in the very grain of the man. [...] The influences of his solitary hut-life were upon him besides, and gave him a savage air that no dress could tame [...]. In all

his ways of sitting and standing, and eating and drinking – of brooding
about [...] in these ways and a thousand other small nameless
instances arising every minute in the day, there was Prisoner, Felon,
Bondsman, plain as plain could be. (Dickens 1965: 352-53)

Pip relates, "The abhorrence in which I held the man, the dread I had
of him, the repugnance with which I shrank from him could not have
been exceeded if he had been some terrible beast" (Dickens 1965:
337).

Debates about transportation from the 1830s onwards had
systematically demonised convicts, accusing them of sodomy, child-
rape and cannibalism, among a range of other unnatural acts.[2] There is
no doubt that Dickens, with a long-term interest in penal reform, was
fully aware of these images and that, against this backdrop, Magwitch
would have been read by some as a symbolic reaffirmation of the
horrors unleashed when the monstrous convict came 'home'. By the
time *Great Expectations* was published, moreover, previously
'liberalising' discourses of moral reform, based upon the belief that
criminals could be reclaimed, had begun to falter. Many
commentators now emphasised the failures of the penitentiary system.
At the same time, transportation was also approaching its end. So
fierce was the debate produced by the prospect of this end to exile that
a moral panic about crime hit Britain. This wave of hysteria further
demonised the convict and more firmly associated the criminal class
with racial otherness by linking convicts with the debased 'rookeries'
of London and, in particular, the Irish.[3] Against this backdrop,
Dickens also shifted ground, publishing articles, for example, in which
he depicted the criminal as irretrievably savage.[4] Imperial as well as
metropolitan events informed his attitudes to race: once a firm
proponent of emancipation, his opinions on slavery became
increasingly ambivalent, and in the wake of the Indian uprising and
the Morant Bay Rebellion, he adopted an increasingly shrill attitude
towards empire and a hardened racist tone, positioning himself, for
example, alongside Thomas Carlyle in the defence of Governor Eyre.[5]

Alternative readings of *Great Expectations* are, nevertheless,
possible and Dickens, indeed, seems to encourage them. Magwitch's
return confounds and undermines supposedly fixed hierarchies of
difference. "Our ways are different ways", Pip tells Magwitch
(Dickens 1965: 334), and yet, from its opening pages, and even in the
depictions of Magwitch as monstrous, *Great Expectations* interweaves
notions of difference with assertions of the universal nature of

humanity. Pip, for example, deploys the spectre of Frankenstein to emphasise the awfulness of his condition now Magwitch has returned:

> The imaginary student pursued by the misshapen creature he had impiously made, was not more wretched than I pursued by the creature who had made me, and recoiling from him with a stronger repulsion the more he admired me, and the fonder he was of me. (Dickens 1965: 334)

But if Magwitch is the Frankenstein who has 'made' Pip, how has Magwitch himself been made monstrous? By the time *Great Expectations* was published, there was more than one answer to this question. Since the 1830s, some proponents for the abolition of transportation had been arguing, with great effect, that the very experience of exile itself deformed the convict. "Unnatural deeds", as one abolitionist put it, emphasising the wrongs committed by the British state, "do breed unnatural troubles" ('P' 1852). In the nineteenth century, matters of penal discipline were increasingly represented as questions for scientific analysis: criminals were to be measured and classified, punishments were to be categorised and calibrated. If Magwitch was a monster, perhaps it was because a Frankenstein-like system had made him so? In *Great Expectations*, this monstrous relationship is read through the lens of individual relationships: "I lived rough", Magwitch exclaims, in a passage which might be read as a wider commentary upon relations between labour and capital, colony and metropolis, "that you should live smooth, I worked hard, that you should be above work" (Dickens 1965: 337).

The possibility that Magwitch has been made, rather than born, a monster becomes ever stronger the more he becomes truly known. Pip initially experiences Magwitch as a "dreadful mystery". The convict, Pip argues, must be made to narrate his story so that his crimes may be fully revealed. Pip expects this process to confirm Magwitch's difference, to fix his character as a man whose very hands "might be stained with blood" (Dickens 1965: 339). But when Magwitch tells his tale, it reveals something altogether different; a human being exiled from society at birth. "I've been carted here and carted there", Magwitch relates of his childhood,

> and put out of this town and put out of that town, and stuck in the stocks, and whipped and worried and drove. [...] there warn't a soul that see young Abel Magwitch, with as little on him as in him, but wot caught fright at him, and either drove him off, or took him up. I was took up, took up, took up, to that extent that I reg'larly grow'd up took up. This is the way it was, that when I was a ragged little creetur as

much to be pitied as ever I see [...] I got the name of being hardened.
(Dickens 1965: 360-361)

Despite this upbringing, Magwitch appears more capable of genuine
emotion and family sensibility than Pip. While the latter has turned his
back on his family, through a false sense of self and a corrupting
pride, Magwitch risks everything to return to his 'son'. Magwitch's
narrative, moreover, explicitly condemns those who judge, as Pip has
done, merely on appearances:

'This is a terrible hardened one', they says to prison wisitors, picking
out me. 'May be said to live in jails, this boy'. Then they looked at
me, and I looked at them, and they measured my head, some on 'em –
they had better a measured my stomach. (Dickens 1965: 361)

Condemned as a mere child, Magwitch has also suffered at the hands
of a class-bound criminal justice system which favours the aristocratic
villain Compeyson precisely because it too is unwilling to penetrate
beneath the surface of how men look.

Finally, the more Magwitch's identity becomes fixed, the less
Pip knows himself. For it is, in fact, Pip, the character whose
autobiographical account the novel ostensibly is, who is a mystery.
Magwitch's return forces Pip to acknowledge his undoing:

I began fully to know how wrecked I was, and how the ship in which I
had sailed was gone to pieces [...] I thought how miserable I was, but
hardly knew why, or how long I had been so, or on what day of the
week I made the reflection, or *even who I was that made it*. (Dickens
1965: 341, 344. Emphasis added)

Biography, historian Theodore Koditschek argues, was "the most
appropriate medium" for the "inherently heroic [...] world vision" of
the nineteenth-century bourgeois man; through biography, the
ideology of the self-made man could be "reified in [...] narrative
recounting(s) of the individual life process" (1990: 182). Biography
thus enabled the intertwined processes of capital accumulation,
metropolitan governance and imperial domination to be naturalised.[6]
Yet Pip has no biography to narrate; he has not made himself, he has
been made. His identity as a 'gentleman' is, moreover, founded only
on surface appearances, dependent upon the symbolic presence of
objects of material value (his watch, his ring, his fine linen) purchased
for him by a convict. Unlike Magwitch, Pip *depends* on being judged
by his appearance.

The "prohibition placed on Magwitch's return", Edward Said
argues,

is not only penal but imperial: subjects can be taken to places like
Australia, but they cannot be allowed to 'return' to metropolitan
space, which, as all Dicken's fiction testifies, is meticulously charted,
spoken for, inhabited by a hierarchy of metropolitan personages'.
(1993: xvii)

But, in *Great Expectations*, Magwitch does return and his otherness is
used not to confirm but to question and undermine this "hierarchy of
metropolitan personages". Magwitch's return to metropolitan space
not only reveals Pip's *self*-deception, but also undermines those
notions of *collective* difference which supposedly separated
'gentlemen', a class which claimed the right to possess *every* place,
from the criminal exiles who had been sentenced to be forever *without*
place.[7]

*

What gave *Great Expectations* such potentially destabilising power
was the extent to which it both drew upon, and was embedded within,
wider cultures of exile. Dickens was ever anxious to encourage a self-
image as a writer of 'high' literature. Unlike his friend, William
Harrison Ainsworth, whose Newgate novels drew openly upon
centuries-old genres of last dying speeches and true accounts of
criminal lives, Dickens was keen to distance himself from such 'low'
associations.[8] He was appalled, consequently, when some critics
linked *Oliver Twist* to Ainsworth's *Jack Sheppard*. The 'authenticity'
of Dickens's fiction came rather, by implication, from his powers of
observation and his ability to 'know' and truthfully 'represent' the
poor.[9] So successful was he, historian Jonathan Rose has recently
argued, that many nineteenth-century working-class readers,
struggling "with the art of recording their lives cited Dickens, more
than anyone else, as the man who got it right" (2001: 112). "Perhaps",
Rose proceeds to argue,

Dickens's most important gift to the working classes was the role he
played in making them articulate [...]. As rules for organising
experience, frames are essential tools for writing stories as well as
reading them. For people who had never been taught how to tell their
own histories, Dickens supplied the necessary lessons. (2001: 114-
115)

The relationship was, however, more multi-directional than this.
Magwitch himself alludes to the shadowy presence of a much wider
cultural 'frame' when he recounts his life: "'I am not a going fur to
tell you my life, like a song or a story-book'", he assures Pip. He then

proceeds to do precisely that, following the well-worn conventions of the criminal biography (Dickens 1965: 360). Many readers 'knew' Magwitch's life *before* he narrated his tale. Through a vast array of songs and story-books, and a deluge of personal letters, biographies, popular prints, mass public meetings and other mediums, transported convicts had, despite their physical banishment, sustained an intimately familiar presence within metropolitan space. Convicts were remembered through broken individual relationships, mourned as lost family and friends. They were also kept alive within collective cultural memories where they served as a dominant recurring motif of exile giving meaningful symbolic form to more broadly experienced processes of exploitation and displacement associated with the profound socio-economic and cultural transformations of the period.

This kind of backchat was not supposed to happen. The perceived terror of transportation was founded on the ability of the imperial state to control and filter communication from the penal colonies, to render the condition of the convict horrifyingly unknowable. Dickens, perhaps revealingly, gives ironic form to this notion in *Great Expectations*. When Pip visits Jaggers, the lawyer, to verify what he has been 'told' by Magwitch, Jaggers cautions him: "'did you say 'told' or 'informed' [...] *told* would seem to imply verbal communication. You can't have verbal communication with a man in New South Wales, you know'" (Dickens 1965: 350). In truth, however, communication with convicts had existed from the outset and much of it was verbal. Convict voices could be heard, albeit only as echoes, through the numerous transportation ballads sung on city streets.[10] Returning political convicts gave individual voice to the experience of the multitude: over many decades, returned exiles like the Chartist leader John Frost went on speaking tours throughout the country, addressing mass audiences on the horrors inflicted by the imperial state. Even letters had an oral quality: addressed to groups of family and friends many were read aloud. Regularly dictated, rather than written, because of the illiteracy of correspondents, their form and structure reflected their spoken provenance. They were frequently colloquial in form and re-reading them even today it is almost possible to 'hear' their voices.[11] While this illusion of orality was partly the product of limited literacy, it may also have reflected the extent to which convict letters, like those of working-class emigrants, sought to simulate conversation in order to create a sense of presence and immediacy (Fitzpatrick 1994: 492-94).[12]

It was, over time, the limited ability of the imperial state to stifle or censor these channels of communication that eventually contributed to the system's demise. The sheer volume of the human flow helped to ensure that this was so. Over 160,000 men, women and children were transported to the Australian penal colonies, and tens of thousands of others went to other sites ranging from Bermuda to Gibraltar.[13] It was a rare neighbourhood, an exceptional community, which did not lose at least one of its members. Personal letters and news from exiled convicts were embedded within these wider collectivities. Neighbourhoods continued to talk of their exiles. When Mary Couard wrote to her husband John, she sought to anchor the truth of recent community chat. "My dear and loving husband", Mary began, "overpowered with grief I sit down to write to you",

> I have been most distracted since Tuesday last when a report was strongly circulated about this town that you was no more, which entirely distracted me. Grantham's wife [Grantham was also a transported convict] and his mother was at my house, on Wednesday morning, and said, she had got no such news in her letter [...]. (Couard 1831)

John Couard was remembered in other ways too: a black sailor, he had worked in the docks at Hull, and a petition was attached to his file, signed by numerous of his fellow workers which asserted: "we think Honorable Sir that he being a man of colour he has been [too] severely sentenced for his crimes were mere trifles" (Anon 1831). Recollections of other convicts lived on within the wider social networks of which they had been part: when Henry Mayhew, the famous nineteenth-century social investigator, visited a lodging house in London in November 1849, he discovered that the men and boys he interviewed there recalled the names of "no less than forty" of their companions who had been transported (Mayhew 1980: 107). Memories were long: letters seeking news of exiles continued to be sent for decades after transportation had ended. The latest of those that survive was postmarked 1908, sent by a Miss Hampson of Lancashire, seeking news of her uncle, Joseph Sudell, transported over half a century before (Hampson 1908).

When convicts thought of home they *too* rooted themselves within broad communities and expansive notions of family. Thomas Harrison was characteristic in writing for an extended audience, sending messages of "kind love" not only to his father and mother, but to "[my] Brothers and Sisters and my Granmother and my Hunkel and Ant and my cusons"(Harrison 1841). When convicts dreamt of return they also pre-figured it in collective terms: "I will stow you away my love and you shall be safe", Henry Dewson promised his convict counterpart Mary Ann Jones, setting out his plans for their escape from Van Diemen's Land, "and I will take you home to my friends in England in triumph" (Dewson 1833: 179-182). Other cultural forms tell similar stories. The arms of many convict women were, for example, decorated with long lists of initials, symbols of kith and kin, at the centre of which were tattooed their own names. Letters, tattoos, tokens – all these forms acted as lifelines, keeping convicts 'alive', defying the power of the state to fully achieve the social and civic death required by transportation.[14]

The folkloric memory of one English village tells the tale of how one woman waited for her convict husband and son to come home. Transported together, her son had been sentenced to seven years, the husband fourteen. As she grew more elderly, the woman continued to wait, sitting all day long outside her home on a chair positioned to face the direction in which *she* believed Australia lay and holding her husband's watch in her hand. Neither of the men ever came back (Thompson 1994: 201). Stories such as these survived into the twentieth century because they formed part of a collective counter-narrative, giving form to wider experiences of rupture and separation. Implicit in some such memories were various strands of political critique. "Monstrous hypocrites", George Loveless, the returned Tolpuddle Martyr, declared of the men who controlled the British state in the 1830s:

> To tear [...] their [...] countrymen from their native land, from the partners of their bosom, and from the arms of their young and helpless families [...] what hypocrisy and deceit is here manifested! (1838: 1, 16)

Loveless, like others, broadened his critique outwards, situating transportation amidst a range of other coercive experiences ranging from the workhouse to pauper emigration which were all too routinely familiar in many plebeian communities. In a pamphlet which achieved wide circulation he wrote:

> those hypocrites who [...] have solemnly pronounced 'What God hath joined together, let no man put asunder' are some of the first to separate man and wife, to send some to banishment, and others to the Poor-law prisons; to oppress the fatherless and [the] widow [. . .]. (Loveless 1838: 23)

"I am now here in my country", Chartist John Frost announced to a packed public meeting in 1856, "for the purpose of showing the good people of England what sort of rulers they have [...]" (Frost 1973: 11). "Never", Frost claimed, striking at the heart of notions of empire as civilising mission,

> in any age or country, has society existed in so depraved a state as I have witnessed in the penal colonies, produced, too, by laws not equalled in severity in any part of the civilized world.

When William Ashton returned from Van Diemen's Land he too related his experiences to a mass audience of working men and women. For theatrical effect he dressed for the occasion in the supposedly stigmatising, parti-coloured convict uniform. Empire, he argued, was the deeply flawed product of the 'blood-stained' British state. This, he concluded, was no surprise. "Look at the annals of [this] country", Ashton counselled,

> keep in mind the Manchester massacre [...] the butcherings at Derby and other places [...] bear in mind [...] the disgusting, cruel and deliberate sacrifice of life under the *New Poor Law Bill*, and then say are there not Englishmen to be found [...] to perpetrate any act that the fiendish heart of man can devise? [...] even English laws at home are not sufficient to protect the poor and weak from the tyrannical despotism of oppressors.

Going further than most, Ashton used the symbol of the transported convict to link the oppression of working people within the British Isles with the experiences of indigenous peoples under colonial rule. The natives of Van Diemen's Land, he told his audience, were also exiles, for they

> have been driven from the land that had hitherto afforded them subsistence, and which they considered as their own, and their children's inheritance [...] they [...] have been hunted like beasts of prey, and murdered by hundreds of those cruel invaders of the soil [...] in some instances, whole nations have been exterminated off the face of the earth [...] refrain from being a supporter of bloodshed, carnage, and violation [...]. (1839: 23)

Exile, Edward Said contends, is "fundamentally a discontinuous state of being" which is experienced "contrapuntally". Empire depended upon the maintenance of rigid divisions and fixed hierarchies between imperial and imperialised populations. Convicts, straddling the fault-lines between metropolis and colony, undermined such spatial and cultural boundaries. Their exilic contrapuntality helped to establish at least the germ of an idea that "there was only one worldly cultural space [...] in which to wage the struggle for liberation and inclusion" (2000: xxviii). "Our strategy", Arundhati Roy told the World Social Forum in Brazil in early 2003,

> should be not only to confront Empire but to lay siege to it. To deprive it of oxygen. To shame it. To mock it. With our art, our music, our literature, our stubbornness, our joy, our brilliance, our sheer relentlessness – and our ability to tell our own stories. (2003)

In their ballads, letters, poems, speeches, folklore, oral memories, and a range of other written, spoken and visual forms, convicts, and those they were forced to leave behind, relentlessly told their own stories throughout the period of transportation and beyond. Magwitch was but a reflection and re-affirmation of such forms.

Notes

[1] For discussion of some of the nineteenth-century novels in which returned convicts appear, see: Patrick Brantlinger, 1988: esp. 120-21, 124, and Lansbury, 1970: esp. 92-93, 100-101, 153.

[2] For a discussion of these issues, see Reid, forthcoming.

[3] See, for example, Davies, 1980: 190-214.

[4] On Dickens's changing attitudes to crime, see Collins, 1962.

[5] On Dickens's attitudes to slavery, see Chaudhuri, 1989: 3-10. On the Governor Eyre case and the politics of race in 1860s Britain, see Hall, 1992.

[6] As Said notes, "stories are at the heart of what explorers and novelists say about strange regions of the world [...]. The power to narrate, or to block other narratives from forming and emerging, is very important to culture and imperialism, and constitutes one of the main connections between them." (1993: xiii)

[7] Many studies of *Great Expectations* position Magwitch as Pip's alter ego. While readings of the novel clearly support this, *Great Expectations* can also be read productively against a much broader geo-political and cultural backdrop. As Brantlinger suggests, both Magwitch and John Edmunds, the returned convict in *Pickwick Papers*, represent a collective or *"sociological* return of the repressed" (Brantlinger 1988: 120-21). The problem of wholly individualistic readings of the Magwitch-Pip dynamic is that they tend to be part of a much wider reluctance to consider Dickens as a writer about empire. As Said notes, most readings of *Great Expectations* "situate it squarely within the metropolitan history of British fiction, whereas I believe that it belongs in a history both more inclusive and more dynamic than such interpretations allow" (1993: xii), Brantlinger's comments are also relevant here: "imperialism", he argues, "influenced not only the tradition of the adventure tale but the tradition of 'serious' domestic realism as well. Adventure and domesticity, romance and realism, are the seemingly opposite poles of a single system of discourse, the literary equivalents of imperial domination abroad and liberal reform at home. In the middle of the most serious domestic concerns, often in the most unlikely

texts, the Empire may intrude as a shadowy realm of escape, renewal, banishment, or return for characters who for one reason or another need to enter or exit from scenes of domestic conflict" (Brantlinger 1988: 12). The tendency to sideline empire in readings of Dickens often persists *even when* his novels are read more broadly. Thus, although, for example, Susan Walsh's fascinating critique of *Great Expectations* situates the novel within contemporary debates about gender and the mid-Victorian economy, it once again tends to downplay the imperial dimension not only of the novel itself but also of these debates (1993-94: 73-98). The insights offered by Brantlinger and Said are yet to be systematically applied to Dickens's studies.

[8] "I got all my patter", Ainsworth openly acknowledged, for *Rookwood*, his novel about Dick Turpin, from James Hardy Vaux's autobiographical account of convict transportation (quoted in Himmelfarb 1984: 422).

[9] The proprietorial and exploitative nature of this relationship is something which Peter Carey powerfully evokes in *Jack Maggs*, his recent reworking of *Great Expectations*. Jack, puzzled by author Tobias Oates's offer to remove the phantoms which haunt his soul, asks, "'what is it to you, Sir? It is my pain after all?' 'I am a naturalist', Oates [for whom read Dickens] replies, 'I wish to sketch the beast within you'. [...] Tobias Oates [...] gazed down at Jack Maggs. He would be the archaeologist of this mystery; he would be the surgeon of this soul" (Carey 1997: 46-47, 54).

[10] On the broader cultural meanings of transportation ballads within the working-class communities in which they were sung, see Eva 1996. Eva suggests that transportation ballads were simply one part of a broader cultural phenomenon and that exile was a more general "pervasive voice in [...] broadside songs". That this was so, he argues, "suggests a sense of dislocation and dispossession as a common condition; the voice of the stranger, the isolated outsider, was that of a shared, general structure of feeling" (1996: 194).

[11] As Tamsin O'Connor notes, the semi-literacy of convicts often meant that "oral and literary cultures collide(d) to reveal the *sound* of an exile's lament" in their letters and petitions (2001: 154).

[12] On the broader cultural functions of orality within epistolary discourse, see Altman 1982.

[13] It is impossible to know how many convicts ever returned. It seems likely, however, that the proportions were tiny. Political exiles were perhaps the main exception: both the Tolpuddle Martyrs and John Frost, the Chartist leader, were, for example, eventually brought home as a result of popular pressure. However, both legal and financial obstacles stood in the way of the majority of convicts. Those transported to the penal settlements in Eastern Australia required an Absolute Pardon to enable them to return within the period of their original sentence. Many of those sentenced to life received a Conditional Pardon. This gave them their freedom in the colonies but permanently excluded them from returning to Europe. To do so, just as to return before one's time was served, was, as Magwitch's story reveals, to invite a death sentence at worst or re-transportation under a new sentence at best. Time-expired convicts (those who had originally been sentenced to either 7 or 14 years) were, unlike lifers, able eventually to become 'free-by-servitude'. At this point they regained their full legal right to return. Nevertheless they still had to pay their own passages home. This was often impossible and was, in addition, harder for women than men. The latter were able, in some cases, to work their passages home by serving as crew on ships. Higher wages for male workers in the colonies presumably also

helped. Finally, by the time many convicts regained the right of return, they had become part of new social, economic and emotional networks within the colonies. Therefore, some probably stayed because to leave would have meant a new round of rupture and loss.

[14] On tattoos and tokens, see: Field & Millett (eds) 1998; Duffield & Maxwell-Stewart 2000: 118-35. On letters, see Reid 2003.

Bibliography

Altman, Janet Gurkin. 1982. *Epistolarity: Approaches to a Form.* Ohio: Columbus.
Anon. Petition. 8 May 1831. Archives Office of Tasmania, Colonial Secretary's Office 1/377/8578/31.
Ashton, William. 1839. *A Lecture on the Evils of Emigration and Transportation, Delivered at the Town-Hall, Sheffield, on July 23rd 1838.* Sheffield: J. Lisgard.
Brantlinger, Patrick. 1988. *Rule of Darkness: British Literature and Imperialism, 1830-1914.* Ithaca: Cornell University Press.
Carey, Peter. 1997. *Jack Maggs.* London: Faber & Faber.
Chaudhuri, Brahma. 1989. 'Dickens and the Question of Slavery' in *Dickens Quarterly* 6(1): 3-10.
Collins, Philip. 1962. *Dickens and Crime.* London: Macmillan.
Couard, Mary. 30 June 1831. Letter. Archives Office of Tasmania, Colonial Secretary's Office 1/377/8578/31.
Davies, Jennifer. 1980. 'The London Garotting Panic of 1862: A Moral Panic and the Creation of a Criminal Class in Mid-Victorian London' in V.A.C. Gatrell *et al* (eds) *Crime and the Law.* London: Europa: 190-214.
Dewson, Henry. 1833. Letter to Mary Ann Jones. 28 November. Archives Office of Tasmania, Colonial Secretary's Office 19/4. 179-82.
Dickens, Charles. 1965. *Great Expectations* 1860-61. Harmondsworth: Penguin.
Duffield, Ian and Hamish Maxwell-Stewart. 2000. 'Skin-Deep Devotions: Religious Tattoos and Convict Transportation to Australia' in Caplan, Jane (ed.) *Written on the Body: The Tattoo in European and American History.* London: Reaktion: 118-35.
Editorial. *Times.* 17 April 1850.
Eva, Philemon. 1996. *Popular Song and Social Identity in Victorian Manchester.* PhD thesis. University of Manchester.
Field, Michele and Timothy Millett (eds). 1998. *Convict Love Tokens: The Leaden Hearts the Convicts Left Behind.* Adelaide: Wakefield Press.
Fitzpatrick, David. 1994. *Oceans of Consolation: Personal Accounts of Irish Migration to Australia.* Cork: Cork University Press.
Frost, John. 1973. *The Horrors of Convict Life.* 1856. Hobart: Sullivan's Cove.
Hall, Catherine. 1992. *White, Male and Middle Class: Explorations in Feminism and History.* Oxford: Polity.
Hampson, J.A. 1908. Letter to the Governor of Tasmania, Australia. 12 November. Archives Office of Tasmania, Governor's Office 39/9.
Harrison, Thomas. 1841. Letter. April 25. Archives Office of Tasmania. Non-State Records 1493/2.

Himmelfarb, Gertrude. 1984. *The Idea of Poverty: England in the Early Industrial Age*. London: Faber & Faber.

Koditschek, Theodore. 1990. *Class Formation and Urban-Industrial Society: Bradford, 1750-1850*. Cambridge: Cambridge University Press.

Lansbury, Coral. 1970. *Arcady in Australia: The Evocation of Australia in Nineteenth-Century English Literature*. Carlton, Victoria: Melbourne University Press.

Loveless, George. 1838. *The Victims of Whiggery. A Statement of the Persecutions Experienced by the Dorchester Labourers; with a Report of their Trial; also a Description of Van Diemen's Land and Reflections upon the System of Transportation*. London: Cleave.

Mayhew, Henry. 1980. 'Letter V, 2 November 1849' in *The Morning Chronicle Survey of Labour and the Poor: The Metropolitan Districts, Volume 1*. Sussex: Caliban: 96-108.

O'Connor, Tamsin. 2001. 'Raising Lazarus' in Frost, Lucy and Hamish Maxwell-Stewart (eds) *Chain Letters: Narrating Convict Lives*. Carlton, Victoria: Melbourne University Press: 148-161.

'P'. 1852. Letter. *Times*, 11 September.

Reid, Kirsty (forthcoming). *Gender, Crime and Empire: Convict Women and Colonial Australia*. Manchester: Manchester University Press.

- - -. 2003. 'Letters from Exile: Communication and the Convict Diaspora'. Paper presented at *The Convicts Research Workshop* (University of Leicester, December 2003).

Rose, Jonathan. 2001. *The Intellectual Life of the British Working Classes*. New Haven: Yale University Press.

Roy, Arundhati. 2003. 'Confronting Empire'. Speech given at the *World Social Forum* (Porto Alegre, Brazil, 28 January). On line at: www.peacewomen.org/resources/voices/declar/arundhati.html (consulted 30.03.2004).

Said, Edward. 1993. *Culture and Imperialism*. London: Chatto & Windus.

- - -. 2000. *Reflections on Exile and other Essays*. Cambridge, Mass.: Harvard University Press.

Thompson, E.P. 1994. 'Sold Like a Sheep' in his *Persons and Polemics*. London: Merlin Press: 193-201.

Walsh, Susan. 1993-94. 'Bodies of Capital: *Great Expectations* and the Climacteric Economy' in *Victorian Studies* 37: 73-98.

10

Exile at the Edges of Empire: Contemporary Writing in Portuguese

Isabel Moutinho

Isabel Moutinho was born and educated in Lisbon, Portugal, and moved to Australia some twenty years ago, for reasons of love rather than exile. Now lecturer in Spanish and Portuguese in the School of Historical and European Studies, La Trobe University, Australia, her main research area is contemporary Portuguese literature, particularly novels dealing with the colonial wars in Africa. She is co-editor of a recent volume, *The Paths of Multiculturalism* (2000).

In this paper, she refers to several forms of enforced displacement of people undertaken in the name of the former Portuguese Empire. These range from the enslavement and transportation of indigenous peoples to the deportation to occupied territories of convicts and others who were burdensome in the metropolis, to, in the Empire's final years, the exile of opponents of the Salazar regime to its colonies. Specifically, she examines three contemporary narratives dealing with exile to Portugal's (former) overseas colonies, two by Portuguese novelists and one by a Timorese author living in Portugal and writing in Portuguese. Both Alexandre Pinheiro Torres's *A Nau de Quixibá* (published in 1977, but written in the 1950s) and Mário Cláudio's *Oríon* (2003) are set in São Tomé and Príncipe. Luís Cardoso's *Crónica de Uma Travessia* (1997) is set in Timor and Portugal. The central character of *A Nau de Quixibá* was sent to São Tomé as a colonial administrator and, while severely alienated, rejects any feeling of nostalgia for his homeland because of his opposition to the Salazar regime and its colonial policies. *Oríon* is an historical novel with a strong metaphorical dimension which treats the lives of a handful of the 200 Jewish children forcibly transported from Portugal to São Tomé in the 1490s, several of whom later became rich from buying and selling slaves. *Crónica de Uma Travessia* recounts the biography of the author's father, a Timorese nurse posted to an island off the main island of Timor, in the context of a wider treatment of political exile by the Portuguese authorities – within the colony, from colony to colony, and from the metropolis to the colony. The paper concludes with a discussion of language issues associated with the writing and publishing of colonial exile narrative.

The basic goals of colonialism — namely enforcing occupation, legitimising political sovereignty, and ensuring the economic exploitation of a territory or state by a foreign country — have been well served over the centuries by regimes which have used their colonies as dumping grounds for citizens who have become burdensome in one way or another to their central government. Portugal, with its long colonial history, is no exception to this coincidence of interests between colonialism and deportation. Portuguese literature, like so many others in the European heritage, is rich in poetry and prose dealing with exile, both in the form of official expulsion from one's homeland with interdiction to return and in the less technical sense of necessary or voluntary expatriation. Nevertheless, the conjunction between exile and colonialism as late as the second half of the twentieth century, often depicted in contemporary literature in Portuguese, makes for a special case within European culture.[1]

Portuguese literature of exile is, of course, not always connected with colonialism,[2] or with the imperial venture at its origin, but this is certainly a capital element in it. Such a combination is not surprising in the case of a country that built its national identity around the experience of voyaging and discovering new lands. Historically, the voyaging of the explorer always implied a feeling of inevitable (though not necessarily undesired) removal from one's home country, with the attendant yearning for the absent homeland. Moreover, the canonical texts of Portuguese maritime history bear witness to the fact that the crown used convicts as the basis for its earliest imperial efforts. So, for example, Camões writes in *The Lusiads* of the Portuguese fleet commander's sending a convict ashore in Calicut, upon arrival in India, in 1498, to obtain much needed information. So, too, does Pêro Vaz de Caminha, in his *Letter* to King Manuel about the finding of Brazil, refer to convicts being left behind for the same purpose of acquisition of knowledge, and consequently power, for the Portuguese authorities. On a more personal note, at the end of the same *Letter*, Caminha begs the King to recall his son-in-law from exile in São Tomé, as a reward for the scribe's good services.[3] But of the feelings of such exiles at the beginnings of empire we know nothing, nor indeed of the despair of those dragged into the most extreme form of exile, not usually included in this category, that of the slaves transported from continental Africa to colonial plantations in Brazil, in Cape Verde, or in São Tomé and Príncipe, islands in the Gulf of Guinea. These two groups, which nowadays often constitute the research focus of historiography, have previously been the most forgotten, for it was not until recent times that literature began to turn its attention to the subjectivity of history's underlings.[4]

Later on, as the newly occupied territories progressively became colonies, the preservation of which turned into an obsession of the Portuguese dictatorship of the middle decades of the twentieth century, the country's literature often reflected the exile experiences of yet another social group: those of twentieth-century opponents of colonialism and of the regime that sustained it well into the mid-1970s despite all the winds of change blowing in Africa.

Contemporary fiction in Portuguese alludes to or focuses on various types of exile, directly or indirectly related to colonialism. These include: self-imposed removal from Portugal in the case of authors who experienced unbearable ideological alienation in their own country; actual political banishment of opponents to Salazar's *Estado Novo* and its colonial policies; the special case of the Portuguese military who fought in the colonial wars and often experienced their conscription to Africa as a deportation; and even various forms of social ostracism perceived as an exile imposed on those who did not conform to the regime's internal and colonial policies.

This study examines three contemporary narratives dealing with exile to Portugal's former overseas colonies, two by Portuguese novelists and one by a Timorese author living in Portugal and writing in Portuguese. Both Alexandre Pinheiro Torres's *A Nau de Quixibá* (1977) and Mário Cláudio's *Oríon* (2003) are set in São Tomé and Príncipe. Luís Cardoso's *Crónica de Uma Travessia* (1997) is set in Timor and Portugal. Tempting as it would be to compare these with a much larger corpus to include also novels of exile set in the heart of Portugal's African empire (Angola and Mozambique), this study concentrates only on narratives set at the very edges of the empire, where the feelings of exile and abandonment are strongest as a consequence of geographical isolation.

Alexandre Pinheiro Torres's *A Nau de Quixibá* (The Quixibá Caravel) was written in 1957 but not published until twenty years later. The long gap between composition date and publication date is indicative of the severity of censorship during the Salazar regime. The book appeared only after the overthrow of the dictatorship, which opened the way to the independence of the former colonies. It is an autobiographical novel, dedicated to the memory of the author's father, whose life it retraces, with the name of the textual author and first-person narrator coinciding with that of the book's empirical author. In *A Nau de Quixibá*, the 17-year old Alexandre, who lives in Portugal with his mother and conservative family, visits his outspokenly anti-Salazarist father, who lives in semi-exile in São Tomé, in 1939. The Portuguese side of the family clearly supports the values of Salazar's regime which considered the colonies to be an inseparable part of Portugal, a right which the country had earned, even a gift from God.

The father's position as a semi-exile is always ambiguous in the novel. Having arrived in the Portuguese colony of São Tomé many years before with his wife and family, he oversees the historical Roça de Monte Café, still an active cocoa plantation. His wife and children have long left him behind and resumed their lives in Portugal. Nevertheless, both he himself and his whole family in Portugal, who thoroughly disapprove of his life, constantly speak of his exile - or Deportation with a capital D, as he calls it. The capital D is important because the father explicitly opposes it to the capital S of everything he hates: the S for Salazar and the S for *saudade*, a Portuguese word with multiple meanings, namely homesickness, nostalgia, and yearning for lost happiness. When the son asks him if he does not feel *saudade*, meaning simply homesickness for family and home in Portugal, the reply is terse: "A saudade [...] é património nacional. [...]. Não: a saudade até se escreve hoje com S grande" (Torres 1977: 37; '*saudade* is the national heritage... What is more: *saudade* is even written with a capital S nowadays', my translation throughout).

The explanation that follows makes the connection between *saudade* (nostalgia) and imperialism clearer, and warns of the danger the father sees for his son's generation of growing up with nostalgia as a national value:

> ... para já, filiaram-te na Saudade do Império [...]. A Saudade, com S grande, sempre com S grande, é a base teórica do nosso Nacional-Socialismo. A Saudade dá a instituição política *saudosa*, o Estado *saudoso*. Saudoso de quê? Do Passado, é claro. E também do Futuro [...]. Mas um Futuro que reedifique o Passado, o reconstrua. (Torres 1977: 38)

> ... to begin with, they enlisted you in the Nostalgia of Empire [...]. Nostalgia with a capital N, always with a capital N, is the theoretical basis for our National-Socialism. Nostalgia produces the *nostalgic* political institution, the *nostalgic* State. Nostalgic for what? For the Past, of course. And also for the Future [...]. But a Future that re-edifies, that reconstructs the Past.[5]

Maria Alzira Seixo writes of exile "as a division felt by the consciousness of the writer concerning space or time," indeed space *and* time, which always implies "developing a specific notion of *parallel time* that opposes the past and the present" (Seixo 2001: 72 and 68). There is no doubt that political militancy in an exile situation is normally associated with an overcoming of adversities suffered in the past, and a living for the present, which amounts to making positive choices for the future. However, in *A Nau de Quixibá*, the father's perception of Portugal's time as being linked to the intoxicating notion of Empire is more complex than a simple rejection of the past, because it corresponds to the evaluation of a specific Portuguese historical conjuncture. The father views this as arrested in time, not only anchored in the past but, worse still, anachronistically prolonged into a present that denies, even now, any possibility of change for the future. This is, no doubt, the reason why this outspoken "anti-monarchist [...], Jacobin, republican, anarchist" ("antimonárquico [...], jacobino, republicano, anarquista"; Torres: 1977: 32) chooses or accepts to remain in the colony in self-imposed exile, because there is no alternative. Even militancy, either in the colony or in the metropolis, ceases to make sense when there is no space for him in a home country that persists in looking backwards in time. Typically, the narrative of exile emphasises a sense of loss and dispossession, but not so for this man, because he would feel even more displaced and dispossessed in a country that is living outside the normal rules of time. Hence his abhorrence of any kind of nostalgia – including the personal homesickness he refuses to feel, as it is too dangerously close to political nostalgia for empire. For this man there is no dream of homecoming, only that need for impassioned raging that Dylan Thomas so vehemently encouraged in his father. The only consolation left for him must be "the fact that the act of withdrawal, perceived as a mode of rejection of the prevailing norms, [is] by nature an act of subversion" (Lahiri 2001: 3).

This time without a future is the borrowed time of Portuguese colonialism in the mid-twentieth-century, as the allegory of the father's obsession with shipwreck history makes abundantly clear. The pictures of wrecked ships, which fill his house and initially puzzle his son, are in fact the visual representation of the father's critique of the regime's imperial delusions and persistence in sustaining a colonialism more and more out of date and untenable. The Empire came with the voyages of the fifteenth- and sixteenth-century caravels, the countless wrecks of which were already then a warning of the precariousness of the enterprise. But five centuries later the regime persists in its blindness, refusing to see the signs of a time inexorably past. So, even Salazar's name, beginning with the S of *saudade*, represents a nostalgia that must, in the end, be read as a morbid attachment to the past.

Nevertheless, this novel of semi-exile, with its recognition of impotence in the face of a regime that institutes the past as a rule for the future, is not devoid of hope, because the son's visit to São Tomé ends with his conversion to the father's opposition to the regime. This deep change is again symbolised by a shipwreck: father and son visit the remnants of a caravel wrecked on the adjacent islet of Quixibá, which gives the book its title. There the son throws a stone, which accidentally sinks the carcass that has withstood for centuries. The torch is thus handed on, as it were, and the son will continue the father's struggle, so that we can say with Antonio Skármeta, about one of his own exiled characters: 'este hombre que viene de la derrota no es un derrotado' (Délano 1978: 3; 'this man, who comes from a background of defeat, is not defeated', my translation).

Mário Cláudio's *Oríon*, published in early 2003, is a striking example of a novel about exile in the service of colonialism. It deals with the lives of a group of Jewish children forcibly transported to the archipelago of São Tomé and Príncipe, by order of the Portuguese King John II in the 1490s. The first-person narrator, one of about two hundred children thus exiled to these unhealthy islands, is supremely conscious of his Jewish origins as well as of the similarities between his personal fate and that of his race, the quintessential victims of mass deportation over more than two-and-a-half millennia. The novel is based on historical, though little documented, events. As São Tomé and Príncipe were uninhabited at the time of discovery, the peopling of the islands became the immediate priority; King John II did indeed arrange for Captain Álvaro Caminha to take with him not only a large number of convicts, but also the children of the so-called Portuguese Jews. The latter had taken refuge in Portugal after their expulsion from Spain, but having overstayed their period of grace in Portugal, they had become subject to slavery.[6]

However, the novel is not primarily historical but metaphorical. Once the basic historical situation is set, the narrator, the most contemplative of the seven children whose lives the book explores, concentrates on the universal fear of the unknown and the yearning for family love and past happiness forever lost, as well as on the excesses which the tropical environment induces these children to indulge in as they grow up. The book raises some disturbing questions: several of these children (Raquel, Caim, Séfora, and in particular Jairo), who all come from the persecuted Jewish minority, soon become persecutors themselves once they adapt to São Tomé's colonial society. Abel (the narrator) and Raquel, his first wife, both buy slaves and become wealthy managers of a sugar-cane plantation. Caim even betrays the leader of the *quilombo*, the king of the runaway slaves who first saved his life. Worst of all, Jairo grows filthy rich as a slave trader and falls into the most abject personal decadence and sexual promiscuity.

Is this a parable referring to present day developments in the conflict between Israelis and Arabs, in which Israeli Jews, historically so subject to persecution themselves, have become the persecutors of the Palestinians? Is it to be viewed rather as a consequence of African excess? Or is it, as one suspects, an allegory of the evils of colonialism? These children were, after all, exiled in the name of the same colonialism which was to thrive on the traffic of slaves and on cruel repression of indigenous populations who rebelled in vain against the imposition of foreign rule. The previously uninhabited island of São Tomé came to be governed and exploited under the same rule as other Portuguese colonies, with slave labour imported from other African regions to establish and work on vast colonial plantations. It would be easy to add to this list of evils the image of the virile metropolis raping the colonised territories, viewed as feminine and weak, which feminist cultural criticism has developed in the wake of Edward Said's *Orientalism*.[7] Indeed, the story of at least one of these Jewish children exiled to São Tomé would support this reading: Débora, raped by the colony's judge, Gonçalo Anes, becomes a prostitute and loses her sanity. Insanity, as Fanon's pioneering work hauntingly exposed, is a common pathological consequence of the colonial encounter. Débora's story, tied as it is with that of one of the few male, Portuguese, historical figures diegetically included in the novel, can thus be seen as a figuration of the rape of the colony itself (though she is not, in fact, a native). But we must not forget that at least two other Jewish young women in this novel, Raquel and Séfora, achieve positions of power within the colony, thereby illustrating women's aptitude both in exile and in the colonial context, when other elements are at stake.

Finally we must look at Perpétua, the only non-Jewish character of the central group, an African slave acquired by Abel, who becomes his constant companion after his wife's death. Whereas all the Jewish children have Biblical names with specific symbolic connotations,

Perpétua has a Catholic saint's name, which already represents the violation of her African identity and religion as a consequence of her enslavement in the colonial plantations. Unlike the Jewish children who either temporarily or more lastingly manage to make a mark in the colonial life of São Tomé and Príncipe, Perpétua remains (perpetually) a slave – Abel's companion, but still a slave, because she dies before manumission. Abel, the exiled Jew, and Perpétua, the African slave, are the meditative characters in this novel of exile and colonialism. Abel, now an old man, writes the stories of the other children, who all pursued active lives. He himself, however, having been a successful plantation manager, has lost everything and prefers to dwell on the past and on his misfortunes. This is a characteristic he shares with Perpétua, who obsessively repeats the tale of her people's disempowerment and enslavement by the European invaders. Abel feels compelled to write this, his book of memoirs, with his written narrative corresponding to Perpétua's oral one, often told and retold. But each finds little therapeutic value, he in his writing and she in her telling: "estava Perpétua muito mais interessada em me guardar como ouvinte do seu fado do que em escutar episódios dos infortúnios que eu padecia" (Claudio 2003: 91; "Perpétua was much more interested in keeping me listening to the story of her fate than in listening to an account of the misfortunes I suffered"). Unfortunately for both characters, this reveals an inability to overcome the past, with both remaining anchored in their self-pity and implicitly accepting exile as a defeat.

Appropriately, then, the book has a circular structure: distant past (departure from Lisbon, arrival in São Tomé) – more recent past (achievements of fellow exiles) – and a present (the moment of remembering and writing) which inevitably leads back to the traumatic memory of the distant past. The act of telling, and especially the act of writing (which gives any narrator a demiurgic power similar to God's), might have become a way of overcoming grief, of engaging with a new environment and finding a positive side in the experience of the new world. But that is not the path chosen by either Abel or Perpétua. Both are irremediably lost in the contemplation of their misfortunes, 'perpetuating' them into the present. Tellingly, in the penultimate chapter, the once again repeated recollection of the moment of departure from Lisbon to exile in São Tomé is now written in the present tense, so that the past becomes present even grammatically, completely obliterating the possibility of any real life in the present.[8] This fictional engulfing of the present by the past is, in the end, in keeping with a common perception of Jewish history. In the unfolding of Abel's experience of deportation, the individual story merges into the collective history of the Jews, seen as the perennial victims of exile.

Unlike *A Nau de Quixibá* and *Oríon*, Luís Cardoso's *Crónica de Uma Travessia* (Chronicle of a Crossing) is not primarily fictional. Maria Luísa Leal sees the book as representative of a tendency in postcolonial prose, that of the "novel 'contaminated' by other registers, namely the non-fictional, which is to be found in the *'récit de vie'*" ("um romance 'contaminado' por outros registos, nomeadamente o não ficcional que se encontra no *'récit de vie'*", Leal 2001: 5). The book reads, above all (initially), as a biographical account of the life of the author's father (not unlike *A Nau de Quixibá*), progressively turning into an *Erziehungsroman* of sorts, becoming also a powerful memoir of Timor's recent history.

There are, in fact, many crossings in this narrative, real and metaphorical: that of the author's family from the main island of Timor to the smaller one of Ataúro; the author's much longer crossing to Portugal, where he goes to further his education and ends up redefining his identity; and finally, that of his parents to the mother-country, in retirement. But the weightier crossing is fundamentally the son's journey from following his father's firm belief in living by the rules and dying under the shadow of the Portuguese flag (*mate-bandera-hum*, in the Tetum expression), to his slow awakening to the cause of political independence for Timor. With this, the son's personal journey of discovery, comes also that of his fellow Timorese, caught in the Indonesian invasion which followed Portugal's withdrawal from its former colony. For them there were difficult choices to make: siding with the ex-coloniser, accepting Indonesian annexation, or fighting for the independence which Timor finally obtained four years after the publication of this book.

Nor is *Crónica de Uma Travessia* a narrative of exile proper. Nevertheless, the reality of political exile in three varieties — namely within the colony itself, from colony to colony, and from the metropolis to the colony — is often mentioned in the book's pages and in such a casual manner that we realise what a common occurrence it is. The first chapter sets the scene. The author's father, a trained nurse, is considered exiled by his profession ("desterrado pela profissão", Cardoso 1997: 20), when he is posted to the island of Ataúro. This, we learn during the family's sea crossing, is a sort of floating prison for all exiles, surrounded by shark-infested waters. On the same boat that carries the family over to Ataúro, there is a real exile, the prisoner Simão, escorted by a *cipaio* (a member of the 'native' police).[9] The convict Simão is Timorese, from the main island, but the connection between colonialism and exile becomes more evident in the reference to the origin of his 'native' policeman, a descendant of Mozambican exiles who realises that he too is being exiled to Ataúro. This implies that the common colonial ruler has the power to exile its subjects from one colony to another, but also, more disturbingly, that all 'natives' from the various colonies are in fact indistinguishable in the eyes of the metropolis, reduced to a common denominator as 'natives'. The secret purpose of this transportation between colonies is revealed: "Embora as autoridades considerassem que um nativo era um bom guarda de outro [...]. Assim se foram livrando também deles aos poucos" (Cardoso 1997: 32; "The authorities [...] [knew] that, when trained for the purpose, one native could be used to guard another [...]. And thus they gradually got rid of them as well", 2000: 23).

Exiles come to Timor from other Portuguese colonies as well: there is an exile from Macau ("um desterrado macaísta", 1997: 81), and, on the island of Ataúro, Mário Lopes, originally exiled from São Tomé and Príncipe, now runs a prosperous business (1997: 33). Success, then, is within the reach of those banished to Timor; the once deported shop-owner is not even barred from some degree of political activity, dealing in "contrabando de livros e ideias subversivas" (1997: 34; "he smuggled books and subversive ideas", 2000: 26), but above all, perorating at funerals, "culpabilizando as autoridades pelos enterrados e desterrados" (1997: 34; "placing the blame fairly and squarely on the authorities for those banished by death or exile", 2000: 26).

No secret is made of the fact that the colony is used for the specific purpose of dumping convicts. Of Timor's Portuguese governor himself (and we must not forget that these are historical, not fictional, figures) we are told:

> Tinha por missão e vontade arrancar os Timorenses e Timor do esquecimento a que fora devotado durante longos anos, então com a finalidade de ser um simples depósito de agentes subversivos. (1997: 78)

> His mission and his desire was to drag Timor and the Timorese out of its oblivion as a dumping ground for subversives. (2000: 71)

Indeed, some of the now internationally known figures of Timor's transition to independence are the children of exiles from the metropolis. Mário Carrascalão, a prominent politician whose name the tragic news of Indonesian massacres in Timor made internationally known, is presented in the book as the son of a man from the South of Portugal, deported to Timor for political activities against the Salazar regime (1997: 83). As a political exile on the island of Ataúro, he is said to have had a very difficult life (1997: 103). But not only did he eventually succeed in making good in Timor as "a prosperous coffee-grower" (2000: 78; "agricultor próspero de café", 1997: 83); he even managed to redeem himself in the eyes of the colonial authorities: "posteriormente recuperado pelas autoridades para funções de presidente da Câmara Municipal de Díli" (1997: 83; "later rehabilitated by the powers-that-be and made the President of the town council in Díli", 2000: 78). José Ramos-Horta, whom Luís Cardoso describes as already then "dotado dum espírito subversivo" (1997: 102; "endowed with a naturally subversive turn of mind", 2000: 97), went to study in Díli, "continuando a exercitar o seu génio de revoltado, herdado do pai, que fora desterrado para Timor por actos anti-salazaristas" (1997: 102; "where he continued to exercise the genius for revolt inherited from his father, who had been exiled to Timor for anti-Salazar activities", 2000: 98). Exiles, then, come to Timor from Mozambique, Angola, Macau, São Tomé, and Príncipe, as well as from Portugal, turning the territory into a multicultural melting pot, which is simultaneously and ironically a hotbed for political insurgency.

Developments in recent Timorese history, from colony to (eventually) independent nation, are thus inextricably bound up with the fact that Timor was used for years and years as a dumping ground for political exiles, especially from Portugal, in that so many of the new country's politicians are the children of deported Portuguese anti-colonialists. Ironically, even those who adopted a pro-Indonesian position during the Indonesian occupation can be seen as deriving their stance from Timor's historical association with colonial exile: Osório Soares, also a public figure, well-known as a pro-Indonesian activist, would distribute "panfletos pró-indonésios [...] como uma forma de se vingar das autoridades coloniais que desterraram o seu tio para os Açores" (1997: 106; "pro-Indonesian leaflets [...] as a way of avenging himself on the colonial authorities for exiling his uncle to the Azores"; 2000: 102). The weapon then can cut both ways, but it clearly shows that there are deep historical reasons why the colony was to feel so profoundly betrayed by a mother-country that eventually granted it independence but behaved rather as a neglectful step-mother: "Mas a mãe-pátria fora sempre distraída com Timor e desta vez tinha o comportamento duma madastra [sic: madrasta]" (1997: 84; "Always neglectful of her maternal responsibilities to Timor, Portugal at this time behaved like a wicked step-mother", 2000: 79).

The author's father, originally from the most rebellious region of Timor (remembered for the Manufahi rebellion against colonial rule), but who was trained in a missionary school and deeply acculturated, is, in the end, the most tragic figure of exile in the book. Indeed, the story of his life stands metonymically for the fate of a people truly exiled from their own sense of identity, estranged from any collective cultural coherence, by centuries of Portuguese colonialism.

*

A final word is due here about the question of language in these narratives of colonial exile. The loss of the mother-tongue, with its concomitant sense of cultural disorientation and deprivation, is a constant element of all literature of exile, which, as a single example, David Malouf has made so palpable to all who have read *An Imaginary Life*. This question, however, partly loses significance in the case of narratives dealing with exile to the edges of a colonial empire, where one common language is — at least officially — in existence. All the characters in these books could, in principle, have continued to speak Portuguese in the remote colonies. In the case of *A Nau de Quixibá*, all characters, being Portuguese by birth and education, would naturally have spoken Portuguese in São Tomé and Príncipe. In *Oríon*, the question is easily brushed aside: if this were history rather than literature, neither the so-called 'Portuguese' Jews (more likely Sephardi speakers of Ladino), nor certainly the African slaves, would necessarily have spoken any Portuguese. But the fiction of exile in the Portuguese colony makes the situation plausible in a literary sense as the few dialogues presented are between people exiled while they were children growing up in Portugal, where they would have learned to speak Portuguese. As to the narration itself, since both novels are by Portuguese authors, the language of narration is naturally Portuguese.

Nevertheless, in postcolonial writing, the matter of estrangement from the mother-tongue acquires special importance. So it is that in *Crónica de Uma Travessia* Luís Cardoso explores the issue discreetly. At the time he wrote this book, the author was living in Portugal, in the ambiguous position of having been born in a distant island which was no longer the Portuguese colony it had been for centuries, nor yet an independent country. But the book reveals aspirations that are common in literatures of postcolonial countries – such as the vindication of a distinct cultural identity – and this is, no doubt, the reason why the issue of the coexistence of several languages gains weight in it. The narrator tells us of each character's different linguistic origins, demarcating Timor as a separate, multilingual entity, thus revealing the "conscience de la multiplicité des langues, expérience d'une manière d'éclatement du discours" which Alain Ricard identifies in other postcolonial literatures (Ricard 1995: 6). But the book is written for a Portuguese-reading public, so that Tetum (and other) expressions used in it appear translated in brief footnotes. That is, the book must be written in Portuguese for practical reasons: the need to be understood, the need to find a publisher, even the fact that the author was educated in Portuguese and seems to have chosen (for the moment) Portugal as his country of residence. But that does not mean that he is prepared to abrogate his right to a different linguistic reality, which still informs his uneasy sense of identity.[10] The claim is made already in the subtitle of the book: *A Época do Ai-Dik-Funam*, which a Portuguese reader can only understand in the very last line of the narrative, and even then only partially. (A footnote in the Portuguese edition explains one of the Tetum words, *Funam*, also giving the botanical name for the untranslated tree-name. The English edition gives a complete translation: "In the season when the coral tree flowers"; Cardoso 2000: 152).

Thematically, narratives of exile are of necessity built upon an axis of physical displacement and cultural dislocation, frequently leading to a questioning of origins and sense of self. Structurally, they almost always intertwine two spatial and two temporal paradigms: the place of origin versus the place of exile, the past versus the present. It is common for narratives of exile to stress situations of hardship and dispossession. However, a shifting emphasis on either of the two locations as well as a preference for the past or the present moment (even looking forward to the future) can determine whether the experience of exile is valued negatively or positively.

The three narratives here examined share a setting at the edges of empire, but each evaluates exile on a different scale. In *Orion*, the memory of the past continues to oppress the narrator, thus preventing any positive overcoming of the deportation. On the contrary, in *A Nau de Quixibá*, the past is all but annulled by the narrator's complete rejection of its memory and any kind of nostalgia: political militancy is not possible for him in exile, but his undeterred dissidence allows for a viewing of exile in the colony as a means of maintaining ideological coherence. In *Crónica de Uma Travessia*, the memory of the past functions precisely as a tool for redefining an identity alienated by the experience of colonialism and, as such, as a springboard for the future. In the early colonial setting, then, and without a political conscience (*Oríon*), the experience of exile is destructive and morally ruinous. In the later colonial settings, however, both *A Nau de Quixibá* and *Travessia* underline the importance of political commitment to a positive evaluation of exile.

Notes

[1] For an introduction to related questions within African literature, see Carvalho, 2001.

[2] Maria Alzira Seixo, 2001, also includes the experience of Portuguese economic migration to richer European countries in her analysis, given the similarities in the feelings of displacement and yearning for return to the home country.

[3] For the text of the letter in Portuguese and English and a discussion of its significance, see: www.auburn.edu/~downejm/sp/cpcmain.htm (consulted 20.03.2004).

[4] For a fascinating account of early colonial circumstance in Luanda, Angola, through the eyes of a slave, see the novel by Angolan writer Pepetela, *A Gloriosa Família*, (Lisbon: Dom Quixote, 1998).

[5] I choose to translate ṣaudade as 'ṇostalgia' because both the N and the S appear in National-Socialism, and the N is in the ṇau (caravel) of the title, as much as the S is in the ṣhipwrecks (ṇaufrágios) mentioned further below.

[6] João de Barros. 1946. *Décadas*, Livro I, Selecção, prefácio e notas de Antonio Baiao. Lisbon: Sa da Costa. See also *Enciclopédia Luso-Brasileira de Cultura* (Lisbon: Verbo, n.d.), 'Judaísmo', 'Judeus em Portugal', and 'São Tomé e Príncipe'.

[7] See, for example, Gayatri C. Spivak. 1985. 'Three Women's Texts and a Critique of Imperialism' in *Critical Inquiry* 12(1), reprinted in Warhol, Robyn R. and Diane Price Herndl, (eds). *Feminisms: An Anthology of Literary Theory and Criticism* (New Brunswick, NJ: Rutgers University Press: 1997): 896-912.

[8] The seventh Jewish child must here be briefly mentioned: Benjamim, a Messianic, mystical character, more magical than real, from whom all others expect salvation. The yearning for his return is remarkably similar to the details of the Portuguese Sebastian myth. The persistent hope for the return of the lost King Sebastian as for that of the disappeared Benjamim, each expected to come back to redeem the Portuguese and the Jewish people respectively, is likewise indicative of a morbid attachment to the past.

[9] Standard Portuguese *sipaio*, English 'sepoy', is normally a person of Indian origin.

[10] It is worth mentioning in passing the example of another postcolonial writer in the Portuguese language, the Angolan José Luandino Vieira: his first book, *Luuanda*, was initially published with a glossary of Kimbundo words used in the text, subsequent editions of the same book dispensed with the glossary, and later, for example in his *Nós, Os de Makulusu*, Kimbundo phrases and sentences appear interspersed in the Portuguese text without any explanation at all, a sign that the author has reached full postcolonial confidence. Similarly, Luís Cardoso no longer includes translations of Tetum or other Timorese expressions in his second book, *Olhos de Coruja, Olhos de Gato Bravo* (2001), thus subtly disempowering readers who have no knowledge of Timor's own languages.

Bibliography

Cardoso, Luis. 1997. *Crónica de Uma Travessia. A Época do Ai-Dik-Funam*, Lisbon: Dom Quixote, translated by Margaret Jull Costa, with a foreword by Jill Jolliffe, as *The Crossing. A Story of East Timor*. London: Granta Books, 2000.

- - - . 2001. *Olhos de Coruja, Olhos de Gato Bravo.* Lisbon: Dom Quixote.

Carvalho, Alberto. 2001. 'Travel and Metaphors of Exile in African Literature in Portuguese' in Lahiri, (2001): 76-85.

Cláudio, Mario. 2003. *Oríon*. Lisbon: Dom Quixote.

Délano, Poli. 1978. 'Antonio Skármeta, un exilio creativo' in *La Semana de Bellas Artes* (México) 35: 3. London: Granta Books.

Lahiri, Sharmistha. 2001. 'Introduction' in her *Inhabiting the Other. Essays on Literature and Exile*. New Delhi: Aryan Books International: 2-15.

Leal, Maria Luísa. 2004. 'Autobiografia e memória em espaços literários pós-coloniais'. Actas do *IV Congresso da Associação Portuguesa de Literatura Comparada* (University of Évora, May 2001). Online at: www.eventos.uevora.pt/comparada (consulted 30.06.2004).

Malouf, David. 1978. *An Imaginary Life*. London: Chatto and Windus.

Ricard, Alain. 1995. *Littératures d'Afrique noire*. Paris: Karthala.

Seixo, Maria Alzira, John Noyes, Graça Abreu and Isabel Moutinho (eds). 2000. *The Paths of Multiculturalism*. Lisbon: Cosmos.

- - - . 2001. 'Faces of Exile in Portuguese Literature' in Lahiri (2001): 68-75.

Torres, Alexandre Pinheiro. 1989. *A Nau de Quixibá*. 2nd edition. Lisbon: Caminho.

11

Audio Installation with Sculptural Images 'Thought Exiled from the Tongue'

Dolleen Manning

A First Nations Canadian scholar and artist of the Anishinaabeg Ojibwe people, Dolleen Manning grew up in an off-reserve context in South Western Ontario with English as her first language, but close to an older generation of Ojibwe speakers. Having studied fine arts at both the University of Windsor and Simon Fraser University, she is now a graduate student in the Centre for the Study of Theory and Criticism at the University of Western Ontario.

Her presentation on the DVD consists of a multi-layered sound recording of the voices of her mother Rose Manning and singer Cody Cardinal from Sad Lake Alberta coupled with a slowly changing sequence of eleven photographs of Rose, Dolleen, and a number of Dolleen's artworks. The two voices, speaking in English and Ojibwe, build into a sensuous chorus of indistinguishable utterances. Evidence of grappling with articulation is subtly woven into the soundscape in the hesitation and pauses of the speaker. This work explores the notion of exile within one's own homeland and the schizophrenic state of thought which arises when the speaker is cut off from her/his own language and strains to communicate with an imposed colonial tongue. The artist depicts the tensions that arise from the de-territorialisation and re-territorialisation of aboriginal people's cultural identities, as they resist, emerge, and recede in relation to traditional, indigenous, western, and hybrid expressions. Dolleen Manning gives abundant thanks to her mother and teacher Ojibwe speaker Rosalie (Elijah) Manning; Cree drummer/singer Cody Gilbert Cardinal; and Toronto-based filmmaker and sound editor Anna Malkin for contributing their time, voices and expertise. The portrait of her mother and herself was taken by Toronto photographer Lorne Fromer. 'Thought Exiled from the Tongue' was originally presented as a sound installation, entitled 'The Transmutation of Language: Ojibwe in Translation', but, for the DVD, sculptural images of separate independent art works by Dolleen Manning have been included to add a visual dimension.

Chi-Miigwech.

See DVD

12

Catastrophe, Memory, and Testimony in Winona LaDuke's *Last Standing Woman*

Hsinya Huang

Hsinya Huang was born in Taiwan, in 1961. Her late father was a Chinese 'forty-niner', who came to Taiwan in 1949 when the Communists took over mainland China, and thereafter lived a diasporic life on the island. When he passed away in 1994 and she had to communicate with his family in China about his funeral, the condition of displacement which he had experienced and recounted to her struck her with belated force of consciousness and assumed inexpressibly poignancy. While the rift separating her father from his native place constitutes an essential sadness, Huang's sense of displacement was reinforced by the fact that she migrated many times in both directions across the Pacific Ocean. Though she finally settled with her husband and their only son in her childhood hometown, migration has nonetheless become a way of thinking, a structure of feeling, and a memory in the blood, which can never be surmounted. She is now Associate Professor of English and Comparative Literature at National Kaohsiung Normal University on Taiwan and has published numerous articles on post-colonial exilic literature. Her monograph, entitled *(De)Colonizing the Body: Disease, Empire, and (Alter)Native Medicine in Contemporary Native American Writings*, is scheduled to be published in September of 2004.

In this paper, Huang details the many dimensions of the involuntary exile of Native Americans from their own territories, resulting from the Euro-Indian wars, land usurpation, and legislative manipulation over five hundred years. This kind of exile, of indigenous people in what are now First World settler nations, has been neglected by scholars in postcolonial studies. Huang writes of the catastrophic decline of Native populations through war and introduced diseases, and the environmental degradation through industrial exploitation and pollution of their traditional lands and modern reservations. She examines here the novel by Native activist Winona LaDuke, *Last Standing Woman* (1997), which traces the history of loss and struggle by her own Anishinaabeg people, over seven generations, from the 1860s to the present and beyond. She shows how LaDuke treats tribal memory over the generations as a means of resistance, of recovering identity in relation to the land to which the tribe is spiritually linked. The oral nature and the circular structure of LaDuke's narrative and its continuation into the future, to the year 2018, counteract the linear pattern and the written basis of first world history.

Winona LaDuke, Anishinaabeg from the Makwa Dodaem (Bear Clan) of the Mississippi Band of the White Earth reservation in northern Minnesota, is a leading spokesperson and activist for indigenous rights. She became involved in Native American environmental issues when she met Jimmy Durham, a well-known Cherokee activist, at Harvard University. At the age of 18 she spoke to the United Nations regarding Native American issues and since then has become well-known as a voice for indigenous environmental and social concerns throughout the US and internationally. LaDuke moved to White Earth after she graduated from Harvard and started to engage in lawsuits to recover lands originally held by the Anishinaabeg and taken illegally by the federal government.[1] After exhausting the resources of the legal system, she founded the White Earth Land Recovery Project to raise funds to purchase original White Earth land holdings. She proclaims the intimate connection between tribal identity and land, maintaining that, to control their own destiny, tribal people must regain control of their land. She has published numerous articles on environmental issues and testified at government hearings. In an article of 1996, she wrote:

> Across the continent, on the shores of small tributaries, in the shadows of sacred mountains, on the vast expanse of the prairies, or in the safety of the woods, prayers are being repeated, as they have been for thousands of years, and common people with uncommon courage and the whispers of their ancestors in their ears continue their struggles to protect the land and water and trees on which their very existence is based. And like small tributaries joining together to form a mighty river, their force and power grows. This river will not be dammed. (LaDuke 1996: 38)

In an interview with David Barsamian, LaDuke contends that Native American ancient rights to the land need to be recognized and protected by the American Constitution. White expansionists created a frontier mythology according to which the lands they seized were an untamed wilderness awaiting civilised cultivation, in the words of Walter Prescott Webb, "a vast body of wealth without proprietors," an "empty land," several times the size of Europe, a land "whose resources had not yet been exploited" (quoted in Arnold 1996: 110). It is clear from research over the last 60 years that the pre-Columbian Americas had a native population of over 100 million, with perhaps 10-18 million living in what are now the United States and Canada (Stannard 1993: 266-268). By the mid-eighteenth century it is estimated that the Native population of these North American territories had dropped to a mere two hundred and fifty thousand.

There has been debate about the extent to which this "great holocaust" (LaDuke 1999: 1) was the direct consequence of war initiated by the colonists and the extent to which smallpox and other diseases served as the cutting edge of European imperialism.[2] While the impact of epidemic diseases may have been the immediate cause of mortality, the ultimate responsibility lies in the rapacity of colonists and their contempt for native tribal civilisation. Native Americans have been largely banished from the American psyche except in the high proportion of states, towns, rivers, and so on, which bear indigenous names. For LaDuke, America has for five hundred years been "in the process of denial of holocaust" (Barsamian 2003: 4).[3]

The prime target for LaDuke's criticism is the colonial destruction of native land and environment. As a renowned native ecologist, LaDuke strategically links natives with other people of colour in the term "environmental racism". While the environmental movement, by and large, emerges out of a white and middle-class preserve, LaDuke underscores environmental threats faced by native communities, as she launches a scathing attack not only on earlier frontier exploitation but on more contemporary ecological catastrophes: two-thirds of the uranium resources in the country, one-third of all the low-sulphur coal, and the single largest hydroelectric project are all on Indian lands, and the federal government is proposing nuclear waste dumps on reservations. In her book *All Our Relations: Native Struggles for Land and Life*, LaDuke associates environmental catastrophe with native trauma. Nonetheless, while over two thousand nations of indigenous peoples have become extinct in the western hemisphere, those who remain, like LaDuke's people, the Anishinaabegs, continue to transform their grief into grievance, affect into active resistance.

*

LaDuke's novel *Last Standing Woman* depicts the history of native loss and resistance. Her story commences around 1862 with the Sioux uprising in Minnesota and its impact on the Anishinaabeg community, and ends in 2018 with the prospect of a tribal future. The year 2018 is seven generations from the Sioux uprising, and seven is a mythical number in North American tribal culture, central to tribal spiritual practices. There are, for instance, "the seven ways of the medicine woman," as indicated in Paula Gunn Allen's *Grandmothers of the Light*,[4] as well as seven sacred rites, which are all common in Plain Indian tribal healing.[5] By extending the temporal frame beyond the time of writing, LaDuke suggests the continuing effort that will be required for tribal survival. She first dramatises a recovery of tribal lands taken by Euro-Americans over the past five hundred years. Upon regaining the tribal home-base, there is then a ceremonial return of the ancestral spirit, which LaDuke envisions as sustaining and continuing the tribal legacy. The novel ends with life in continual regeneration. As the narrator, Last Standing Woman, writes at the end of a 2018 journal entry: "What carries us through is the relationship we have to creation and the courage we are able to gather from the experience of our *aanikoobijigan*, our ancestors, and our *oshkaabewisag*, our helpers" (1997: 299). At the centre of the present discussion of LaDuke's chronicle of Native land loss and recovery, consequently, is a demonstration of how home as 'root' is transmuted into 'route' in a quest for tribal identity, of how a homing desire is inscribed through a wish to return to a place of origin, of how the dynamics of history and memory work to regain a native home-base, and of how LaDuke's distinctive form of story-telling testifies to tribal exilic experience.[6]

In *Writers in Exile*, Andrew Gurr highlights the way in which "colonialism has peopled the world with exiles, whether through the forcible deracination of the middle passage into slavery, or through the subtler forms of colonial provincialism" (Gurr 1981: 27). While the work of Edward Said, Homi Bhabha, Nico Israel, and the like has ensured that the subject of post-colonial exile in the Middle East, India, and the Caribbean has been well studied, the specificity of the indigenous experience needs to be more fully articulated. It is important, as Arnold Krupat points out, not to conflate the experience and writings of indigenous peoples, who have been overwhelmed by European settlement within so-called First World countries, with those of Third World peoples. Native Americans, for instance, suffer continuing internal colonialism or domestic imperialism, which results in their being strangers at home, forever exiled in their homeland. George Manuel and Michael Posluns define this different experience as that of "the Fourth World": "The Aboriginal World has so far lacked the political muscle to emerge; it is without economic power, it rejects Western political techniques; it is unable to comprehend Western technology" (Manuel and Posluns 1973: 6).

Behind the exilic experience of American Natives lie US government policies, including: the removal of tribes west of white settlement areas (1830), involving dislocation from ancestral lands; the allotment of land into individual rather than tribal ownership (1887), thereby discouraging the maintenance of larger tribal communities; the reorganisation of traditional tribal leadership into 'democratically' elected Tribal Councils (1934), which allowed little self-government on reservations; and the termination of Native American nations (1950), which encouraged further dislocation into urban centres. All this federal action, as Susan Forsyth suggests, has aimed at resolving the problem that Native American Nations pose to the US, of these "vanishing Americans [...who] stubbornly refuse to disappear" (Forsyth 2000: 146).

According to Forsyth, the first collection to include an essay by a Native American writer about native displacement was *Dangerous Liaisons: Gender, Nation, and Postcolonial Perspectives*, an anthology of post-colonial critical writings, published in 1997. James Clifford's ethnography of travel and cultural traffic of the same year, *Routes*, also engages questions of Native American exilic experience. Ward Churchill, a few years earlier, had perceived and pursued "strategies and courses of action designed to lead to decolonization within the colonizing 'mother country'" (Churchill 1993: 24-26) – the most spectacular of these strategies include the occupations of the Bureau of Indian Affairs building in Washington, D.C. and the AIM (American Indian Movement) armed resistance at Wounded Knee in 1973, which drew world attention to the resonantly symbolic site of tribal protest.[7] All this resistant history is dramatised in LaDuke's *Last Standing Woman* and establishes the core of her representation of tribal exilic experience. Strikingly, therefore, tribal exilic discourse discloses not only 'loss', but the recovery of a sense of 'history' and 'home'. It shows how the "unhealable rift forced between a human being and a native place" (Said 1987: 357) may, after all, be healed by a re-connection to tribal history and native home through memory/story-telling as testimony.

LaDuke represents the tribal milieu in its historical and geographical specificity, with precise dates and places. Beginning in 1862, her tribal vision extends through the intervening years and into the future as far as the year 2018. In chronicling more than 150 years of conflicts between cultures and peoples, and the imposition of a violent system of governance and legal campaign, LaDuke in effect provides a paradigm for baring the roots of five hundred years of American history since 1492. She underscores the subject of tribal land loss under expansionist usurpation by enumerating the states, rivers, lakes, and numbers of acres as evidence, in a way that white historians have not done. She 'maps' the tribal lost lands:

> The Dakota had lost over thirty million acres of Iowa, Minnesota, and the Dakota Territory due to the treaties and papers which they didn't understand. They had retained only a "reservation" ten miles wide and one hundred and fifty miles long bordering the Minnesota River. (LaDuke 1997: 29)

> The government would terminate the *Anishinaabeg* reservations of Gull Lake, Sandy Lake, Pokegama, Oak Point, and others because of the Dakota's Little Crow's War with the government and Bugonaygeeshig's raiding the white men as revenge for white men's invasion and cheating. (LaDuke 1997: 32)

LaDuke takes up the argument of Michel Foucault and others that, rather than a single history, there are always contradictory histories or 'counter histories'. To reclaim history for Native Americans means to challenge the ruling race's ideology in order to reconstruct and re-write their own tribal history. Official American history starts in 1492 when Christopher Columbus discovered the New World, or rather, in 1607 when John Smith arrived on the banks of James River. But what Europeans took to be an 'empty land' with an uncultivated landscape has now been shown to have been inhabited and worked by Native Americans for thousands of years before the arrival of the white men. There was a pre-European landscape that represented the achievements of tribal generations, and it is upon this landscape, both geographical and cultural, that Euro-American patterns of land use and settlement have been superimposed. LaDuke has responded to distorted official documentation and the unfair treatment of Native Americans by presenting a colonial history in the voice of the conquered, in what Homi Bhabha refers to as "the native subject's cultural resistances" (Bhabha 1994: 152). Or rather, it is tribal memory woven together through LaDuke's story-telling that should eventually substitute History with an upper-case H.

Pierre Nora makes a distinction between *history* and *memory*. He contends that history is:

> the reconstruction always problematic and incomplete, of what is no longer [...]. History is a representation of the past [...]. History binds itself strictly to temporal continuities, to progressions and to relations between things. (Nora 1989: 8-9)

History always responds to and represents dominant ideology. By contrast, according to Nora,.

> memory is life, borne by living societies founded in its name. It remains in permanent evolution, open to the dialectic of remembering and forgetting [...]. It is a perpetually actual phenomenon, a bond

> tying us to the eternal present. [...]. Memory takes root in the
> concrete, in spaces, gestures, images and objects. (Nora 1989: 8-9)

By referring to "the concrete, in spaces, gestures, images and objects" (Nora 1989: 9), LaDuke appeals to her tribal memory. Memory is needed not merely to realise the past, but to relate one to the present: "memory is a crucial tool and agent for insisting on the identity and the place in the world" (Weissberg 1999: 10). Memory as resource of resistance and identity has been confirmed and repeatedly examined by post-colonial exilic writers and critics (Hall 1997: 52). Homi Bhabha asserts "remembering is never a quiet act of introspection or retrospection. It is a power re-membering, a putting together of the dismembered past to make sense of the trauma of the present" (Bhabha 1994: 63). Through remembering, LaDuke retrieves the traumatic indigenous past, retrospects and introspects tribal land history, and re-presents the disjointed/fragmented homeland as a unified map in her chronicle of tribal exilic experience. To remember is to give life to the disjointed past, which not only forms identity but engenders healing power:

> the loss of identity [...] only begins to be healed when the forgotten
> connections are once more set in place. Such texts restore an
> imaginary fullness or plenitude, to set against the broken rubric of our
> past. They are resources of resistance and identity. (Hall 1997: 393)

To retrieve the past, by remembrance, is an act of rebellion against forgetting. It is how we understand tribal exile as tragic, yet with a potential for salvation. This fits well with the Anishinaabeg, as well as Cherokee and Pueblo, notions of balance between positive and negative aspects of spiritual power. *Last Standing Woman*, in chronicling tribal loss and resistance, reconstructs a communal/tribal consciousness oppressed, buried, and threatened with being lost. By retrieving her tribal past, LaDuke spotlights a legitimate cause to recover the land long lost to European colonizers, to go back 'home', so to speak.

The significance of home can never be overstated. Home is one source of identity, a powerful source of continuity in the sense of self. Referring to the experience of the West Indies, Antonia MacDonald-Smythe points out that "home is more than a house-physical structure. Home is more than a bundle of one's skin. It is an idea, one laden with associations of belonging, of connectedness, of physical wholeness, and spiritual growth" (MacDonald-Smythe 2001: 99). This sense of home is "the goal of the voyages of self-discovery and self-identification" (Gurr 1981: 18); in other words, through the identification of home, one can find his/her proper location and cultural being. On the other hand, for those who are deprived of secure dwelling places, or those who leave their homelands whether voluntarily or not, home becomes the landscape to be recovered. For Third World exiles who determine that a return is no longer possible, home is more readily fixed in a mental landscape.[8] But for tribal exiles, home is the actual geography.

It is crucial to acknowledge that tribal home is rooted in nature, in land. Native Americans believe the land has a spirit, it has energy and power, and humans grow out of it like trees. To be precise, while tribal generations inhabit the land, the land embodies the ancestral spirit that protects and continues life to come. As Paula Gunn Allen emphasizes, "[w]e are the land. To the best of my understanding, that is the fundamental idea that permeates American Indian life; the land (Mother) and the people (mothers) are the same [...]. The earth is the source and the being of the people, and we are equally the being of the earth" (Allen 1992: 119). The intimate association between land and tribal people constitutes LaDuke's thematic concern, as she elaborates on the ownership of America: "The reality is [...] if you do not control your land, you do not control your destiny" (LaDuke 2002: 143). The separation of tribal people from their native place thus amounts not only to native exile but also to genocide, as Western expansionists continue to steal tribal land in the name of civilisation. The tribal history (memory) of land loss is retrieved as testimony of tribal catastrophe after the Discovery. Even more significant than this, in land/nature as home, Native Americans find strength to go beyond and above. The Native legacy in the American landscape transcends Western ideas of historical process, the history of colonisation, joining the mundane (the present life) with the arcane (the ancestral spirit). Home deeply rooted in land is both the margin and the centre, a site of oppression, repression, and expression, which tribal exilic writers yearn to articulate.

The land recovery episodes in the novel interweave actual tribal history with fictional accounts. The White Earth Land Recovery Project founded by LaDuke in the early 1990s has regained one thousand acres and set its sights on thousands more as over 90 per cent of the original 837,000 acres, now owned by Whites, were transferred over the years by theft, fraud, treaties, and federal legislation. LaDuke represents the White-Red confrontation over land in a well designed and orchestrated 'Standoff at White Earth'. The

'Protect Our Land Coalition' was formed in 1990, and launched an occupation to reclaim lost tribal land (LaDuke 1997: 159-220). The federal government then agreed to negotiate with White Earth about the halting of logging (LaDuke 1997: 218); finally, in 2000, the federal government financed the re-acquisition of more than ten million acres of Indian land across the Nation, enabling White Earth to purchase fifty thousand acres of land so that, combined with other acquisitions they had made, the tribe came to own over half of their reservation (LaDuke 1997: 285).[9] In chronicling not merely the loss but the recovery of land, LaDuke manages to alter the chaotic and grotesque world of violence and conflict, which was earlier depicted by the Ojibwe author Gerald Vizenor in his *Darkness in Saint Louis Bearheart* and by Louise Erdrich in *Tracks*. LaDuke, furthermore, moves beyond the White Earth of the Chippewa, aligning the Anishinaabeg with other Indian Nations for native coalition: she refers to uranium mining at Acoma, for instance, which is familiar to readers of Native American literature from Leslie Marmon Silko's *Ceremony*. By drawing upon native solidarity, LaDuke offers a progressive version of the tribal land history found in the White frontier thesis, only with the direction reversed.

Progress in tribal terms is never as linear as the progress prescribed in the White frontier thesis. LaDuke's tribal narrative possesses a circular structure, incorporating one individual event within another, piling meaning upon meaning, until the accretion finally results in a story which is collective and tribal. LaDuke's book is composed in four parts, each of which takes on historical complexity. She titles the four portions: 'The Refuge', 'The Re-awakening', 'The Occupation', and 'Oshki', to chronicle seven generations of tribal contestation against White supremacy, from 1862 to 2018. Both seven and four are significant numbers in tribal spiritual practices.[10] The individual threads are tied together in Part IV as a revelation of the tribal future. The prevailing idea is summarized in the Epilogue, in a diary written by the narrator. The diary both begins and ends the novel, configuring a distinctive tribal voice: "I wrote this because I am called to write. I have done the best I could, and have tried to tell some of our story from my mother's words and from the words of my relatives" (LaDuke 1997: 299). As she continues to write, the diarist pins much hope on the "memories and principles" which are tribal: "There is a great deal I have omitted, but in the least, I tried to be honest with the memories and the principles" (LaDuke 1997: 299). The third Last Standing Woman takes up the role of tribal historian as well as story-teller that Nanpush performs in Erdrich's *Tracks*.

Consequently, LaDuke's yearning for home is inscribed not only through land recovery projects but through a wish to recover "our story from my mother's words and from the words of my relatives" (LaDuke 1997: 299). Uncovering generational continuity in genealogy is emblematic of a return to the place of origin. John Docker investigates the meaning of searching for genealogy: "In exploring our family tree we immerse ourselves in history and in the process we transform it and make it personal. This is our history. This is part of our identity. We can never know how our ancestors lived, but we can imagine and give it life" (Docker 2001: 21). The yearning for home permeates the narrative of exile. In LaDuke's case, family history and tribal landscape, home and memory, intertwine to fabricate Native lost identity. Through the never-ending stories, transformed with each retelling, LaDuke relies on the oral ritual of her Anishinaabeg tribe to reclaim tribal lost heritage.

LaDuke opens the novel with a telling of the migratory history of the Anishinaabeg tribal people:

> There were many migrations that brought the people here. *Omaa, omaa*, here. Here to the place where the food grows on the water. *Anishinaabeg Akiing,* the people's land, the land where the *manoomin,* the wild rice, grows. It had been perhaps a thousand years since the time the *Anishinaabeg* had left the big waters in *Waaban aki,* the land of the east. And they now turned *Ningaabii'anong,* to the west. . . They traveled by foot on the land and by canoe on the rivers, traveling farther and farther to the west until they turned home. *Giiwedahn.* So it was that the families, the clans, and the head people of the *Anishinaabeg* came to the head waters of the Mississippi. Here, *Gaawaawaabiganikaag,* White Earth, named after the clay, the white clay you find here. It's so beautiful, it is. Here the people would remain, in the good land that was theirs (LaDuke 1997: 23, italics in the original).

LaDuke recovers tribal woodlands by tracing the ancestral migratory past. The passage intermingles English with a rhythmic tribal language filled with oral story-telling markers. Drawing upon tribal orality, LaDuke recovers the lost memory of the home-base as she recounts migration. The italicized tribal words chanted represent both the 'route' of the migration and the 'root' of migratory people. Tribal history/memory is embodied in the land and traced with stories, with magic, with the presence of ancestors and spirits. This is their law, to be rooted in land, "the one law for them that is the Creator's"

(LaDuke 1997: 23). By retrieving tribal memory through storytelling, LaDuke bypasses the white man's 'paper' law.

Last Standing Woman commences, notably, with a chapter entitled "The Storyteller": "The story, though, was all of our story [...]. But when the story flew into my ears, it made a picture in my mind I could never forget" (LaDuke 1997: 18). The story is the testimony. The narrator, the third Last Standing Woman, tells stories, even when she is still a foetus:

> Each month as the child grew, the stories came forth with more force. And soon, they formed a web that surrounded them both and linked them from past to future. While before there seemed to be no time, now there seemed to be nothing but time. (LaDuke 1997: 295)

The baby-girl's coming "was signalled by the departure of the oldest person in the village, Mesabe. He was at once the story and the teller." Mesabe's passage "appeared to open the door for her entrance into life. It was also his life that brought forth the work of hers" (LaDuke 1997: 296).

While Mesabe is the tribal elder who knows the stories of the previous three generations, and those of the following three generations, this power line is continued in the name of Last Standing Woman. There are, in fact, three figures of Last Standing Woman, who continue to transmit stories and, in so doing, sustain tribal tradition in a feminine continuum. Each of the tellings becomes not just a repetition of the tale, but a metamorphosis of a past lost, in a present lived, and a future foreseen. Each story gives rise to a strategic disclosure and enhances self-empowerment and self-creation. Tribal history is synonymous with memory, and story becomes a testimony. Drawing upon a vital feminine line, LaDuke's novel, in the form of a tribal history, is a testimony that embodies significant cultural and political repercussions. This testimony has involved a potency to communicate oppression and repression, poverty and subalternity, imprisonment as well as the struggle for survival. Exile is understood as tragic yet with a potential for salvation.

Last Standing Woman is, thus, double-faced, addressing both loss and gain. While the frame story of loss and oppression is organized according to the time of 'linear history' (that is, history as imposed by the colonists), tribal continuance and survival relies on the time of 'ceremonial history' or rather "monumental time", to borrow post-structuralist Julia Kristeva's terminology.[11] Multiple modalities of time permeate the novel. Ceremonial/monumental time retains eternity by repetition. There are cycles, gestations, the eternal recurrence of a biological rhythm which conforms to that of nature and whose regularity corresponds to what is experienced by tribal people as cosmic time and vertiginous visions. As the narrator, the third Last Standing Woman, puts it:

> I do not believe that time is linear. Instead, I have come to believe that time is in cycles, and that the future is part of our past and the past is part of our future. Always, however, we are in new cycles. The cycles omit some pieces and collect other pieces of our stories and our lives. That is why we keep the names, and that is why we keep the words (LaDuke 1997: 299).

The linear (the chronological structure of the novel) and the cyclical time of nature, land, and stories intertwine to embody a tribal world where the material and mundane merge with the spiritual and arcane, which LaDuke describes thus: "The Anishinaabeg world undulated between material and spiritual shadows, never clear which was more prominent at any time" and Native life is "not a life circumscribed by a clock" (LaDuke 1997: 24).

To explicate further, the ceremonial history is carried on by a name. The recurrence of the name, Ishkwegaabasiikew, 'Last Standing Woman', informs tribal survival. There are three women called Last Standing Woman, representing the past, the present, and the future respectively. The baby-girl, the narrator as she grows up to be the embodiment of the tribal voice, is related to Lucy, the second Last Standing Woman "by name and by spirit" (LaDuke 1997: 18), who is in turn related to the first one who gave and passed down the name. As the narrator, the third Last Standing Woman, testifies so as to retain tribal history, "Lucy St. Clair who named me was afraid we would forget [...]. And a picture of how we had these gifts we should keep" (LaDuke 1997: 18). This tribal consciousness, as articulated by the narrator, spotlights the danger to tribal identity of losing memory of their location of origin as they lost their land, their common territory, to the Whites. Last Standing Woman, in the repetition of the name, maintains the dynamics of remembrance and commemoration. There are, indeed, three things that guide tribal direction, as the narrator claims: "our name, our clan, and our religion" (LaDuke 1997: 299). As there is always a woman called "Last Standing," the tribe will never perish and its culture moves on through the keeping of the "names," and thus, "the words" (LaDuke 1997: 299). Last Standing Woman is by no means 'last' but rather symbolic of "the continuation and the rebirth of her people, something that is indigenous to White Earth" (Matchie 2001: 71).

LaDuke's collective, tribal story is therefore the cure/medicine for the tribal traumatic past. As Paula Gunn Allen avers, in her *Grandmothers of the Light*, "every medicine path has its attendant stories, and medicine people, also known as shamans, wise women, conjurors, adepts, mages, practitioners, or masters, teach apprentices through story" (Allen 1991: 3). Through stories told, the buried tribal past is revived and land recovered. In the end, the ancestral bones are reburied in the White Earth, which not only symbolically reclaims tribal land but, as McConney says, signals "the lost pieces from the opening histories [coming] home for the people to be whole" (McConney 2003: 2).

Last Standing Woman writes in her journal toward the end of the novel: "For all the pain and heartache we have felt, there has been, and will be, an equal amount of joy. That is how everything works. There is always a struggle to maintain the balance" (LaDuke 1997: 299). In the end, stories are retold about the history of migration and the old ways of hunting; the ancient bones are returned from a museum showcase to the reservation while a character called Moose hums an old rhythm to greet them—"Slowly, death chants, lullabies, love songs, and war songs became a composite of music, chants in his mind and ears" (271); drums are now returned to White Earth—"the *Midewiwin* water drums and the big drums" (1997: 273). Finally, Moose feels the ancestors are singing in the back of his car. In fact, it is their spirits that sing (279). Exile becomes an occasion for potential salvation in that the exiled tribal self continues to resist definition and categorisation. Returning to the way of life of her people before colonisation is impossible, so "making do" (as Betty Louise Bell describes the strategy of another Native American writer) is important: "a recognition of ordinary lives, the lives of Native Americans, fragmented and forever affected by extraordinary losses"; under the pressure of loss, the survival of tribal people depends on the "adaptations to loss that discover continuity and affirm life" (Bell 1994: 3). These two things are not only ordinary, but also divine, for Native Americans. The oneness of ordinary and divine, which has been forfeited by Western thought because of the dominant concept of dichotomy, becomes the lesson of salvation that Native Americans teach the whole world, which is, according to Andrew Gurr, "peopled with exiles" (1981: 27).

Notes:

[1] The Anishinaabeg are also known as the Chippewa and Ojibwe (English and French versions of the name given them by Euro-American colonists and other tribes).
[2] See, especially: J.R. McNeill and Alfred W. Crosby, 1972, *The Columbian Exchange: Biological and Cultural Consequences of 1492* (Westport: Greenwood Press), and Donald Joralemon, 1982, 'New World Depopulation and the Case of Disease' in *Journal of Anthropological Research* 38.
[3] That this denial continues to this day is shockingly illustrated by the fact that the latest edition of the *Encyclopedia Britannica,* employs research from 1939 to support its assertion that there were hardly more than one million Natives in North America in pre-Columbian times, thereby ignoring more than 60 years of subsequent research that makes absolutely clear that the real figure was at least ten times higher. 'Native American', *Encyclopædia Britannica.* 2004. Encyclopædia Britannica Online. (consulted 17.01.04).
[4] They are, according to Paula Gunn Allen, "the way of the daughter, the way of the householder, the way of the mother, the way of the gatherer, the way of the ritualist, the way of the teacher, and the way of the wise woman" (1991: 9-15)
[5] The seven sacred rites foretold to the Lakota by White Buffalo Calf Woman, a holy woman who appeared among the people, include: the sweat lodge ceremony, the vision quest, the ghost keeping ceremony, the sun dance, the hunka ceremony ("the making of relatives"), the girls' puberty rite, and the throwing of the ball ceremony (Hirschfelder 2001: 263-264).
[6] LaDuke's *Last Standing Woman* is not the sole fictional work that deals with Anishinaabeg land loss; Louise Erdrich's *Tracks* is another prominent example. While in *Tracks*, the Chippewa lose their trees in a period when the ancient magic power is diminishing, LaDuke dramatises the White-Red conflict over land in a confrontation to prevent lumber men from cutting more trees. Even so, the Anishinaabegs are indeed forced from their woodland reservation and driven into the 'civilized' West where the Whites threaten to exterminate them. Not all Native American tribes, however, have been completely exiled from their homelands: the Pueblos and the Navajo are strong examples. They too have experienced degradation of their land, though — the story of uranium mining at Acoma, for instance, is familiar to readers of Native American literature through Leslie Marmon Silko's *Ceremony*. The Navajo and the Pueblos have partially lost their sacred land spirits even as they have maintained control of villages and homesteads.
[7] In December 1890, at Wounded Knee Creek in South Dakota, around three hundred Lakota (Sioux) were killed by the US army, an incident which became emblematic of governmental military aggression toward Native Americans. This event is the historical basis on which LaDuke initiates her narrative of the first-generation Anishinaabeg Last Standing Woman's friendship with Lakota woman Situpiwin. While LaDuke's novel is a recent literary representation of tribal resistant history, this incident is the title and the last chapter of Dee Brown's 1970 popular history of the defeat of American Indian armed protest against white expansion, *Bury My Heart at Wounded Knee: An Indian History of the American West* (New York: Holt, Rinehart and Winston) (quoted in Forsyth 2000: 144). LaDuke obviously picked up where Dee Brown left off and used this symbolic incident to usher in her chronicle of tribal exilic

experience. Coincidentally, the 1970's saw a resurgence of Native American resistance, whose high point came in the 1973 siege of Wounded Knee for 71 days in protest against the white government's victimisation of Natives. Mary Crow Dog's autobiography *Lakota Woman* (New York: Harper Perennial, 1991) is one of the famous renditions of this historical incident. For details concerning the siege of Wounded Knee, refer to Forsyth's essay, "Writing Other Lives," which draws on *Lakota Woman* exclusively to deploy Native American autobiographical representation of Euro-American coloniality.

[8] Such hallmark figures of post-colonial studies as Edward Said, Salman Rushdie, Stuart Hall, Homi Bhabha, and V. S. Naipaul seem to have turned themselves into permanent exiles. Unlike classical wanderers who are exiled from the centre to the margin, these Third World critics migrate from the periphery to the metropolis to write back on the empire. For them, the locality of home is problematic; neither the place they were born in nor the place they leave for is home. Home could be here, there, everywhere, and nowhere. The dynamics of their cultural positioning assists to forge a detached stance, on which they acclaim their vision as well as salvation.

[9] Nevertheless, in 'Who Owns America?', a speech on White Earth Reservation land recovery, delivered in 2001, LaDuke criticised the function of the 'Indian Claims Commission', through which the federal government acknowledged that they had taken land and not paid for it, and thus secured 800 million dollars to compensate the Indian community. LaDuke asks whether this is not an even worse act of theft: "Which is pretty darn cheap real estate, is what it is. What does it average out to? [...] 11 cents an acre? 17 cents an acre? 5 cents an acre?" (LaDuke 2001: 146). That the American government actually gets to set the price which they will pay in compensation for something that they stole must have some redress in terms of justice, as LaDuke insisted in her speech (2001: 146). In the novel, the armed take-over of White Earth's tribal offices by the Protect Our Land Coalition is a dramatisation of the process of the land recovery. The weeks-long occupation serves as a catalyst for what follows in the novel: two National Guardsmen are taken hostage and the FBI botches a dawn raid and ends up crawling to the negotiating table. The tribe wins its land back through the government's financing. It becomes clear then that *Last Standing Woman* is also LaDuke's *roman à clef*—a chronicle of the turbulent times on White Earth and her own direct-action role in counteracting the imperial abuse of land and power.

[10] In addition to the four parts, there are also a prologue and an epilogue to *Last Standing Woman*, both of which employ the word 'storyteller' in their title. Storytelling is a familiar Native American tradition, as one can see from Silko's *Ceremony and Storyteller*. Jamie Marks thus calls *Last Standing Woman* "a storyteller's tale of White Earth" (1998: 1A). While storytelling is an important aspect of the novel, that warrants a lengthy discussion later in the paper, the significance of the numbers, four and seven, should be stressed. In tribal numerology, four is perhaps the most sacred number, with its power stemming from four cardinal directions and four seasons. Four therefore symbolises full circles or wholeness. Two early Native Renaissance representative works, Scott Momaday's *House Made of Dawn* and James Welch's *Winter in the Blood*, both consist of four parts, echoing spatial and seasonal circles. Edith Swan's interpretation of symbolic geography in Silko's *Ceremony* also pivots around the number four.

[11] The concept of 'monumental history' is originally used by Friedrich Nietzsche in 'On the Advantages and Disadvantages of History for Life': "That the great moments in the struggle of individuals form a chain, that in them the high points of humanity are linked through millennia, that what is highest in such a moment of the distant past be for me still alive, bright and great—that is [...] *monumental history*" (Nietzsche 1997: 68).

Bibliography

Allen, Paula Gunn. 1991. *Grandmothers of the Light: a Medicine Woman's Sourcebook*. Boston: Beacon Press.
- - - . 1992. *The Sacred Hoop: Recovering the Feminine in American Indian Tradition*. Boston: Beacon Press.
Arnold, David. 1996. *The Problem of Nature: Environment, Culture and European Expansion*. Oxford: Blackwell.
Barsamian, David. 2003. 'Being Left: Activism on and off Reservation: David Barsamian Interviews Winona LaDuke' in *Z Magazine* 19 May. On line at: www.zena.secureforum.com/Znet/zmag/articles/being_leftja98.htm (consulted 03.04.2004)
Bell, Betty Louise. 1994. 'Introduction: Linda Hogan's Lessons in Making Do' in *Studies in American Indian Literatures* 2.6.3: 3-6.
Bhabha, Homi. 1994. *The Location of Culture*. London: Routledge.
Churchill, Ward. 1993. *Struggle for the Land: Indigenous Resistance to Genocide, Ecocide and Expropriation in Contemporary North America*. Monroe, Maine: Common Courage Press.
Clifford, James. 1997. *Routes: Travel and Translation in the Late Twentieth Century*. Cambridge, Mass.: Harvard University Press.
Cook-Lynn, Elizabeth. 1996. *Why I Can't Read Wallace Stegner & Other Essays: A Tribal Voice*. Madison: University of Wisconsin Press.
Docker, John. 2001. *1492: The Poetics of Diaspora*. London: Continuum.
Dorris, Michael. 1987. *A Yellow Raft in Blue Water*. New York: H. Holt.
Duffy, Shannon. 'The Americas on the Eve of the European Invasion'. On line at: www.loyno.edu/~seduffy/aztecs.html (consulted 09.01.2004).
Erdrich, Louise. 1988. *Tracks*. New York: Henry Holt.
- - - . 2003. *Books and Islands in Ojibwe Country*. New York: National Geographic.
Forsyth, Susan. 2000. 'Writing Other Lives: Native American (Post)coloniality and Collaborative (Auto)biography' in Bery, Ashok and Patricia Murray (eds) *Comparing Postcolonial Literatures: Dislocations*. New York: Palgrave.
Gurr, Andrew. 1981. *Writers in Exile*. New Jersey: The Harvester Press.
Hall, Stuart. 1997. 'Cultural Identity and Diaspora' in Williams, Padmini and Laura Chrisman (eds) *Contemporary Postcolonial Theory: A Reader*. New York: Harvester Wheatsheaf Press: 392-403.
Hirschfelder, Arlene and Paulette Molin. 2001. *Encyclopedia of Native American Religions*. New York: Checkmark Books.
Israel, Nico. 2000. *Outlandish: Writing Between Exile and Diaspora*. Stanford, California: Stanford University Press.

Kristeva, Julia. 1986. *The Kristeva Reader* (ed. Toril Moi). Oxford: Blackwell.

Krupat, Arnold. 1996. 'Postcolonialism, Ideology, and Native American Literature' in *The Turn to the Native: Studies in Criticism and Culture*. Nebraska: Nebraska University Press: 30-55.

LaCapra, Dominick. 1996. *Representing the Holocaust: History, Theory, Trauma*. Ithaca: Cornell University Press.

- - - . 2001. *Writing History, Writing Trauma*. Baltimore: The Johns Hopkins University Press.

LaDuke, Winona. 1999. *All Our Relations*. Cambridge, MA: South End.

- - - . 1997. *Last Standing Woman*. Stillwater: Voyageur.

- - - . 1996. 'Like Tributaries to a River: The Growing Strength of Native Environmentalism' in *Sierra* (Nov-Dec): 38-46.

- - - . 2002. 'Who Owns America? Minority Land and Community Security' (2001) in *The Winona LaDuke Reader: A Collection of Essential Writings*. Foreword by Ralph Nader. Stillwater, MN: Voyageur Press: 138-47.

McClintock, Anne, Aamir Mufti, and Ella Shohat, (eds). 1997. *Dangerous Liaisons: Gender, Nation, and Postcolonial Perspectives*. Minneapolis: University of Minnesota Press.

McConney, Denise. 2003. Review of Last *Standing Woman* by Winona LaDuke. On line at: www.usask,caa/native_studies/NSR/Frames/Book%20Review/-121/ 12-1LaDuke.html (consulted 05.06.2003).

MacDonald-Smythe, Antonia. 2001. *Making Homes in the West/Indies: Constructions of Subjectivity in the Writings of Michelle Cliff and Jamaica Kincaid*. New York: Garland Press.

Manuel, George and Michael Posluns. 1973. *The Fourth World*. New York: Schocken Books.

Marks, Jamie. 1998. '*Last Standing Woman*: A Storyteller's Tale of White Earth' in *Becker Country Record* 30 September: 1A.

Matchie, Tom. 2001. 'Fighting the Windigo: Winona LaDuke's Peculiar Postcolonial Posture in *Last Standing Woman*' in *FEMSPEC* 2.2: 66-72.

Momaday, Scott. 1999. *House Made of Dawn*. New York: HarperCollins.

Nelson, Emmanuel. 1993. 'Fourth World Fictions: A Comparative Commentary on James Welch's *Winter in the Blood* and Mudrooroo Narogin's *Wild Cat Falling*' in Fleck, Richard (ed.) *Critical Perspective on Native American Fiction*. Washington D.C: Three Continents Press: 57-63.

Nietzsche, Friedrich. 1997. 'On the Advantages and Disadvantages of History for Life' in *Untimely Meditations* (ed. Daniel Breazeale, tr. R. J. Hollingdale) Cambridge: Cambridge University Press: 57-124.

Nora, Pierre. 1989. 'Between Memory and History: Les Lieux de Mémoire' in *Representations* 26: 7-25.

Said, Edward. 1987. 'Reflections on Exile' in Ferguson, Russell *et al* (eds) *Out There: Marginalization and Contemporary Cultures*. Cambridge: MIT Press: 357-66.

Silko, Leslie Marmon. 1977. *Ceremony*. New York: Penguin.

- - - . 1981. *Storyteller*. New York: Arcade.

Stannard, David E. 1993. *The American Holocaust: The Conquest of the New World*. Oxford: Oxford University Press.

Swan, Edith. 1988. 'Laguna Symbolic Geography and Silko's *Ceremony*' in *American Indian Quarterly* 12.3: 229-49.

Vizenor, Gerald. 1978. *Darkness in Saint Louis Bearheart*. St. Paul, MN: Truck Press.

Webb, Walter Prescott. 1964. *The Great Frontier*, Austin: *s.n.*

Welch, James. 1974. *Winter in the Blood*. New York: Harper & Row.

Weissberg, Liliane. 1999. 'Introduction' in Ben-Amos, Dan and Liliane Weissberg (eds) *Cultural Memory and the Construction of Identity*. Detroit: Wayne State University Press: 7-26.

13

American Literary Exiles: The Escape from Anguish[1]

Peter Karsten

Peter Karsten was born in Connecticut, earned a BA from Yale in 1960 and served for three years on a cruiser with the US 6th Fleet in the Mediterranean. He earned his PhD in history at Wisconsin, and teaches at the University of Pittsburgh. He has spent several semesters conducting research or teaching in Cambridge, England, the Algarve, Dublin, Sydney, Wellington, and Augsburg. He has published books and articles on a wide range of subjects. He is serving as Academic Dean of the Fall 2004 round-the-world voyage of the "Semester-at-Sea's" SS Universe Explorer, a floating college for some 600 undergraduates and 30 faculty. He is currently editor-in-chief of a three-volume Encyclopedia of War and American Society. He describes himself as a 'comparativist'.

In this paper, he studies several generations of American self-styled 'literary exiles', most of whom went to Europe, and finds that very few could legitimately claim that title in the sense that writers who have been banished by oppressive political regimes, or have fled from religious persecution in other countries, can. (In this *strong* sense, the US has, of course, been more often a goal for exiles than a source of exiles). The possible exceptions are some victims of McCarthyism, homophobia, and racism, such as Richard Wright and James Baldwin. Most could not even be referred to as economic migrants, in that they were almost never fleeing poverty. American literary exiles generally fall into three or four main categories: 'exiles at home', such as Edgar Allen Poe and Emily Dickinson; the many 'sojourners' and 'expatriates', such as James Russell Lowell and Gertrude Stein, who spent a period away from their native land, but without any conscious high purpose; 'self-exiles' from James Fenimore Cooper to T.S. Eliot, who went to live in Europe to imbibe what they saw as the culture of their ancestors, or those, such as Ezra Pound and Djuna Barnes, who sought to distance themselves from the puritanical and/or materialistic features of American life. While some clearly flourished in exile, others (such as John Dos Passos) found either that they were less in tune with European culture than they had expected, or that the great works they had planned to write did not materialise. In the meantime, some of the most powerful portraits of American life in the 1930s were composed, not by the Lost Generation, but by those who had stayed behind, such as John Steinbeck, Carl Sandburg, Erskine Caldwell, and documentary filmmaker Pare Lorenz.

The title 'literary exile' has been claimed by, or accorded to, a number of American-born writers who have worked outside their country of origin. These include members of the so-called 'Lost Generation', many of whom chose to relocate (at least for a number of years) to European settings (particularly Parisian ones).[2] Yet very few have the characteristics of the exiled writers whose work is presented and described in the other parts of this volume. With the exception, as we are reminded in the two immediately preceding contributions, of Native Americans displaced in very large numbers from their tribal lands,[3] no American creative artists can truly be said to have been 'banished' from their homeland. Only a few have fled political or cultural persecution as victims of McCarthyism and homophobia, or victims/critics of racism (such as Richard Wright and James Baldwin). Where are the refugees from persecution, comparable to an Émile Zola, an Isabel Allende, or a Yilma Tafere Tasew?[4] Where are the religious refugees?[5] Moreover, very few have been driven by impoverishment to become refugees. Indeed, some of our self-proclaimed exiles chose to settle into cheap digs abroad partly because of what the then-almighty dollar could buy. While the United States has played host to creative people in exile from many other countries over the last two hundred years, it has hardly been a breeding-ground for exiled writers in the strong sense of that term.[6] Perhaps all of this is only to say that the United States has never been as tyrannical (or economically destitute) a place as the homelands of many *true* literary exiles, but it is still worth saying.

Since the terms 'banishment' and 'flight from persecution' can hardly be used of American literary exiles, it becomes necessary to sort our American literary exiles using the simple prepositions *within, from,* and *to*.

The first category I shall refer to are those who have been described as 'exiles within' (or 'exiles at home' in Daniel Marder's words, a group that includes Edgar Allen Poe, Emily Dickinson, perhaps Robert Penn Warren (Hendricks 2000), and possibly even Herman Melville, for, despite his early nautical experiences in the South Seas, Melville spent most of his days within the United States, and, late in life, after suffering personal losses, retreated into solitude and has the hero of *John Marr and Other Sailors* tell us that "lone in a loft I must languish/ Far from closet and parlour and strife/ Content in escape from the anguish/ of the real and the seeming in life" (Melville 1888: 10).

Another category consists of those who *did* spend several years abroad, but cannot be said to have had any particular spiritual purpose that would constitute 'self-exile'. They might more appropriately be called either sojourners, or expatriates, or even *re*-patriates. Here I have in mind James Russell Lowell, Nathaniel Hawthorne, Edith Wharton, Eugene O'Neill, Sinclair Lewis, Archibald MacLeish, F. Scott Fitzgerald, and perhaps Gertrude Stein and Henry Miller.

Lowell spent fifteen months in Italy with his family in the early 1850s, an experience "to which he had been looking forward for more than a decade", as one Lowell scholar put it. He "studied Italian manners and customs, the language and the art of the country", and "attempted to keep a journal", but "the expatriate company in Rome, which included a number of old friends and at least seven other Lowells" was too tempting, and his journal was of little future literary value to him (Howard 1950: 312-313). Hawthorne's European sojourn began in 1853, at the age of 49, when he was rewarded by the in-coming Pierce Administration with the consulship at Liverpool; after four years in that post, during which time he produced no literary work, he moved his family to Florence for two years before returning to the United States for good.

Wharton's childhood had been spent in Europe; her expatriation was, consequently, more in the nature of a return to roots; and, in any event, she never abandoned her dedication to American society. Sinclair Lewis spent time in Berlin in 1928, but this was prompted by his desire to be with his lover, the journalist, Dorothy Thompson.

O'Neill sailed for Europe 'quietly' in 1928, hoping to keep his departure (with his lover, Carlotta Monterey) from his wife. He then moved secretly from London to the Pyrenees, thence to Shanghai, trying to keep the two from scandal-hunting reporters, before his divorce became final and he married Ms Monterey and settled into a chateau in the Loire Valley for two years. Hiding from the literary and social scene in Britain and France, O'Neill did allow to George Jean Nathan that the seclusion he enjoyed was providing him with "more strength to put into one's job" than he had found "in the U.S.A" and he did manage to write the trilogy *Mourning Becomes Electra* while there, but Europe's primary appeal for O'Neill appeared to be the chance at privacy, coupled with "the obvious financial reasons": "You can live so much better here on so much less money," he told his son, Eugene Jr., in September 1928. In any event, he cut his trip to the Far East short principally because "I couldn't write a line there", and by April 1931, he and Carlotta were on their way back to the U.S.

"Europe is fine," he wrote to Agnes Brennan, "but I don't see how any American can ever settle here for good" (Gelb 1960: 663, 668, 680; Bogard and Bryer 1988: 288, 296, 311, 313, 337, 343, 381).

Gertrude Stein was essentially a bored medical-school student when she moved to Paris on a whim (though she certainly 'found' herself there). Henry Miller moved there, not so much as a self-exile seeking new direction, as one fleeing personal and occupational failure. His first attempts to pull himself away from his Brooklyn roots (moves to Florida and California) had left him floundering. The steamship ticket for France appears to have been presented to him by his philandering wife as a means of getting him out of the picture (Kennedy 1993: 143-114).

But others *do* appear to have consciously exiled themselves to foreign shores (at least for substantial periods of time) *with* a spiritual purpose. Lloyd Kramer's insightful observation comes to mind: "The experience of living among alien people, languages and institutions can [significantly] alter the individual's sense of self. [...] Intellectual exiles frequently respond to their deracination by describing home (idealistically) or rejecting home (angrily) or creating a new definition of home (defiantly)" (Kramer 1988: 9-10). This passage serves well as a description of the experience of a number of American literary 'exiles'.

Writers like James Fenimore Cooper, Henry Adams, Henry James, and T.S. Eliot, none of them exiles-by-compulsion, appear to have 'returned' to the Mother Country with a kind of imagined nostalgia. Cooper, for example, complained of a "poverty of original writers" in his antebellum United States, as well as a poverty "of materials [...] no annals for the historian; no follies for the satirist; no manners for the dramatist; no obscure fiction for the writer of romance" (Cooper 1960: I, 287; II, 107). Hawthorne, in *The Marble Faun*, offered a similar verdict: "Romance and poetry, like ivy, lichens, and wallflowers, need ruins to make them grow" (noted in Marden, ch. 8). An unsuccessful artist in Henry James's *The Madonna of the Future* bemoans what he regards as the fact that "we are the disinherited of Art [...] excluded from the magic circle! The soil of American perception is [...] as void of all that nourishes and prompts and inspires the artist as my sad heart is void of bitterness in saying so! We poor aspirants must live in perpetual exile" (James 1962, 3: 14-15). Thus, many of James's American heroes and heroines were constantly "looking to see something original and beautiful" (Levin 1966: 75-76) in England, France, or Italy. But it is only fair to note a certain ambivalence on James's part towards these characters; after all, the narrator of *The Madonna of the Future* responds unsympathetically to the artist's plaint: "You seem fairly at home in exile... Florence seems to me a very easy Siberia... Nothing is so idle as to talk about our want of a nutritive soil, of opportunity, of inspiration, of the things that help. The only thing that helps is to do something fine!" (James 1962, 3: 15)[7]

Others, like Ezra Pound, e.e. cummings, John Dos Passos, Ernest Hemingway, Richard Wright, Djuna Barnes, and James Baldwin, appear to have sought to escape from their familiar American roots, not in order to imbibe the culture of their ancestors so much as to distance themselves from either the puritanical or materialistic aspects of the US (or both) in the hopes of acquiring greater levels of literary awareness and creativity in unfamiliar surroundings.[8] In this regard, they echo the experiences of their English predecessors, Keats, Shelley, Byron and Robert and Elizabeth Barrett Browning. (Barnes and Baldwin were also escaping homophobia.)

For some, it was the Great War that had "dislodged them from their homes and the old restraints, given them an unexpected and disillusioning education, and left them entirely rootless," in Alfred Kazin's formulation (Kazin 1956: 240). The proceedings of the ensuing Peace Conference at Versailles was noted as well, as in Dos Passos's account of the "three men shuffling the pack, dealing the cards: the Rhineland, Danzig, the Polish Corridor, the Ruhr, self-determination of small nations, the Saar, League of Nations, mandates, the Mespot, Freedom of the Seas, Transjordania, Shantung, Fiume, and the Island of Yap; / machinegun fire and arson / starvation, lice, cholera, typhus; / oil was trumps" (Dos Passos 1930: 248). Similarly, the heroine of Dorothy Canfield's *The Deepening Stream*, becoming aware of the behind-the-scenes wheeling and dealing at Versailles, "began to cry. She felt her way to a bench and sat on it, burying her face in her hands and sobbing....She felt a hand on her shoulder....A gaunt old man, shabbily dressed, a refugee.... 'Pardon...I see that Madame is in trouble. Madame is a refugee?' 'No,' said Matey, and then, 'Yes!'" (Canfield 1930: 336).

At home there were, on the one hand, flappers, bobbed hair, bootleg gin, and speakeasies; jazz, blues, and the movies; the Model T, Freud, Havelock Ellis, and the Sexual Revolution; and news of a strange new European artistic movement, Dada; on the other hand, there were Prohibition, the deportation of alien radicals, a widespread crack-down on Unions, Sacco & Vanzetti, the Immigration Restriction Act, racism, the eugenics movement, the Ku Klux Klan, and a resurgence of religious fundamentalism. Malcolm Cowley tells us (in *Exile's Return: A Literary Odyssey of the 1920s*) of a symbolically significant moment: In 1921 Harold Stearns proclaimed that the U.S. was a "maladjusted" mess and that "the futility of a rationalist attack" on the mess was "obvious". He decided to abandon the United States, and when he left for Paris, with some fanfare, in July 1921, "he was seen," says Cowley, as "Byron shaking the dust of England from his feet." Reporters "came to the gangplank to jot down his last words. Everywhere young men were prepared to follow his example [...]. 'I'm going to Paris' they said at first, and then, 'I'm going to the South of France [...]. I'm sailing Wednesday – next month – as soon as I can scrape together money enough to buy a ticket... I'm sick of this country. I'm going abroad to write one good novel'" (Cowley 1951: 78-79, 175).

Ezra Pound called to them from abroad as well. In 'The Rest' (1917) he writes:

> O Helpless few in my country,
> O remnant enslaved,
>
> Artists broken against her,
> Astray, lost in our villages,
> Mistrusted, spoken-against,
> [...]
> You of the finer sense,
> [...]
> Hated, shut in, mistrusted;
>
> Take thought:
> I have weathered the storm,
> I have beaten out my exile.
>
> (Pound 2003: 272)

Of course their new European homes had social, economic, and political shortcomings as well. Moreover, others of those who had exiled themselves in the 1920's ("myself included," Cowley adds) disregarded "the Ruhr, *fascismo*, reparations, the New Economic Policy, the birth of prosperity, as they bedazzled themselves with the future of their art" (Cowley 1934: 78-79, 175, 214).

But for Afro-American literati, these shortcomings seemed less significant than the racism they confronted constantly at home. Richard Wright, who left the States permanently in 1947, has the hero of *The Long Dream* reflect on a conversation he has just had with an Italian-American on a flight the hero is taking to exile in Europe, having been released from prison after over two years for a crime he had not committed: "That man's father had come to America and had found a dream; he [Fish Tucker] had been born in America and had found it a nightmare" (Wright 1958: 380).

Some clearly flourished during their 'exile'. One thinks especially of Hemingway, Pound, Eliot, Stein, and Miller. Italo Calvino describes a paradox in *Invisible Cities*: "Arriving at each new city, the traveller finds again a past of his that he did not know he had; the foreignness of what you no longer are or no longer possess lies in wait for you in foreign, unpossessed places" (quoted in Kennedy 1993: 27). "One of the things that I have liked all these years", Gertrude Stein writes in her *Autobiography of Alice B. Toklas*, "is to be surrounded by people who know no English. It has left me intensely alone with my eyes and my English. I do not know if it would have been possible to have English be so all in all to me otherwise" (Stein 1990: 70). Similarly, Hemingway suggests in *A Moveable Feast* that writers like himself and his fellow exiles may benefit from their 'transplanting' like other life forms. But things can, at times, be 'relative': while European critics were impressed by Richard Wright's 'transplantation' in French existentialism (evident in *The Outsiders* and *Savage Holiday*) his countrymen were not.

In any event, they became, in Alfred Kazin's words, "specialists in anguish" (1956: 241). Dos Passos's anguish over the way things were is evident throughout his *U.S.A.* trilogy, as when he sighs in his 'Camera's Eye' account of the struggle over Sacco and Vanzetti: "all right we are two nations" (Dos Passos 1930: 462). Consider also Thomas Wolfe's angst: "Naked and alone we came into exile [...] What doors are open to this wanderer? And which of us finds his father, knows his face, and in what place, and in what time, and in what land?" (quoted in Kazin 1956: 368-9). Henry Miller willingly grants, in *Tropic of Cancer* that "we are doomed", but he recommends an "agonizing, blood-curdling howl, a screech of defiance, a war-whoop!", a "last expiring dance" around "the rim of the crater [...] but a dance!" (Miller: 1, 98-99, 257). (And, for all its chauvinism, *Tropic of Cancer is* one-hell-of-a-successful literary dance.)

If some flourished, many others (perhaps most) of these self-styled exiles were disappointed; either their sojourns abroad did *not* stimulate their creative selves, *or* they concluded that their vision of a superior European culture had been just that – a vision, with little basis. Mark Twain's *A Tramp Abroad* is a screed assailing European (especially German) culture. His *Connecticut Yankee in King Arthur's Court* displays little mercy for English social structure and customs. James Fenimore Cooper's sojourn abroad dissuaded him from any further "truckling" to "European opinions" (Cooper 1960: 1: 287). It is true that Cooper returned "out of step with his country," in the words of his biographer. Europe had "unfitted him for life in America" in that he would continue to identify with a culture of "gentility" (albeit an American one) (quoted in Marder 1984: 35). Nevertheless, his most enduring hero, one to whom he returned again and again, Natty Bumpo ("Leatherstocking"), is a homespun democrat, and one who is constantly retreating to the moving frontier, exiling himself from an encroaching American society. Just so, Cooper wrote to a friend that "now my longing is for a Wilderness – Cooperstown is far too populous and artificial for me and it is my intention to plunge somewhere into the forest [...]" (1960: II, 89). Moreover, Cooper then created the *first* literary 'Ishmael' in nineteenth-century American literature, Ishmael Bush, Leather-stocking's counterpart in *The Prairie*. This "semi-barbarous squatter" (Cooper: 1960 364) thought little of 'exiling' countless *native* Americans, but Cooper was not completely unsympathetic towards Ishmael Bush, whom he characterizes as basically honest - if stubborn - an impoverished child of democracy, a self-exile on the vast prairie, seeking little more than a new chance for his ever-growing family (see Marder 1984: 45, for such an interpretation, with which I agree).

Many of those who had exiled themselves in the 1920s may have "escaped from all the things they hated"; they may have made it to a "café looking out across" a "sun-hallucinated square" in France or "the Tripolitanian coast," or Dalmatia; to a place "where one could lie abed all day and work through the night," where one could "write without thought of editorial deadlines or critics asking what it meant; [where] one could write exactly as one pleased," but the "days passed by and the great novel or poems was not even started. The refugees were undergoing a peculiar experience," Malcolm Cowley observed: "Here [...] there were no distractions whatever, nothing to keep them from working except the terrifying discovery that they had nothing now to say" (Cowley 1951: 242-43). Cowley, to be sure, distinguishes between what could generally be accomplished in Paris, where most were able to write *something*, and this emptiness that came upon those who retreated to more isolated sites.

So many of these 'exiles' returned to the United States. Harold Stearns wasted eleven years in Paris, borrowing from friends in the Montparnasse colony, and selling tourists racetrack tips as 'Peter Pickem' for the *Paris Tribune,* before returning to the States in 1932 to reverse his earlier general condemnation of American culture with *The Street I Knew* and *America: A Reappraisal.* John Dos Passos, furious at the Communist purges within some of the battalions of the International Brigade in Spain, during that country's Civil War, plunged back into the American mainstream, as did Archibald MacLeish, who championed Franklin Roosevelt and turned from Ars Poetica to a Poetry of Commitment. Similarly, James Baldwin, returning in 1956, would engage himself productively in the Civil Rights movement over the next decade (although he retreated for 'Relief and Recovery' to his favourite abode, Istanbul).

In the meantime, those who had *not* declared themselves to be exiles – talents like John Steinbeck, William Faulkner, Carl Sandburg, Stephen Vincent Benet, Robert Sherwood, James Agee, Erskine Caldwell, and the documentary film-maker, Pare Lorenz – would, in the thirties, produce powerful portraits of American culture and life, some of which may endure at least as long as those of the 'Lost Generation'.

America's literary 'exiles' were *not* archetypical. No American literati could truly be said to have been 'banished'; few were truly victims of political or cultural persecution, despite Ezra Pound's claim. Few were driven by impoverishment to become refugees – in fact, some may have become impoverished *because* of their self-exile. Some writers who never left the States, like Emily Dickinson, and perhaps William Faulkner, *could* be said to have been true 'spiritual' exiles, while others who *did* leave, including some of those who virtually *emigrated* to France, were actually mere sojourners, inasmuch as their fealty to the United States, its culture and its literature, remained fixed. Among those who *do* appear to have exiled themselves, some acted out of a sense of veneration for the Old World, others were simply escaping the New in order to find new voices. Some of the latter found those voices in exile; many others did not, and had to return to their roots in the States in that quest.

Is there a message in any of this? Would it be that, for most of those writers who have a real *choice*, physical self-exile is neither a necessary nor a sufficient step to discover one's talents or stimulate one's creative juices? But one must allow that it is impossible to

know, at the outset, whether one is likely to be the *exception* to this
generalization, or the *rule*.

Notes

[1] This paper draws, in part, on Peter Karsten, '"Escape from the Anguish": A
Historical Typology of Exiles with Particular Attention to American Literary Exiles'
in Helmut Koopmann and Klaus Dieter Post (eds) (2001) *Exil: Transhistorische und
Transnationale Perspektiven*. Paderborn: Mentis: 147-158.
[2] Among the several studies of American writers in Paris, see George Wickes, 1969,
Americans in Paris; Shari Benstock, 1986, *Women of the Left Bank, Paris: 1900-
1940*; J. Gerald Kennedy, 1993, *Imagining Paris: Exile, Writing and American
Identity*; and Jean Méral, 1989, *Paris in American Literature*.
[3] For a recent account of the treatment of Native Americans that incorporates the
notion of exile, see Oren Lyons, et al., 1992, *Exiled in the Land of the Free:
Democracy, Indian Nations and the U.S. Constitution* (Clear Light Pub., Santa Fe).
See also: James Merrill, 1989, *The Indian's New World: Catawbas and Their
Neighbours from European Contact through the Era of Removal* (Chapel Hill:
Published for the Institute of Early American History and Culture, Williamsburg, Va.,
by the University of North Carolina Press) 185; Colin G. Calloway, 1995, *The
American Revolution in Indian Country: Crisis and Diversity in Native-American
Communities* (Cambridge, New York: Cambridge Univ. Press).
[4] The 'Loyalists' of the 1770s and '80s, who would flee the 'Patriot' governments of
the thirteen rebellious North American colonies to new homes in the British Canadian
provinces, the West Indies, or the British Isles themselves; certain defeated supporters
of the 'Confederacy', who emigrated to Mexico and elsewhere after 1865; Radicals
expatriated (that is, deported) during the 'Red Scare' of 1919 and 1920; some home-
grown U.S. Reds who elected to exile themselves in the 1920s and '30s by emigrating
to the Soviet Union; as well as draft-resisters during the Vietnam War who chose to
move to Canada, Britain, or Sweden. One source for the views of certain of these self-
exiles is the newsletter of the Union of American Exiles, *American Exile in Canada*,
published in Toronto for at least two years (1968 and 1969). See also Marcia
Freedman, 1990, *Exile in the Promised Land: A Memoir* (Ithaca: Cornell University
Press), a feminist's account of self-exile to Israel.
[5] In this connection, mention should perhaps be made of the followers of Joseph
Smith and the Church of Jesus Christ of the Latter-Day Saints (Mormons), who
abandoned homes in Illinois and Missouri (when local opposition to their religious
and social ways reached fever pitches), for their God-given 'State of Deseret', where
they promptly made exiles of some of that place's aboriginal inhabitants.
[6] Emma Lazarus' famous poem about the Statue of Liberty styles her "the Mother of
Exiles," and Lazarus did not have only political or religious refugees in mind (*Poems
of Emma Lazarus*. 2 vols., Boston: Houghton Mifflin, 1899, "The New Colossus"
Vol. 1: 202-03).
[7] Compare Marder 1984: 14 with a somewhat more insightful analysis of *The
Madonna* by Harry Levin in his 'Literature and Exile' chapter in *Refractions: Essays
in Comparative Literature* (1966: 75-76).

[8] Andrew Gurr believes that the condition of expatriation by writers in the twentieth century became so commonplace that exile seemed "the essential characteristic of the modern writer" (1981: 14). While true, this actually describes a number of American authors of the *nineteenth* century, as well as most of those of the twentieth century.

Bibliography

Benstock, Shari. 1986. *Women of the Left Bank, Paris: 1900-1940*. Austin: University of Texas Press.

Canfield, Dorothy. 1930. *The Deepening Stream*. New York: Harcourt Brace.

Cooper, James Fenimore. 1960. *Letters and Journals of J.F. Cooper* (ed. James Franklin Beard). Cambridge, Mass: Belknap Press of Harvard University.

Cowley, Malcolm. 1951. *Exile's Return: A Literary Odyssey of the Nineteen Twenties* New York: Viking.

Dos Passos, John. 1937. *USA: Trilogy, including The Forty-Second Parallel, 1919, and The Big Money*. New York: Modern Library.

Gelb, Arthur and Barbara Gelb. 1962. *O'Neill*. New York: Harper.

Grossman, James. 1949. *James Fenimore Cooper*. New York: W. Sloan.

Gurr, Andrew. 1981. *Writers in Exile*. Sussex: Harvester.

Hendricks, Randy. 2000. *Lonelier than God: Robert Penn Warren and the Southern Exile*. Athens: University of Georgia Press.

Howard, Leon. 1952. *Victorian Knight-Errant: The Early Literary Career of James Russell Lowell*. Berkeley: University of California Press.

James, Henry. 1962. *Complete Tales of Henry James* (ed. Leon Edel). 3 vols., Philadelphia: J B Lippincott.

Karsten, Peter. 2001. '"Escape from the Anguish": A Historical Typology of Exiles with Particular Attention to American Literary Exiles' in Koopmann, Helmut and Klaus Dieter Post (eds) *Exil: Transhistorische und Transnationale Perspektiven*. Paderborn: Mentis: 147-158.

Kazin, Alfred. 1956. *On Native Grounds: An Interpretation of Modern American Prose Literature*. Abr. ed. with a new postscript. Garden City, N.Y.: Doubleday.

Kennedy, J. Gerald. 1993. *Imagining Paris: Exile, Writing and American Identity*. New Haven: Yale University Press.

Kramer, Lloyd S. 1988. *Threshold of a New World: Intellectuals and the Exile Experience in Paris, 1830-1848*. Ithaca: Cornell University Press.

Levin, Harry. 1966. *Refractions: Essays in Comparative Literature*. New York: Oxford University Press.

Marder, Daniel. 1984. *Exiles at Home: A Story of Literature in Nineteenth-Century America*. Lanham: University Press of America.

Méral, Jean. 1989. *Paris in American Literature* (tr. Laurette Long). Chapel Hill: University of North Carolina Press.

Melville, Herman. 1888. *John Marr and Other Sailors*. Boston, private printing of 25 copies.

Miller, Henry. 1961, *Tropic of Cancer*. New York, Grove Press.

O'Neill, Eugene. 1988. *Selected Letters of Eugene O'Neill* (ed. Travis Bogard and Jackson Bryer). New Haven: Yale University Press.

Pound, Ezra. 2003. *Ezra Pound: Poems and Translation* (ed. Richard Sieburth). New
    York: Library of America.
Stein, Gertrude. 1990. *The Autobiography of Alice Toklas*. New York: Vintage.
Wickes, George. 1969. *Americans in Paris*. Garden City, New York: Doubleday.
Wright, Richard. 1958. *The Long Dream*. New York: Doubleday.

14

Interview, Poems, and a Short Story: 'Fingers', 'Kyrenia', 'Don't Forget', and 'Ledra Street'

Nora Nadjarian

Nora Nadjarian is an Armenian Cypriot. Her grandparents arrived in Cyprus as refugees from Asia Minor in the early part of the twentieth century. She grew up in a Greek-speaking community in Limassol and was just seven years old when, in 1974, the partition of the island nation into a Turkish north and a Greek southern portion took place. She and her family experienced, in effect, a second exile, as Greek Cypriots living in the north were forced to move south and Turkish Cypriots living in the south had to move north. Since 1974, Cypriots of both communities have been unable to move freely within their own country. In April 2003, the first moves towards relaxation of the partition occurred. Nora undertook most of her formal education in the UK and writes in English. She has won several international awards for her writing, including prizes in the Scottish International Open Poetry Competition in 2000, and again in 2003. Her story 'Ledra Street' was a runner-up in the Commonwealth Short Story Competition in 2001. Her work has appeared in magazines in the UK and US, and a volume of her poetry, *The Voice at the Top of the Stairs*, was published in Cyprus in 2001.

In an interview for the accompanying DVD, she talks of her personal experience of partition and reads and comments on poems and a short story deriving from that experience. The poem 'Fingers' recalls her sense of childhood confusion on the day in 1974 when partition took place. In 'Kyrenia' (written in 2001) she can only imagine herself in the beautiful northern port town, about which she heard so much but, like all other Greek Cypriots, could not visit – until 2003. The poem 'Don't Forget' (2003) takes up the mantra which Greek Cypriots have been repeating for almost thirty years, as if fearful that they might surrender their memories of locations, including their former homes, which they have not seen for all that time. For the short story 'Ledra Street', Nadjarian created a fictional fatal accident whose absurdity mirrors the tragic lack of logic with which a street in Nicosia has been cut in half by the partition of the capital city. In the interview she talks of the occasion, very recently, when she first came face-to-face with Turkish Cypriot writers.

See DVD

Fingers

(Cyprus, 1974)

You clasp and cling onto that hour,
like a baby; that one hour in summer when
everything happened. And changed.

There was music on the radio.
In the kitchen Mum and her mum
tailed ladies' fingers, on the hour
(about an hour to cook); and you cycled
or read about Alice whose fingers shrank
in the Land of Wonder. Fifty minutes.

The hour in July grew hotter.
Ants climbed your toes while you blew
gum bubbles onto the bark of the fig tree
with its leaves like big, green hands.
Grass underneath your sandals crunched
just like fire crackling. Thirty-five.

Ten minutes and your ice cream
melted vanilla onto a stray cat's ears and
something droned out of the blue in the sky
and the music stopped. Mum came
and took you, pushed you till your fingers
gave and the ice cream dropped.

Dad was back with shouting eyes;
it was too early to see him. Mum was not setting
the table with forks but tears. The saucepan
had boiled over but nobody cared. And you cried
because of the vanilla which you loved
and the whole kitchen wailed. Five.

And you were in the car, leaving. Five.
The cat was licking its vanilla paws. Four.
Ladies' fingers were sobbing in the kitchen. Three.

The fig tree's leaves were waving goodbye. Two.
You were letting go, finger by finger. One.
You never knew the island was dividing.

You never knew an hour could be so cruel.

Kyrenia

Imagine it, says my mother. Kyrenia.
Standing at the edge of ripples,
an orange sun on my hair,
zest on my skin.

Boats dancing in water, floating
like smiles at a wedding, on white light.
Mermaid voices gliding in and out
of nets, shimmers of songs.

Like my youth, she says, out of reach.
At times, she weeps; till sun meets moon,
till mermaids scream and boats turn
to rocks about to sink.

Don't Forget

The past came to visit again last night,
wrapped her arms round my neck
and whispered: It's me. Don't forget.

I knocked at a door which a woman opened.
She said in Turkish: Come in. Welcome.
Hoşgeldiniz. Hoşgeldiniz.

She handed an album of photos of me,
my husband, our children, this house,
pre-1974. The blue album. My living room.

I kept these for you, she said.
I thanked her in Greek. *Efcharisto poli.*

A tiny space the size of a pinhead

between each word, stung the air, the moment,
the dream. She offered coffee and sweets.
One of us was guest, the other hostess – but which?

Oh, there are some dreams which make no sense.
Turn over the cup, she said. I will tell you
your fortune, and we will learn the future.

Yes, I said, yes. We leant like two friends over a secret,
and the patterns of the future on the walls of the cup
made us weep on each other's shoulders –

all those thirty-year old tears, finally, belatedly;
two sisters who were mothers, wives, daughters,
so long ago. Then the past came and sat between us

and woke me with a whisper:
It's me. Don't forget.

Ledra Street

I would like to tell you about the *kafenion*[1], about the cat that lived
there, and the cheese rinds I fed it. About the coffee-shop owner who
was hit by a car, and the tray and the glasses and the coffee which
flew. These are the less important things.

   More importantly, there was a time Ledra Street was a whole,
non-pedestrianised, and we still called Turkish coffee, Turkish. But
that was a long time ago.

   I can find the spot even now where the coffee-shop owner tried
to cross, and the car hit him and the glass and the cups and the coffee
flew. He died in hospital later. The tyres screeched, the men gathered
round and my father ran out of his shop with a pic-measure in his hand
to see if it was me, panic written in his eyes and a pic-measure in his
hands, as if to measure the life or death left in the body on the tarmac.
I read panic again in my father's eyes one hot July day, the day I grew

---

[1] *kafenion* – a traditional Cyprus coffee-shop

up. The day my memory was divided into important and less important things.

Today I walked on Ledra Street and counted the steps from where the *kafenion* stood, all the way to the checkpoint. It was fifty-two steps. Fifty-two steps to freedom, fifty-two steps to captivity. I can only imagine the other side. My father's shop hidden in a souk. Labyrinths of spices, hands dripping gold, a tree of idleness, Bellapaix, *la belle paix*. When the *hodja*'s[2] voice clings to the clammy summer evenings, I try to imagine his face and weigh the importance of his syllables. What is he asking God, and how carefully is God listening?

I secretly mourned the coffee-shop owner's death for years. It was my fault he died. "Don't feed it on the table," he would say. "Not on the table. A cat has nine, I have only one. If anyone comes in and finds a cat on the table in my kitchen, I will not have any custom. I will not have a life." And the day he lost his life, he made three coffees on the pale blue flame. The bubbles of the coffee rose and subsided, rose and subsided in the *brikki*.[3] He lined up the little cups, filled them, picked up the aluminium tray, that special swaying pyramid of a tray, and left his shop, the cat, and me.

It was my fault. I would like to say this to the sky in the evening, like the *hodja*: it was my fault. But somehow it doesn't seem important any more. It sounds silly, even. I had been feeding the cat on the table, when I thought I heard a noise. I took the cat and threw it on the floor. Frightened, it ran into the street and got tangled in his feet. The brakes screeched, too late. So he died, because of me and a stupid cat.

It was in the paper the next day. My father made his lips small enough to pull in the coffee from the little cup, and read – possibly to himself, possibly to my mother: "Andreas Demetriou, 41, killed by driver on Ledra Street." My mother said: "And his wife? And his children? Don't they ever write about those that are left behind?"

I am now the one left behind. Behind a wall, behind a checkpoint, looking for my father's shop, looking for my childhood, dismissing a man's death, mourning the division of a city. Counting the steps to the other side. Wondering where unimportance ends and importance begins.

---

[2] *hodja* – a muezzin, who calls Muslims to prayer from a mosque
[3] *brikki* – a small pot used for making traditional Cyprus coffee

15

The Poetics of Exile in the Inter-war Novels of Irina Odoevtseva

Xenia Srebrianski Harwell

Xenia Srebrianski Harwell was born in a displaced persons' camp in West Germany into a Russian and Lithuanian/German family. After emigrating to the United States she and her parents settled first in Harlem, and eventually in the Bronx, and became part of New York's large and dynamic Russian émigré community, attending Russian school on Saturdays for twelve years. She studied at Barnard College, the University of Vienna, Vanderbilt University and University of Tennessee-Knoxville. She later worked at the US Consulate in St. Petersburg, Russia. Srebrianski Harwell has taught Russian and German language, literature, and culture at colleges in the South and Midwest of the US. She is the author of *The Female Adolescent in Exile in Works by Irina Odoevtseva, Nina Berberova, Irmgard Keun, and Ilse Tielsch*, Peter Lang, 2000). As an inveterate wanderer, she has travelled throughout the US, Canada, and Mexico, as well as in the Caribbean, Eastern and Western Europe, Russia, Africa, Mongolia, China, and New Zealand.

In this paper she examines the writings of Irina Odoevtseva, a member of the first wave of Russian émigrés after the revolution, who settled in Paris and, over the next sixty years, wrote novels and poetry in Russian, few of which have been translated. She returned to Russia with celebrity status in 1987 and died in 1990. The three novels discussed here centre on the lives of young Russian women, living in Paris, who negotiate in different ways the gaining of erotic experience and the loss of connection with their Russian cultural origins. The first novel, *Angel Smerti* (1927, Angel of Death), depicts the inner life of Ljuka, a young girl, whose memories of the violent events surrounding her emigration from Russia come to taint her newly awakening sexuality. The second novel, *Izol'da* (1929, Isolde), is a psychological thriller involving three young Russians involved in a robbery and murder, which Srebrianski Harwell sees, on a metaphorical level, as a study of the instability of émigré identity. The third novel, *Zerkalo* (1939, The Mirror), returns to the central character of *Angel Smerti*, as she abandons her husband to penetrate the brilliance and glamour of the French film-making world. Herself later abandoned, she attaches herself to a Soviet traveller and briefly contemplates the possibility of a return to the Soviet Union, soon realising that such a plan is unrealistic. Odoevtseva prided herself on not living in the past and on adapting to the community she found herself in. The melodramatic

depiction, in these three novels, of the psychic agonies of exiles who
fail both to adapt and to maintain a full sense of their Russian identity,
suggest unacknowledged exilic anxieties in the author herself.

Irina Odoevtseva was a member of the 'first wave' of Russian
émigrés, those who left Russia following the revolution and civil war.
Born in Riga in 1895 and raised in St Petersburg, she became a
student of the poet Nikolaj Gumilev and a member of the acmeist
Guild of Poets. In 1922 she published her first collection of poetry,
and the following year she settled in Paris, where she was an active
member of Russian cultural circles. She published four novels and six
collections of poetry, but became best known for her memoirs, *Na
beregakh Nevy* (On the Banks of the Neva, 1967) and *Na beregakh
Seny* (On the Banks of the Seine, 1983). In 1987 she returned to St
Petersburg at the invitation of the Writers' Union and enjoyed
celebrity status there until her death in 1990.

The three novels Odoevtseva completed during the interwar
period – *Angel smerti* (Angel of Death, 1927), *Izol'da* (Isolde, 1929)
and *Zerkalo* (The Mirror, 1939) – are the subject of this paper. At the
time of their publication these novels were quite popular, and *Angel
smerti* was translated into English as *Out of Childhood* (1930) and into
German as *Ljuka der Backfisch, Roman* (1930). However, they have
never been republished, and are available in few libraries.
Consequently, today they are little known and have been the subject of
scant scholarly attention.

Odoevtseva dismissed her novels as "chisto zhenskikh"
(Kedrova 1988: 4; 'purely women's writing'), that is, dealing with
love. It is true that, with young women as central characters, love is an
integral part of each plot. However, each work also participates in the
discourse about exile, touching on some of the issues facing Russian
émigrés in Odoevtseva's time. Taken together, the novels appear to
follow a progression that reflects different stages in the emigration and
assimilation process. Mutating family relationships, and the changing
mix of the heroines' love interests, mark the stages of transition. In
Angel smerti, published just a few years after Odoevtseva's departure
from Russia, we have a present mother (there are no fathers in these
works—they perished in Russia) and a cohesive family. Evening
conversation focuses on Russia, and both love interests are Russian. In
Izol'da, which was written two years later, we find a vanishing mother
who abandons her children. Family life is on the verge of a complete
breakdown, and discussions of Russia are avoided. There are two love

interests – one Russian and one French. In the last novel, written a decade later, both mother and family have disappeared. A Russian husband has been abandoned in favour of the major love interest, who is French. It should be noted that the heroine's movement away from Russia, family, and Russian boyfriends does not constitute progress – at each stage there is failure in terms of personal fulfilment and integration into the new society.

One of the issues Odoevtseva is able to touch upon, by featuring adolescents as protagonists, is that of the retention of Russian culture in the younger generation. Members of the Russian émigré community in Paris made extensive efforts to create the social structures that would enable Russian children to continue their Russian education and knowledge of native culture, with the expectation of an eventual return to the homeland (Harwell 2000: 103). None of Odoevtseva's protagonists are integrated into such structures, and the loss of Russian culture among them is evident. Although they speak Russian, they are not completely familiar with Russian literature, nor do they have a firm religious foundation. In *Angel smerti*, an aunt appears to criticize the mother for not raising the girls to be more culturally Russian, to which the mother replies that her primary concerns are economic (Odoevtseva 1928: 77-8). In fact, the mothers pragmatically encourage their daughters to do well at French, rather than Russian, schools. Additionally, each novel individually foregrounds and poetizes other aspects of the exile condition, and it is these that I will focus on now.

In *Angel smerti*, Ljuka, a lively fourteen-year old, eager to grow up, falls in love with Arsenij, the boyfriend of her older sister, Vera. Vera marries a rich Russian for reasons of economic survival, but continues her affair with Arsenij and is carrying his child. Through a misunderstanding, Ljuka believes that Arsenij loves her. In order to keep her from learning of the affair with Vera, Arsenij feigns love for Ljuka and kisses her. Vera sees them, and in her shock falls down some stairs, and is fatally injured. Not understanding that Ljuka is innocent, Vera curses her before she dies.

Much of the novel is devoted to describing Ljuka's inner life, and in particular her preoccupation with death, a state of mind that appears to have had its inception during the period of the revolution and emigration. Thinking back to that time, Ljuka remembers the dark empty mirrors in her house that gave her a sense of foreboding, and reflects that the idea of a happy childhood is just a myth (Odoevtseva

1928: 10). She dwells on thoughts of her dead father, who was murdered by the Bolsheviks.

Ljuka's memory of Russia is part of a private and separate world that is not to be shared with outsiders. When a French acquaintance asks Ljuka to tell her about Russia (Odoevtseva 1928: 17), Ljuka pretends not to remember anything about it, although later she thinks to herself: "Pomnit li ona? Razve mozhno zabyt'? Tak bol'no. Tak grustno....No ob etom nel'zja razskazyvat' glupoj, chuzhoj zhenshchine" (1928: 17; "Does she remember? How can she forget? So painful. So sad...But one should not talk about this to a stupid, foreign woman"; this, and all other translations, with no source indicated, are my own).

Ljuka's departure from Russia is tainted with violence. When she is forbidden to take her cat, which she loves above all else, she places its neck in a noose and hangs it. As she watches its death twitches, she sees Azrail, the Angel of Death, with huge black wings, swoop in to take the cat's soul (Odoevtseva 1928: 49). In Paris, Ljuka continues to struggle with the deaths of her father and her cat, through surrealistic visions that blend reality and the projections of her mind.

To Ljuka, Azrail, and therefore death, continues to be equated with departure. Ljuka finds herself on the shore of the Black Sea (the location of the mass evacuation of Russians following the failure of the White Army), waiting to be evacuated. As she looks across the water, the ominous image of Azrail floats before her eyes. Later in Paris she makes the same connection between death and departure in a poem she recites on her way home from school: "Est' Angel Smerti v groznyj chas/ Poslednikh muk i razstavan'ja/ On krepko obnimaet nas,/ No kholodny ego lobzan'ja" " (Odoevtseva 1928: 55; "There is an angel of death at the terrible hour of last suffering and separation. He embraces us tightly, but cold are his kisses"). These lines refer to the journey into physical death, but to Ljuka they also represent the journey into exile. Not without significance also is the fact that the Angel of Death is among the fallen angels banished from heaven, and therefore is in exile himself (Bethea 1994: 38).

In the poem quoted above, a connection is also made between death and sexual images – the embrace and the kiss. This too is related to Ljuka's experience. The image of the Angel of Death is so firmly embedded in Ljuka's subconscious that her awakening sexuality is also expressed through his image. In a dream, Ljuka lies nude on a couch, feeling both shame and pleasure. She sees black wings, feels cold and death, and recognizes Azrail. He caresses her breasts and kisses her. As before, we see Ljuka between the realms of reality and vision: when she awakens from the dream, she 'sees' Azrail sitting on her bed, and asks him to return every night (Odoevtseva 1928: 51-52). Furthermore, she conflates the images of Arsenij and Azrail (Odoevtseva 1928: 135) into the surrealistic erotic/death-bringing figure that she sees at the church door at Vera's funeral. Thus it is the process of emigration and exile that has permeated Ljuka's consciousness with a pathological hyperawareness of, and obsession with, death.

Odoevtseva was criticized by some members of the Russian community for portraying Russian youth negatively in her second novel, *Izol'da* (Bobrow 1996: 43; Harwell 2000: 23), which recounts the experience of three Russian adolescents living in Paris – Liza, her brother Nikolaj, and her boyfriend Andrej.

An English student, Cromwell, falls in love with Liza, and indulges the Russian threesome in the night life of Paris. Greedy for more, Nikolaj and Andrej devise a plan to steal Cromwell's mother's jewels. They murder Cromwell, dispose of his body, and run off with the jewels. Liza, an unwitting accomplice to the plot, seeks refuge in a hunting lodge belonging to Cromwell's cousin, Leslie. She returns to Paris in time to commit suicide with Andrej.

The title of the novel, *Izol'da*, alludes to the heroine of the medieval story of *Tristan and Isolde*, and suggests the theme of tragic love. But Odoevtseva does more than invoke the medieval work. A copy of the book becomes an actual prop in the novel in that this is what Cromwell happens to be reading when he looks up and sees Liza. With her long dress and blonde hair, Liza appears like a vision to him, and he is induced to call her 'Isolde'. Moreover, he hands Liza the book itself, which she then passes on to Andrej, calling him "her Tristan". This gesture accomplishes two things. First, on the symbolic level, it represents the intrusion of a 'western text' into the lives of the Russians. By accepting it and her new name, Liza symbolically agrees to become part of this western narrative. Secondly, what the text contains, the story of the Mark-Isolde-Tristan triangle, is now replicated in the newly established triangle of Cromwell-Liza-Andrej (Harwell 2000: 33). There are some other relevant similarities between the Russians and Tristan and Isolde – both groups are living as foreigners (Harwell 2000: 33). Tristan is 14, Liza's age, when he is kidnapped and brought to England. Cromwell, like Mark, is English, and although he has no kingdom, he does have possessions – a car and money – for which he is admired (Harwell 2000: 33). Finally, Isolde's suggestion that her friend Brangane be killed, even though she saves Isolde's life (Hatto 1960: 22), finds its parallel in the Russians' murder of a person who has been nothing but a good friend.

Nikolaj, who orchestrates the murder, violates morality on several other levels as well. Neither friendship nor family are sacred to him. He sets up an exchange: he offers Cromwell Liza's virginity if he promises to bring his mother's jewels to their house, and then he coerces Liza into spending the night with Cromwell. He lies to Liza about the purpose of the jewels, telling her that they will finance a trip to Russia (Harwell 2000: 34-5). Both he and Andrej, sixteen-year old males without prospects, illustrate the negative extreme of life in exile. They are victims of what Robert J. Lifton calls "psychohistorical dislocation" (Lifton 1979: 296), which involves the "breakdown of symbolizations around family, religion, authority in general, and the rites of passage of the life cycle" (Melton 1998: 82).

Whereas Nikolaj is completely alienated from his mother, and from both his past and present lives, Liza is not. She attempts to maintain normality in family relationships and is integrated into her school life at the French *lycée*. Most importantly, she continues to love Russia, even though this love is based on vague, nostalgic, childhood memories and a romantic imagination (Harwell 2000: 28). Liza's effort to reformulate Russia in her mind by assimilating the memories of older people, and by reading Russian literature and fairy tales, and her idealization of the Russian childhood, common to the Russian émigré sensibility, represents the "trope of the lost paradise" (Melton 1998: 86). Another characteristic that Liza shares with some émigrés is that of messianism. Her childhood fantasy of single-handedly rescuing her homeland through sacrifice and suffering parallels the adolescent Liza's fascination with the suffering figures of Joan of Arc and the Christian martyrs, and is projected into a dream, in which an angel confirms to Liza that she has been charged with a holy mission (Harwell 2000: 29). Her willingness to sacrifice her virginity for 'the cause', while an extension of her messianic thinking, is also, on another level, a distortion of the saintly ideal – a distortion arising, perhaps, from the irregular state of exile itself. Even so, if we wish to find in this novel the equivalent of the medieval work's love potion, which stands for something "that threatens to overwhelm [...], something that infects [the] whole being" (Hatto 1960: 7), then Liza's passion for Russia is that equivalent.

Liza's reaction to the crime, to the treachery of her brother and her boyfriend, to her abandonment by her mother and other adults, all of which occur simultaneously, is to retreat physically – to the remote country setting of the hunting lodge – as well as psychologically – into a state of amnesia and catatonia. The new, but alien, name – 'Betsy' – she is given by Leslie, another Westerner, reflects Liza's alienation from herself and the world, as do the robot-like repetitive speech patterns and the precise, unwavering daily routine of the lodge. Lifton terms this phenomenon, often a characteristic among exiles, as "psychic numbing" – a response to excessive psychic disruptions, in which "the mind [...] stops creating symbols and becomes deadened to external stimuli" (Melton 1998: 18).

On a metaphoric level, *Izol'da* explores the émigré's struggle between two cultures. Liza willingly accepts the manipulation of her identity by others (specifically, by Westerners) because, as a young émigré, she has difficulty in establishing her own. She is torn between her old love – Andrej/Russia, and her new love – Cromwell/the West, until she comes to understand that her attraction to the West is just a flirtation and that her place is at the side of the former. At the same time, she realizes that the choice of Andrej/Russia means continued hopelessness and the knowledge that no real choices remain.

Odoevtseva's third novel, *Zerkalo* (The Mirror), appearing about a decade after the first two, returns to the character Ljuka, who is now twenty-one and has left her Russian husband to live with the French filmmaker, Thierry Rivoire, who has promised to make her a film star. The couple lead a glamorous life and, in time, Thierry falls in love with her. He decides she should have his child, but when he learns of Vera's deathbed curse, he abandons Ljuka. She commits suicide, then he does the same.

The novel paints a psychological portrait of Ljuka as she gains and then loses love. The mirror imagery that is referred to in the title of the work is a device that reflects Ljuka's psychological state and plays on the novel's theme of image versus reality. Ljuka at 21 is more detached and hopeless than her fifteen year-old self in *Angel smerti*. One scholar has noted a discontinuity in the depiction of the character between the two books (Bobrow 1996: 65). While this discontinuity may be a literary flaw, it is also possible that Odoevtseva is updating the protagonist's character based on the girl's continued struggle with life in exile. Ljuka is less assimilated into French society as an adult than she was as a schoolgirl, for example, and her economic situation has not improved. She believes that the fact that she is Russian, and therefore poor (Odoevtseva 1939: 9), makes her an outsider: at the theatre she feels like an "oazis[om] bednosti " (1939:

6; 'island of poverty') among the well-off French moviegoers. When she seizes upon Thierry's promise of fame, she immediately thinks not only of penetrating the 'insider' society, but also of becoming distinctive within it: "Eto Parizh, kotoryj skoro budet poklonjat'sja ej" (1939: 24; This is Paris, which will soon be bowing before me), she says. Like Liza, Ljuka is unsure of herself and her identity. Throughout the novel, at emotional and important moments in her life, Ljuka repeatedly glances into mirrors, unreal surface reflections, as if searching for or confirming her own emotional response in the unreal surface that is the mirror, instead of from within.

The 'insider' Thierry is glittering, machine-like (he drops off to sleep and awakens instantly, as if at the flip of a switch), and unemotional, and wears a huge ever-present artificial smile. He suggests illusion, impermanence, and superficiality. On the symbolic level, there is an implicit criticism of the West in his portrayal.

This criticism becomes explicit in the scene in which Ljuka meets the Soviet Russian on a train as she returns to Paris. She is distraught after having been turned away by Thierry, even though she is pregnant with his child. The Soviet traveller, as a true son of the revolution, rejects outright the notion of love (Odoevtseva 1939: 158), and deems extreme Ljuka's emotional reaction to the loss of Thierry. To the traveller, Ljuka's made-up appearance and emotionally-charged singing style, which he calls 'European', are excessive and artificial (1939: 160, 161). He compares Paris to an operetta, an inauthentic place, and draws a parallel between it and Ljuka's grief, which to him seems theatrical (1939: 167). The traveller offers a solution to Ljuka's problems – a return to the Soviet Union.

Talking about Russia calms Ljuka's hysteria and dissipates her grief (1939: 162). The day she spends in Paris with the Soviet traveller is filled with a sense of harmony (1939: 165). On the symbolic level Odoevtseva is speaking of the desired union of the émigré with native land, and it is true that the idea of returning to the Soviet Union was one that occupied the minds of many émigrés during the interwar period (Raeff 1990: 43). Yet, after the traveller goes home, Ljuka realizes that a return to Soviet Russia would not solve her problems. As in *Izol'da*, the discourse concerns the difficulty of the choices given to the émigré – old Russia (the former husband) has disappeared, the Soviet Union (the traveller) is an unrealistic option, and the West (Thierry) is unreliable, lacking in real values, and has rejected her even with the knowledge of the pregnancy, that is, of the fact that a union has been created between them.

Joseph Brodsky said of the exiled writer: "his head is forever turned backward and his tears, or saliva, are running down between his shoulder blades" (Brodsky 1995: 27). Odoevtseva, however, prided herself on not living in the past (Kolonitsaja 2001: 146) and on being a part of whatever community she found herself in. She stated that she "never considered herself an émigré, but a Russian" (Kedrova 1988: 3), and that she always adapted easily to new surroundings (Kedrova 1998: 5). She was also known to be of a generally optimistic disposition (Bobrow 1996: xvii). All the more striking, then, are the melodramatic aspects of her works, as well as the psychic agonies of her protagonists – their fears, anxieties, and loneliness, their lack of choices, and the ease with which they are seduced into new identities. Whether her work reveals unconscious exilic anxieties can only be a matter of conjecture. According to Bethea, Kristeva postulates the possibility of such subconscious exilic trauma:

> A secret wound, often unknown to himself, drives the foreigner […] however, he does not acknowledge it: with him, the challenge silences the complaint […]. He is dauntless: "You have caused me no harm", he disclaims. (Bethea 1994: 41)

Regardless of what Odoevtseva herself proclaims, it appears that the poetics of her three interwar novels proclaims otherwise.

Bibliography

Andrew, Joe. 1993. *Narrative and Desire in Russian Literature, 1822-49.* New York: St. Martin's Press.
Bethea, David M. 1994. *Joseph Brodsky and the Creation of Exile.* Princeton: Princeton University Press.
Bobrow, Ella. 1996. *Irina Odoevsteva: Poet, Novelist, Memoirist. Oakville, ON.:* Mosaic Press.
Brodsky, Joseph. 1995. *On Grief and Reason: Essays.* New York: Farrar Straus Giroux.
Harwell, Xenia Srebrianski. 2000. *The Female Adolescent in Exile in Works by Irina Odoevtseva, Nina Berberova, Irmgard Keun, and Ilse Tielsch.* New York: Peter Lang.
Hatto, Arthur. Thomas. 1960. 'Introduction' in von Strassburg, Gottfried *Tristan.* Harmondsworth, England: Penguin: 7-35.
Johnston, Robert H. 1988. *"New Mecca, New Babylon": Paris and the Russian Exiles, 1920-1945.* Kingston, Canada: McGill-Queen's University Press.
Kedrova, K. 1988. 'Vozvrashchenie Iriny Odoevtsevoj' in Odoevtseva, Irina *Na beregakh Nevy.* Moskva: Khudozhestvennaja literatura: 3-8.
Kolonitskaja, Anna. 2001. *'Vse chisto dlja chistogo vzora...': (Besedy s Irinoj Odoevtsevoj).* Moskva: Voskresen'e.

Lifton, Robert Jay. 1979. *The Broken Connection: On Death and the Continuity of Life*. New York: Simon and Schuster.
Melton, Judith M. 1998. *The Face of Exile: Autobiographical Journeys*. Iowa City: University of Iowa Press.
Odoevtseva, Irina. 1928. *Angel smerti*. Paris: Izdatel'stvo "Montparnasse" (translated as *Out of Childhood*, tr. Donia Nachshen, London: Constable, 1930).
- - -.   1929. *Izol'da*. Paris-Berlin: Izdatel'stvo knizhnago magazina "Moskva".
- - -.   1930. *Ljuka der Backfisch, Roman* (tr. Wolfgang E. Groeger). Berlin: Rembrandt.
- - -.   1967. *Na beregakh Nevy*. Washington: Victor Kamkin.
- - -.   1983. *Na beregakh Seny*. Paris: La Presse Libre.
- - -.   1939. *Zerkalo*. Bruxelles: Les Editions Petropolis.
Raeff, Marc. 1990. *Russia Abroad: A Cultural History of the Russian Emigration, 1919-1939*. New York: Oxford University Press.
Sabov, Aleksandr. 1988. 'Snova na beregakh Nevy' in Odoevtseva, Irina *Na beregakh Nevy*. Moskva: "Khudozhestvennaja literatura": 314-322.
Struve, Gleb. 1996. *Russkaja literatura v izgnanii*. Paris-Moscow: YMCA Press/Russkij put'.

16

Interview and Poems: 'Refugees', 'Coming to Paradise', 'Immigrant Architectures', 'My Life in Two Parts', 'In the Shadow of the Bridge'

Kapka Kassabova

Kapka Kassabova was born and spent her childhood and adolescence in Bulgaria. Declining the title of *exile*, she refers to her family as *economic migrants*, who left their homeland in 1989 first for Britain, where she attended high school for a year, then for New Zealand, where she undertook her university studies and has established herself as a leading poet, novelist and essayist in English. Her debut novel *Reconaissance* won the 2000 Commonwealth Writers' Prize for best first novel in the South-East Asia and Pacific region. Her first book of poetry won the 1999 Montana Best First Book of Poetry award. Her second novel is *Love in the Land of Midas* and she was the 2002 and 2004 New Zealand Cathay Pacific travel writer of the year. In 2003 she published her latest book of poetry, *Someone Else's Life*, and held the Creative New Zealand Berlin residency. In addition to Bulgarian and English, she speaks fluent French and some German and Spanish.

In an interview for the accompanying DVD, Kapka recalls her feelings of alienation as a young teenager living in Bulgaria, and the challenges associated with writing in a new language (English) and new countries (England and New Zealand). She explains that she first properly found her voice as a poet in English as she sought to capture the experience of migrants, displaced persons, and other people who feel themselves to be in exile. We see her reading two poems of that kind, 'Refugees' (a recent poem) and 'Coming to Paradise' (from a group 'The Immigrant Cycle', 1998) at a live public performance. She then meditates on the question of where she now belongs, where home is, concluding that, unlike many migrants, she takes a strange kind of comfort from not being tied to a single location. Being displaced, she says, serves as a motivating factor in her creativity. She explains that she uses Bulgarian and English for different purposes and in different aspects of her life. She ends by reading three poems: 'Immigrant Architectures', 'My Life in Two Parts', and 'In the Shadow of the Bridge'. All of these poems can be found in Kapka's latest volume of poetry, *Someone Else's Life*, Auckland: Auckland University Press, 2003.

See DVD

Refugees

Look: the poverty of rain
Let's gather it in thimbles of patience
then pour it out in the mud

Meanwhile
we'll count all the worlds
to which we'll never go

We must remember – memory is hope.
But quietly, for words can cut out gaps in us
so wide we'd find
too many bodies lying there

Forget, we must forget
the memories – they open up and blossom
like switch-blades in the guts

Look: this is the world we have
Too poor to hide in
Too dark to cross, too single to forget

Coming to Paradise

We came and found paradise but something
was missing in the water, in the sky,
in the movement of hands
that couldn't embrace or punish

Our children have the large
moist eyes of wounded deer
but must betray no sign of weakness
they must be winners or nothing

Our children know all the songs
all the shows all the jokes
they try to learn the memories too
our children are like the rest

It's a sign of fluency to dream in a language
but we dream wide-awake
we think about our dreams
in broken silences

We stand alone and stubborn
we spend years looking for a crack
in the neighbours' wall
but only find a key

We came looking for paradise and paradise
we found, but it wasn't enough
so we wept and talked about leaving
and never left.

Immigrant Architectures

These days, you feel uneasy
about closing your eyes.
You are afraid of finding

your native city so familiar
and so aloof
you'll wonder if you've really
been there.

You'll find the restored
front of a palace
and behind it
the ruins of your neighbourhood.

Boulevards paved
with familiar faces
watch you and cry out
in a chorus of displeasure.

All-embracing loves
close in on nothing,
like dancing with yourself.

And the sea, the sepia sea
inside your glass head
that everybody sees
and no one understands.

And what you've known mutates.
And what you've known
is something else,
something like the shadow
of a predatory bird gliding
into the great stillness
before a great storm

which is only the storm
of your blood
in the cracked cup of memory.

My Life in Two Parts

1
Outside my window is a row of poplars
growing from the turf of childhood.
Poplars grow in rows, never on their own.
It is Christmas. The sky is full of stars,
the branches are bare,
the wolves distant and menacing.
Now is the only time for oranges.
Their brisk fragrance fills the nails
as we lie in cold rooms high in the Balkans
dreaming of palm trees and the world.

2
Outside my window is a palm tree.
It is winter. The sky is enormous
and the ocean follows the moon.
Oranges are on the window-sill with other
tropical fruit no longer of interest.
Bright-plumed parakeets sway in the palm tree
and that's the only time I look up.

I lie in the low, stuffy rooms of adulthood
dreaming of poplars and the world.
Always they come in rows.

In the Shadow of the Bridge

Wherever we went, something else
was on our minds.
It was too hot, it was too cold.
We were tired, we were not in the mood.
We had been there. It wasn't what we wanted.
We were the constant witness of ourselves.

One evening, the moon rose from the horizon
like we'd never seen it:
enormous and yellow.
We drove towards it in the falling night.
We knew it was a rare chance.

We stopped at the roots of a bridge.
We stood in the giant shadow,
pierced by the headlights of passing cars above.
Across the black, wind-combed water was a city
and all its alien lights. We had come from that city.
Your camera on a tripod by the edge of the water.
I sat inside the vintage car.
The moon bulged right above us.

We had everything that night.
So we took a picture and drove away.

17

The Myth of the Great Return: Memory, Longing and Forgetting in Milan Kundera's *Ignorance*

Fiona J. Doloughan

Fiona Doloughan was born in Northern Ireland where she spent her childhood and adolescence before moving first to England and then to the USA to pursue her education. After completing her PhD in Comparative Literature at Chapel Hill, she returned to the UK where she has held appointments in both French and English at a number of universities. She is currently a Lecturer in English in the Department of Linguistic, Cultural and International Studies at the University of Surrey. Her publications reflect her interdisciplinary and cross-cultural background. Recent publications have focused on texts produced by writers who have access to more than one set of linguistic and cultural resources, such as Ariel Dorfman, Milan Kundera and Ben Okri.

In this paper, she argues that Milan Kundera, in his recent novel *Ignorance* (2002), explores the condition of exile in ways which go against readerly expectation. On the literal level, he portrays two characters for whom the longed-for return to their Czech homeland offers little fulfilment, as they discover that life in their adopted countries (Denmark and France) has more reality for them than what they have returned to find. Moreover, they realise that other people's perceptions of them as displaced or in exile run counter to their own sense of being *at home* in their new countries. Doloughan suggests, however, that Kundera is equally interested in the themes of exile and return on a metaphorical level. Through repeated allusions to the *Odyssey* he poses the question of whether, especially in the modern world, not only any notion of return to an unaltered homeland, but the possibility of recovering memories of the past with any accuracy and completeness, are always illusory. Both on the actual and the metaphorical level, the exilic condition is one where past and present, old and new, co-exist and intermingle. Structurally, too, in this novel Kundera interweaves the lives of the characters and narrative threads in such a way that none of them can be followed without reference to another.

"For a man who no longer has a homeland, writing becomes a place
to live" (Adorno 1951, cited in Said 1994: 43).

In *Representations of the Intellectual,* Edward Said treats exile as both
an actual and a metaphorical condition. He conceives of the exile as
someone who exists "in a median state, neither completely at one with
the new setting nor fully disencumbered of the old, beset with half-
involvements and half-detachments, nostalgic and sentimental on one
level, an adept mimic or a secret outcast on another" (Said 1994: 36).
Translated into the metaphoric domain, exile is, for Said, characterised
by "restlessness, movement, constantly being unsettled, and unsettling
others. You cannot go back to some earlier or perhaps more stable
condition of being at home; and, alas, you can never fully arrive, be at
one with your new home or situation" (Said 1994: 39).

In discussing Milan Kundera's treatment of exile in his recent
novel *Ignorance* (2002), I wish to view it, following Said, as a
metaphorical as well as an actual condition. Insofar as the novel is
concerned with the plight of the émigré(e) and what s/he encounters
on a return visit to his/her native land, it may be considered to be a
material and thematic representation of the exilic condition. At the
same time, the manner in which the themes of exile and return are
structured – i.e., in relation to and against the grain of references to
Odysseus and his (eventual) return to Ithaca – can be seen to
interrogate notions of exile which are culturally and historically
available. In addition, Kundera's own status as a Czech exile who has
lived in France, his second homeland, since 1975 and whose recent
novels, including *Ignorance,* have been written in French, serves to
underscore the fact that for this novelist exile and loss of homeland are
live issues of which he has experience rather than being merely
imagined or represented conditions.

At the level of material representation, therefore, I shall argue
that Kundera is questioning the myth of the Great Return both in
relation to his characters' experiences and by means of the narrator's
interrogative, and often ironic, comments. With respect to its
metaphorical dimension, I shall view exile as what Michael Seidel
calls "an enabling fiction … a fiction enabling me to address the larger
strategies of narrative representation" (Seidel 1986: xii). For, insofar
as Kundera's novel reflects "a double perspective that never sees
things in isolation" (Said 1994: 44) but always in relation to "what has
been left behind and what is actual here and now" (Said 1994: 44), it
may be seen as, in effect, the product of an exilic imagination. Living
and working in France, but representing changes, real or imagined, in

his homeland, Kundera possesses what Hana Píchová refers to as "the contrapuntal vision in which countries, shores, and languages are held in dual focus" (Píchová 2002: 9).

The counterpoint and dual focus in *Ignorance* stem partly from the fact that the novel is concerned with whether or not it is still possible to speak of exile and return in the same terms as in the past or whether, in fact, the modern world is one where such notions assume different, and perhaps contradictory, meanings. In the fourteenth section of the novel (there are fifty-three in total), the narrator speculates about whether in today's post-Communist, post-Cold War world, with its rapid transformations, the writing of an *Odyssey* is still possible. He conjectures that given our contemporary experience of time, notions such as exile and return, which depend for their impact on constancy and lack of change, may well be inconceivable:

> The gigantic invisible broom that transforms, disfigures, erases landscapes has been at the job for millennia now, but its movements, which used to be slow, just barely perceptible, have sped up so much that I wonder: Would an *Odyssey* even be conceivable today? Is the epic of the return still pertinent to our time? When Odysseus woke on Ithaca's shore that morning, could he have listened in ecstasy to the music of the Great Return if the old olive tree had been felled and he recognized nothing around him? (Kundera 2002: 54)

Throughout the novel, references to Odysseus and his plight act as a kind of touchstone against which Irena's and Josef's experience of exile and return are set. As early as section 2, Homer's account of Odysseus's adventures is cited. For the narrator, the *Odyssey* is "the founding epic of nostalgia" (Kundera 2002: 7) which glorifies a return to the known and the finite rather than the infinitude of adventure and the unknown. According to the narrator, it sets up "a moral hierarchy of emotions" with Penelope "at its summit, very high above Calypso" (Kundera 2002: 9). In a way, the *Odyssey* sets a cultural standard against which other stories of exile can be measured. In Kundera's novel, it serves as a kind of grand narrative which emplots a powerful set of cultural myths, which, however attractive they may be, seem ultimately to be at odds with the modern condition.

Thus, for Irena and Josef, the return to Prague and Bohemia after their 'adventures' abroad fails to constitute the joyous and longed-for return but places them both, in different ways, in situations where the life they have been leading in France and in Denmark seems more 'real' to them than what they have returned to find. Neither character conforms to the expectations which others have for them; in their case, the return to the homeland is not willed but a product of the wishes of others. In the case of Irena, for example, it is her French friend, Sylvie, who pushes her to return; in addition, Gustaf, her Swedish lover, is keen to open a new office in Prague so that Irena will have a connection once again with her native land.

For Irena, however, the view that other people have of her as "a young woman in pain, banished from her country" (Kundera 2002: 24) is far from her vision of self. As she chats with Milada in Prague, she realizes that her life in France after her husband Martin's death was, in fact, a happy time, a time when she was in control of her own destiny. Her life in Prague had been under her mother's watchful eye; to escape, she had married Martin, an old friend of her mother's. Even her emigration had been prompted not by herself but by the need for Martin to escape the secret police. Only in Paris, in the years following Martin's death, did she enjoy a sense of independence, despite the difficulties of bringing up children alone.

Josef, too, has returned to Bohemia at the behest of his wife (now dead) rather than at his own instigation. During his few days revisiting landscapes and family members from the past, what intrudes on his consciousness from time to time, like a beacon, is an image of home – the home he and his Danish wife had set up together in Denmark:

> ... he sees two easy chairs turned to face each other, the lamp and the flower bowl on the window ledge, and the slender fir tree his wife planted in front of the house, a fir tree that looks like an arm she'd raised from afar to show him the way back. (Kundera 2002: 143)

For Josef, then, the home-fires that continue to burn are not those of his native land but rather those of his adopted land where he has spent his adulthood. In fact, reading through a high school diary which outlines his adolescent relationships, he finds it difficult to identify with the exploits and emotions of the young boy he finds represented there. His past life does not seem to have substance for him, since he fails to recognize his former self. Only when he copies out a sentence from his adolescent diary in his adult handwriting is he forced to confront the fact that they are one and the same.

> The resemblance is upsetting, it irritates him, it shocks him. How can two such alien, such opposite beings have the same handwriting? What common essence is it that makes a single person of him and this little snot? (Kundera 2002: 83)

What seems to be at issue here, and in the novel as a whole, is the nature of memory and the passage of time. Josef wrestles with representations of the past – in his diary, in the minds of his brother and sister-in-law, in his own head – which would appear to be at odds with the 'facts' around him. He has no truck with the adolescent that he appears, from his diary, to have been; indeed, he is distinctly antagonistic towards his former self and has either forgotten episodes from his past or remembers things differently.

> He goes on reading and remembers nothing. So what has this stranger come to tell him? To remind him that he used to live here under Josef's name? (Kundera 2002: 72)

His chance encounter with Irena at Paris airport is illustrative of the gap between memory and experience. For Irena, this encounter is charged with meaning; she remembers Josef as someone with whom she almost had an affair before leaving Prague and she is keen to renew his acquaintance:

> From the moment she ran into Josef at the Paris airport, she's been thinking of nothing but him. She constantly replays their brief encounter long ago in Paris. (Kundera 2002: 98)

Josef, on the other hand, has no memory of this pleasant and interesting woman, though he covers up his ignorance in order to prolong their conversation.

> He enjoyed the encounter, too; she was friendly, charming, and agreeable; forty something and pretty; and he hadn't the faintest idea who she was. (Kundera 2002: 48)

Indeed, when, back in Prague, they finally make love in Josef's hotel room, Irena becomes aware that Josef has no idea who she is and, in her drunken state, accuses him of being a bad man.

> You don't know who I am! You picked up a strange woman! You made love with a stranger who offered herself to you! You took advantage of a misunderstanding! You used me like a whore! I was a whore to you, some unknown whore! (Kundera 2002: 187)

For the narrator, it is in the very nature of human beings to forget and to try and reconstruct the past from the paltry fragments retained in the annals of memory. But why one fragment and not another? No one knows, he replies,

> since in each one of us the choice occurs mysteriously, outside our will or our interests. We don't understand a thing about human life, if

> we persist in avoiding the most obvious fact: that a reality no longer is
> what it was when it was; it cannot be reconstructed. (Kundera 2002:
> 124)

Yet we continue to try and make sense of the past by inserting our
memories into causal chains which help to make them intelligible for
us – and, indeed, for others – but these causal chains are, in fact,
necessary fictions, since we cannot actually remember the events
leading up to and following a fragment from the past. According to
the narrator, our narratives of the past are approximations, intended to
provide a plausible explanation of events which we no longer fully
remember. "Josef", he writes, "could not claim that his anecdote was
identical with what he had actually experienced; he knew that it was
only the plausible plastered over the forgotten" (Kundera 2002: 126).

In addition, the narrator points to the perspectival nature of our
memories; we (necessarily) see things from our subjective viewpoints,
which may or may not correspond to the viewpoint of other people. So
for Irena and Josef, who spent time together in the past, their
recollections of events are not at all the same.

> The same recollections? That's where the misunderstanding starts:
> they don't have the same recollections; each of them retains two or
> three small scenes from the past, but each has his own; their
> recollections are not similar; they don't intersect; and even in terms of
> quantity they are not comparable: one person remembers the other
> more than he is remembered; first because memory capacity varies
> among individuals [...] but also [...] because they don't hold the same
> importance for each other. When Irena saw Josef at the airport, she
> remembered every detail of their long-ago adventure; Josef
> remembered nothing. From the very first moment their encounter was
> based on an unjust and revolting inequality. (Kundera 2002: 126)

This injustice and inequality continue until their frenzied love-making
in Josef's hotel room. Even in the midst of passion, Josef is already
thinking about his return flight to Denmark. If he is able to enjoy, to
the full, this erotic encounter, it is because he sees it as his last:

> As he is making love, from time to time Josef looks discreetly at his
> watch: two hours left, an hour and a half left; this afternoon of love is
> fascinating, he doesn't want to miss any part of it, not a move, not a
> word, but the end is drawing near, ineluctable, and he must watch the
> time running out. (Kundera 2002: 184)

So he leaves the by now drunk and still sleeping Irena in his hotel
room, which he secures on her behalf until noon the following day.
Alone, he heads for the airport and boards his plane, the image of

home still etched on his brain: "Through the porthole he saw, far off in the sky, a low wooden fence and a brick house with a slender fir tree like a lifted arm before it" (Kundera 2002: 195). This image of home has run through the novel like a leitmotiv; Josef's few days in Bohemia have confirmed him in the view that Denmark, rather than Bohemia, is where he recognizes himself and his life. The price of returning to Bohemia would be the loss of his life in Denmark. It becomes clear to him, while visiting his brother, that were he to stay in Bohemia, all trace of his wife would soon be gone. For his brother and sister-in-law know nothing of her, neither her age, nor her profession; their initial caution, for security reasons, has given way to a complete lack of interest. By contrast, Josef's life in Denmark is full of reminders of his (dead) wife's presence; his memory of her remains intact.

Both of Kundera's main characters, then, serve to undermine the notion of the Great Return. In Josef's case, his expectations of people and places are not met and he fails to identify with his former self and his former life. His duty done, he cannot wait to leave Bohemia and return to Denmark.

For Irena, things are slightly more complicated. The evening she organizes for friends in the restaurant in Prague is fraught with tensions and misunderstandings – she orders wine on behalf of her friends, for example; they express their preference for beer. Initially, her friends seem uninterested in her new life; their interest lies, rather, in Irena's memories of their past life together. Yet, by the end of the evening they are showering her with questions about her present, thereby, she feels, depriving her of her recent past, "[a]s if they were amputating her forearm and attaching the hand directly to the elbow; as if they were amputating her calves and joining her feet to her knees" (Kundera 2002: 43).

Later, in bed, reviewing the evening in her mind, she realizes how much she misses her French friend, Sylvie, and how she would like to be able to take her out and explain to her the price to be paid for the Great Return:

> And you know something, Sylvie – now I understand: I could go back and live with them, but there'd be a condition: I'd have to lay my whole life with you, with all of you, with the French, solemnly on the altar of the homeland and set fire to it. Twenty years of my life would go up in smoke, in a sacrificial ceremony. And the women would sing and dance with me around the fire, with their beer mugs raised high in their hands. That's the price I'd have to pay to be pardoned. To be accepted. To become one of them again. (Kundera 2002: 45)

Nevertheless, there are moments when Irena feels at home in Prague. While waiting for her rendezvous with Josef, she goes walking through a part of Prague she loves, a quiet, leafy neighbourhood far from the downtown area. At that moment, comparisons with Paris are in Prague's favour: she contrasts the intimacy of Prague with the "chilly geometry" (Kundera 2002: 133) of Paris. In fact, the Prague she revisits on her walk is emblematic of her lost country: "Little houses in gardens stretching away out of sight over rolling land" (Kundera 2002: 134). She feels happy and recognizes how difficult it must have been to have left the city. Her stroll through Prague becomes a kind of farewell, since at the time she emigrated she didn't have time to take her leave properly. Walking and reflecting on her life, she becomes certain that she will leave this city and the life it is weaving for her:

> She moves on, and she reflects that today she is finally carrying out the farewell walk she failed to take last time; she is finally saying her Great Farewells to the city that she loves more than any other and that she is prepared to lose once again, without regret, to be worthy of a life of her own. (Kundera 2002: 138)

Through his characters and through the narrator's comments on their thoughts and actions, Kundera represents the exilic condition as one where past and present, old and new, co-exist and intermingle; France and Denmark are viewed through the lens of Prague and Bohemia and Irena's and Josef's lives as émigrés are given value in relation to their present experience of return to the homeland. Indeed, the experience of return, where the characters live in a kind of no-man's-land with "half involvements and half detachments" (Said 1994: 36), helps to cement their attachments to the lives they have been living in their adopted homelands. The return that Josef desires is to an image of home which has attached itself to the house he shared with his wife in Denmark, thus confirming Seidel's view that "[t]he memory of home becomes paramount in narratives where home itself is but a memory" (Seidel 1986: 11).

For Irena, what is clear is that she wishes finally to enjoy a life of her own choosing; such a life requires that she leave Prague and all that it represents. Whether she returns to Paris or moves elsewhere is left in abeyance. For while talking to Josef over lunch, she offers him her future, a future which he is keen to avoid: "Not here. In France. Better yet, somewhere else. Anywhere" (Kundera 2002: 170).

At one level, then, Kundera's novel is structured around the themes of exile and return; references to the *Odyssey* which underpin the work serve to highlight the myth of the Great Return. At the same time, Kundera's focus on memory, longing, and forgetting reflect more general concerns about (self-) knowledge and the nature of time. The émigré is emblematic of those who move, usually for political reasons, from one land – and language and culture – to another. The journey they have undertaken is literal as well as metaphoric. Yet, as Said suggests, exile in the sense of existing in a median state is not the prerogative of the émigré. The intellectual, he claims, needs to be able to adopt the standpoint of the exile insofar as s/he represents what he calls "a spirit in opposition rather than in accommodation" (Said 1994: xv). For Said, this means that "an idea or experience is always counterposed with another, therefore making them both appear in a sometimes new and unpredictable light" (Said 1994: 44).

It is precisely this dual focus and juxtaposition of ideas and experiences that Kundera achieves in *Ignorance*. The novel is structured in such a way that characters are seen not in isolation but in relation to one another; their individual perspectives are always compared and contrasted with the perspective of others. Josef's memories, for example, are set against those of Irena and of Milada; Irena's life is situated in relation to that of her husband, Martin, and that of her lover, Gustaf. Moreover, the novel's division into fifty-three sections, with overlapping and interwoven storylines, reflects the contingent and perspectival nature of perception and experience. One narrative is interrupted by, and set against, another such that the reader is aware of the limitations and self-delusions of each of the characters. In addition, commentary from the narrator and the extended 'philosophical' passages serve as counterpoint to, and explanatory framework for, the experiences of individual characters, thereby raising them to a more abstract and generalisable level. In other words, 'theory' is seen to inform 'practice' and the particular is shown in relation to broader and more universal concerns. For, as Peter Kussi points out, Kundera is concerned that literature transcend national and parochial boundaries (Kussi 1978: 30).

Indeed, it is at this more abstract level that we may view writing as an exilic condition and representation as the product of an exilic imagination. Given that, for Said, intellectual representations (and here he includes talking, writing, teaching, appearing on television) "are the *activity itself*" (Said 1994: 15), and that for Kundera the novel is "a living, evolving source of form and inspiration as well as a repository of accumulated knowledge" (Kussi 1978: 20), it becomes possible to view Kundera's work as a meditation on loss and return which ultimately constitutes his true homeland.

As long ago as 1971, Kundera bemoaned the fact that "[i]n our society it is counted a greater virtue to guard the frontiers than to cross them" (quoted in Kussi 1978:16). Throughout his life, Kundera has crossed countless frontiers and, in his fiction, interrogated "the stereotypes that are so limiting to human thought and communication" (Said 1994: x). He has used his double vision as an exile, or what Kussi calls "the effects of 'extraterritoriality'" (Kussi 1978: 29), to question accepted truths both at home and abroad. I shall give the last word to Píchová who sums up Kundera's view of the novel as an interrogative mode embodying a spirit of questioning and of opposition:

> Kundera calls upon a broader history of the novel, defining it as a genre of questioning, placing his own work into a broad sweep of the history of the novel as a kind of bridge, as a way of preserving a spirit of questioning that resists accepting any one truth as the only truth. (Píchová 2002: 13)

Bibliography

Kundera, Milan. 2002. *Ignorance*. London: Faber and Faber.
Kussi, Peter. 1978. *Essays on the Fiction of Milan Kundera*. PhD thesis. Columbia University: University Microfilms International.
Píchová, Hana. 2002. *The Art of Memory in Exile: Vladimir Nabokov and Milan Kundera*. Carbondale and Edwardsville: Southern Illinois University Press.
Said, Edward. 1994. *Representations of the Intellectual*. London: Vintage.
Seidel, Michael. 1986. *Exile and the Narrative Imagination*. New Haven: Yale University Press.

18

Exile in Redemption: S.Y. Agnon's *Only Yesterday*

Arnold J. Band

Arnold Band was born in Boston, Massachusetts and was educated at
Harvard University, with study years abroad in both Jerusalem and
Paris. He has taught at UCLA since 1959, but has been a visiting
lecturer at Yale University, the Hebrew University, Tel Aviv
University, and Brandeis University. While living in Los Angeles on
the Pacific Rim, he has travelled much to Europe, Israel, Mexico, and
East Asia. He is best known for his pioneering research on Agnon
and other Jewish authors. A collection of his leading essays was
recently published as *Studies in Modern Jewish Literature*.

In this paper, he discusses a novel by S.Y. Agnon, the leading
Hebrew writer of the twentieth century, who won the Nobel Prize in
1966. In many of his novels, but specifically in *Only Yesterday*,
Agnon deals with the aspirations for redemption from exile generated
by the Zionist movement. In this novel, Band suggests, Agnon insists
that the secular redemption from exile embodied in the re-creation of
the ancestral home of the Jews as a modern national state does not
solve the religious problem of exile, which, following both Biblical
and Kabbalistic notions, treats exile as a metaphysical condition
remedied only by some sort of messianic event. *Only Yesterday*, set
in Jerusalem and Jaffa in the first decade of the twentieth century,
explores this theme through the tragic experiences of the hero. The
Biblical echoes add to the historical depth of the plot. The novel,
written between 1936 and 1945, against the bloody background of
the times, is a sober reflection on the failings of secular, nationalistic
aspirations.

In the Western literary tradition, exile as an event and a recurring
theme has its foundational origins in the books of the Hebrew Bible
(the Old Testament). The historical experience of Ancient Israel left a
record of two major historical exiles, that of 722 BCE and that of 586
BCE. These, in turn, shaped both contemporary historiography and
prophecy, on the one hand, and major mythic structures, on the other
hand. The cardinal paradigms of sin and punishment through exile
that we encounter in the first eleven chapters of Genesis reflect this
experience. Adam and Eve expelled from Eden, Cain driven from his
home, and the builders of the Tower of Babel dispersed over the face

of the earth are examples that have educated many peoples for centuries. It was not inevitable that exile would be regarded as punishment for sin rather than the result of drought or, conversely, that sin would be punished by exile rather than by pestilence, but the joining of exile and sin was what the Hebrew prophets and historians deduced from their experience – and bequeathed to us.

Furthermore, the exile-sin nexus, well established by the seventh century BCE, was accompanied by a concomitant promise or hope for redemption as a reward for repentance, for the mending of one's ways. Again, this was not inevitable. One can conceive of a variety of different reactions to an exilic situation: a type of quietism, or a rejection of this world, or a violent militancy. But the pre-exilic prophets and the Deuteronomic historians formulated a theology of redemption that includes concepts of repentance and messianism. Redemption implied two types of return: return to the ways of the Lord and return to the ancestral homeland. This powerful cluster of ideas which generations have taken for granted was well formed even before the exile of 586 BCE, and has come down in a rich variety of possibilities throughout history. While this cluster of concepts has been the heritage of all the western monotheistic religions, Judaism, because of its historical circumstances, has emphasized the exile component to a degree unknown in other religions. Reconstructed during the Babylonian exile of the sixth century BCE (see the book of Ezekiel), Judaism entered the Hellenistic period with its dispersion of populations, called 'the Diaspora', that found meaning – if not pleasure – in exile.

This notion of exile informed all of Jewish writing until the modern period and, even in the twentieth century, continued as a powerful theme in the works of many writers, specifically those with training in traditional texts. Among these, the leading figure is the Hebrew writer S.Y. Agnon (1887-1970) who was awarded the Nobel Prize for Literature in 1967. Agnon's life spanned the great events in the Jewish world during the twentieth century. Born in 1887 in Galicia, then part of the Austro-Hungarian Empire, he settled in Palestine in 1908 and, apart from a sojourn in Germany between 1912 and 1924, lived in Jerusalem until his death in 1970. He was thus a witness to major events such as: the acculturation of European Jewry, the Zionist-inspired return of Jews to their ancestral homeland, and the violent destruction of the European Jewish Diaspora in World War II. Well read in both traditional Jewish and modern European literature, he was superbly equipped to render these experiences in compelling literary form.

Among his many works of fiction, the novel *Temol Shilshom* (*Only Yesterday*) is particularly well-suited for discussion in the context of a volume on the poetics of exile. Published in its full scope in 1945, it deals with the adventures of a young Jewish *halutz* ('pioneer') from Galicia who tries to settle in Jaffa and Jerusalem during what is known as the Second *Aliya*, the second wave of Jewish immigration to Palestine between 1904 and World War I. Though this time is often treated, in literature, as the heroic period of the Zionist return from exile to homeland, Agnon's portrayal of it is radically dissonant with this literary paradigm. His hero, Yitzhak Kummer, never settles on the land as a farmer (the Zionist ideal), but works as a house-painter in both Jaffa and Jerusalem and finally dies a violent death after having been bitten by a rabid dog in Jerusalem. The journey from exile to homeland ends in death, the ultimate exile from a life of self-fulfilment -- and this is not the only exile that we find.

This plot or *fabula*, even in its bald form, should suffice to intimate the potential vectors of exile-homeland implications, which are far more complex when we study the *sujet*. But before I do, I want to return to my basic formulation of the original, biblical cluster of exile-redemption notions outlined above. When one speaks of redemption in traditional Jewish texts, one refers either to a spiritual redemption, the return to the life under God's law and the concomitant state of peace on earth, or to the territorial return. Within the world of traditional Jewish messianic aspirations, the two forms of redemption, the spiritual and the territorial, are usually combined, and the normative term for either redemption was the same, *ge'ulah*. What makes this term so powerful in Hebrew is that phonetically it resonates with its opposite, the term *golah* or *galut* - the standard term for exile. The movement from *galut* to *geulah* was one of the clichés of the period, inviting rampant over-determination.

The term *ge'ulah*, in fact, was so ubiquitous that by the time of the Second *Aliya* (1904-1914), of Israel (the Jewish people) from exile to their ancestral homeland (Zion), it was used in a secular sense for a gamut of activities relating to the Zionist activities in resettling the Land of Israel (Palestine) during the Ottoman Turkish occupation: buying land, draining swamps, irrigating deserts, and building institutions of all sorts. These secular *ge'ulah* activities were promoted in essays, speeches, songs, and slogans all designed to mobilize the potential *halutzim* ('pioneers') who would hopefully come to execute the Zionist program. The entire project, fuelled by the harsh realities of exilic life in Czarist Russia with its pogroms and discriminatory laws, assumed such mythic proportions in Zionist circles, that it far outstripped the realities on the ground. While some writers of the Second *Aliya* did write glowing accounts of the lives of fulfilment the pioneering youth were supposed to be living, there were contemporary writers like Yosef Hayyim Brenner who wrote more sober, often devastatingly pessimistic, accounts of real events of the time. Without understanding the dissonance between the myth and the harsh reality, one cannot possibly understand what Agnon, writing his novel *Temol Shilshom* (*Only Yesterday*) a generation later in the late 1930s and early 1940s, was striving to express in this major novel. To say that the return from exile to homeland was a failure is a simplification, since the terms were so endlessly over-determined. The dissonance between avowed constructed myths and lived realities is, of course, one of the great themes in the modern novel and Agnon examines the exile-to-homeland theme within this rubric.

To do so he created a protagonist, Yitzhak Kummer, a naïve, idealistic, young man from a pious family in Galicia, a young man with no experience in life, the type one would expect to grow through his experiences if he were placed in the traditional *Bildungsroman*. But this novel is not the traditional *Bildungsroman*. Given the irreconcilable gap between constructed myth and reality which no experience can bridge, the novel becomes not a *Bildungsroman*, but its negation, an anti-*Bildungsroman*, in which the hero does not grow, but floats aimlessly and actually regresses to the point where he dies a violent, meaningless death. In the homeland he cherishes and dreams about, he is never free of exile. This death is a logical consequence of his exile from all possible meaningful communal associations: he does not belong to the new world of Zionist pioneers; he imagines he might belong to the traditional pious life of the Old Yishuv (the pre-Zionist settlement) in Jerusalem, but he is considered an outsider, an exile there.

This fusion of central theme and character construction is evident in the very first, signature sentence of the novel. Often discussed, it cannot be understood without our prefatory explanation of the exile-homeland nexus, and the dissonance between constructed myth and lived reality.

> Like all our brethren of the Second *Aliya*, the bearers of our salvation
> (redemption), Isaac Kummer left his country and his homeland and

> his city and ascended to the land of Israel to build it from its
> destruction and to be rebuilt by it. From the day our comrade Isaac
> knew his mind, not a day went by that he didn't think about it. A
> blessed dwelling place was his image of the whole Land of Israel and
> its inhabitants blessed by God. (Agnon 2000: 3)

A close reading of this short passage will demonstrate all the points
made above. First, when the ostensibly omniscient narrator begins to
tell us about his hero Isaac (Yitzhak) Kummer, who was "like our
brethren of the Second *Aliya*" (Agnon 2000: 3), he situates both his
hero and himself as part of a specific historical movement of
"brethren" with all that implies. He also establishes the close bond
between himself and his hero, so close, in fact, that in certain
passages which use 'combined speech' they merge. Secondly, these
brethren are referred to as "the bearers of (the men of) our Salvation
(redemption)" in what at first sounds like a traditional, pious flourish,
but is actually ironic. They, and those who wrote about them, might
have believed they were 'redeemers', i.e. bringing redemption to the
Jewish people through their settlement of the Land of Israel, but they
never achieved this goal.

Thirdly, the page is studded with terms taken from pious texts:
"*beney ge-ulah*" ("bearers of redemption"); "*heni'ah et artzo ve'et
moladeto*" ("he left his land and homeland", taken from Genesis 12);
"*alah le'eretz yisrael*" ("he went up [on pilgrimage] to *Eretz
Yisrael*") etc. The density of this religious terminology must alert
Agnon's reader to the fact that he or she is reading a deliberate
parody, not a pious declaration. (It is also possible that one finds here
an echo of the opening line of H. N. Bialik's famous poem, '*Be'ir
haharega*' ('In the City of Slaughter'), an angry lament over the
Kishinev pogrom of 1903.

Fourthly, "*Livnot ota mehurbana*" ("to build it from its
destruction"), starts as a parody of a biblical phrase, but goes on to
mouth, and mock, the Zionist cliché found in songs and posters:
"*livnot ulehibanot*" ("to build and be built"), that encapsulates the
entire Zionist ethos. By going to the Land of Israel to build it, the
exilic Jew would rebuild or rehabilitate his disintegrated exilic (*galut*)
personality. In Zionist ideology, the exilic personality was considered
decadent, and needed to be cured or redeemed by leaving exile for the
Land of Israel, to go from *galut* to *ge'ulah*.

The phrase "from the day our comrade Isaac knew his mind"
("*amad al da'ato*") is satirical since Isaac never really reaches the
maturity of one who knows his mind, i.e. has independence of
thought. Throughout the novel he has no independent thought and

this is adumbrated in the rest of this passage in which we see that Isaac's mind is simply an extended pastiche of other people's clichés - recalling Flaubert's description of Charles Bovary's mind, "the sidewalk on which everyone else's thoughts walked".

Apparently sensing that Yitzhak Kummer, basically a simpleton, might not be able to carry the complex tangle of ironic messages he would want to convey, Agnon joined to him a second character which acts as a sort of alter ego: the dog Balak. While Balak is not a name in common use since he was the hostile king of Moab in Numbers 22:2, the name is actually Agnon's whimsical creation: when one reads backwards the word for dog in Hebrew, *KeLeV*, one gets *BaLaK*. Reading the Hebrew letters from left to right rather than right to left is a powerful marker of alienation and of exile since that is the way a gentile would ordinarily read Hebrew letters. In the novel, it is the director of a diasporan organization in the Land of Israel who first reads the name that way. The letters in Hebrew were whimsically painted on the dog by Yitzhak himself; as he wanted to clean his paint-brush one day he wrote on the dog: *Kelev Meshuga*, 'Mad Dog', in Hebrew. The dog, actually considered mad by the Jewish residents of Jerusalem who read this message, is driven away with sticks and stones and wanders the city, an exile in his own home. In his exilic wandering, he contracts rabies, the disease of the exilic dog, and, returning to his original neighbourhood, bites Yitzhak during the latter's wedding week. Yitzhak contracts rabies, goes mad, and dies bound to his bed – in a modern Binding of Isaac. Unlike the biblical Binding of Isaac which ends in a glorious redemption in that Isaac is saved and a ram is substituted for him, this modern Isaac dies a meaningless death, alone on a foul bed.

We, the readers, are treated to a prolonged journey through Jaffa and Jerusalem of the Second *Aliyah*, seen either through the eyes of Yitzhak or the dog, Balak - his alter ego. The travelogue, well integrated with the plot, renders such a detailed series of scenes of these two centres of Jewish habitation during the Second *Aliyah* that many readers read the novel as a historical novel about the Second *Aliyah* when it is actually the opposite. It is a novel written a generation later. In it Agnon employs the deadly tensions between the ideals of the Second *Aliyah* and the impossibility of their realization as a paradigm of the human tragedy involved in believing in powerful myths that one cannot realize in life situations. Yitzhak fails to become a productive pioneer working the soil, and becomes instead a mediocre housepainter superficially painting over old houses. He tries to become a secular member of the new pioneering society, but ends up returning to the traditional life among pious Jews in Jerusalem who reject him as an outsider – an exile from the secular world in the pious world in Jerusalem. He dies, bitten by the dog which becomes rabid when exiled because he has on his back the words 'Mad Dog', painted, on pure whim, by Yitzhak. Yitzhak is, thus, an exile from meaning, from a redeemed world which might endow meaning to human life.

While the novel is graphically situated in Jaffa and Jerusalem of 1908-12, it reflects the thinking of its author at the time of its composition. We have abundant documentation of Agnon's concerns at this time since this was the peak of his creative life. Without running through his entire bibliography of the period, item by item, we can point to three salient works.

From 1930 on, Agnon published a series of surrealistic stories – often dubbed Kafkaesque – reflecting a profound spiritual crisis. Though situated in traditional religious settings, they manifest an agonized struggle with doubt and a sense of inner exile from religious equanimity.

In 1938-39, he published serially his novel *A Guest for the Night* (*Oreah nata lalun*), in which a narrator, with many of the distinctive features of the writer Agnon, tells of a year-long visit to the town of his childhood, Shibush (a fictive equivalent of Buczacz), that had been devastated during the hostilities on the Eastern front in World War I. This home, abandoned during many centuries of exile in Galicia, had been destroyed with no possible hope for reconstruction or redemption. Though the novel describes the devastation of World War I, it reflects the anxieties of the late thirties, fuelled by the rise of Nazism and the murderous riots in Mandatory Palestine between 1936 and 1939.

During the months of the final composition of *Only Yesterday*, news of the murder of Polish Jewry by the Germans began to reach Jerusalem. During this period Agnon wrote and published such Holocaust stories as 'The Lady and the Peddler' (*HaAdonit veharokhel*) and 'The Sign' (*HaSiman*).

While I would not call *Only Yesterday* a Holocaust novel, the historical context of the time of its composition is that of the late 1930s and early 1940s, not the Second *Aliyah* of 1904-14, when the novel's action takes place. To call it a novel of the Second *Aliyah* is naïve. The realization that territorial redemption from exile does not necessarily entail spiritual redemption is something Agnon certainly knew early in his career, perhaps as early as 1908, but it is in the complex prose of *Only Yesterday* that we really find the obsessive vision that the Exile he was brought up with in Galicia was destroyed and the Land of Israel, the goal of the Zionist dream, was far from a satisfying redemption, if anything, an exile within redemption. Finally, he is telling us that exile is never over, that it is perhaps the lot of all mankind.

Bibliography

Agnon, Shmuel Yosef. 2000. *Only Yesterday* (tr. Barbara Harshav). Princeton, N.J.: Princeton University Press.
Band, Arnold J. 1968. *Nostalgia and Nightmare: a Study in the Fiction of S.Y.Agnon.* Berkeley and Los Angeles: University of California Press.

19

Exile and Revolt: Arab and Afro-American Poets in Dialogue

Saddik Gohar

Saddik Gohar was born in Egypt and holds MA and PhD degrees from Indiana University of Pennsylvania. He has taught English language and literature at universities in Egypt and Saudi Arabia, and has several times been a visiting professor at the Indo-American Centre for Studies and Research at the Hyderabad campus of Osmania University, India. He is currently an associate professor in the Department of English Language and Literature, Faculty of Humanities and Social Sciences, United Arab Emirates University. Five collections of his poetry in Arabic have been published, and he is currently translating two of them into English. He is a human rights activist, calling for the rights of minorities and oppressed groups in the Arab world, and a peace activist working for peaceful coexistence between all Arab countries and the Israeli people. He has published extensively in the fields of English/American literature, comparative literature, and translation theory. Among his many publications is *A Singer in the Ghetto: A Study of Le Roi Jones/Amiri Barak's Revolutionary Poetry* (1998).

In this paper, he explores the motifs of exile and revolt in the poetry of contemporary Palestinian writers. Exile, both physical and spiritual, is a traditional theme of poetry in Arabic, but the subject of exile has become more acute since 1948 with the forced exodus of Palestinians from their homeland and the emergence of dictatorial regimes in many Arab countries. He explores work by some of the outstanding poets who have remained in their homeland (such as Mahmud Darwish), as well as those who have left the country (such as Kamal Nasir). This poetry communicates powerfully the pain of exile, anger at the injustice of their situation, and the hunger for return, while subverting the widespread image in the West of the Palestinian as terrorist. Gohar makes the parallel between these poets and radical black American poets of the 1960s, who wrote of the enslavement and transportation of their African ancestors and the ongoing discrimination against Afro-Americans, and highlights the support offered to Palestinians by later generations of Afro-American poets, such as June Jordan, who have delved into their own experience of exile and alienation to develop a dialogue with the writers in Arabic. Nevertheless, whereas for most Afro-American poets the idea of a permanent return to Africa is no more than a dream, for Palestinians the hunger to return to their rightful homeland does not diminish.

In an article entitled, 'Real Wounds, Unreal Wounds: The Romance of Exile', Ian Buruma argues:

> Exile as a metaphor did not begin with the Jewish Diaspora. The first story of exile in our tradition is the story of Adam and Eve. No matter how we interpret the story of their expulsion from the Garden of Eden — original sin or not — we may be certain of one thing: There is no way back to paradise. After that fatal bite of the apple, the return to pure innocence was cut off forever. The exile of Adam and Eve is the mark of maturity, the consequence of growing up. An adult can only recall the state of childlike innocence in his imagination; and from this kind of exile a great deal of literature has emerged. (Buruma 2001: 3)

Whether associated with the Jewish Diaspora or the fall from Eden, exile may be viewed as the forced or self-imposed moving away from one's homeland. Thus, exile becomes a signifier not only of living outside one's place of origin but also of the inner condition caused by such a physical absence. At the same time, exile may also connote the exclusively spiritual, intellectual or even existential condition of someone who is alienated from the surrounding community. In whatever form, exile has always been a source of inspiration for poets and writers. As Buruma argues, the exilic experience has triggered a great deal of literature characterised by "the melancholy knowledge that we can never return to Eden" (Buruma 2001: 3).

Historically, the theme of exile has occurred as a basic motif in Arabic poetry from the pre-Islamic era up to the modern time. For example, in the early twentieth century, Egyptian Ahmad Shauqi, known as 'the prince of poets', explored the theme of exile in his poetry. In 'An Andalusian Exile', he says:

> O bird crying on the acacia tree, alike are our sorrows
> should I grieve for your troubles or lament my own?
> what tale have you to tell me? — only that the self-same hand that
> laid my heart waste has pinioned your wind
> Exile has cast us both, fellow strangers
> in a grave not our own, where our kind never meet
> parting has struck us — you with a knife, me with a barbed arrow
> child of the valley, nature has set us apart
> and yet affliction has brought us together.
>
> (Jayyusi 1987: 102)

Shauqi's romantic image of the Andalusian exile was replaced by new images in post-Second World War poetry, following major political and social changes in the Arab world. For instance, the rise of Arab nationalism as a reaction against European colonialism and Zionism and the subsequent revolutions which erupted in many Arab countries were among the radical changes that greatly affected Arab people. The anti-colonial and anti-Zionist revolutions in countries such as Egypt, Syria, Iraq, and Algeria were associated with the emergence of dictatorial regimes which committed many atrocities against their own peoples, turning these countries into prisons and places of exile. Due to lack of democracy and freedom, many Arab intellectuals and representatives of religious and ethnic minorities in the Arab world, such as the Kurds, the Shi'ites, and the Copts, were forced to leave their countries and live in diaspora.

Furthermore, the Palestinian tragedy which resulted in the exodus of Palestinian refugees after the 1948 and 1967 wars between the Arabs and Israel deepened the wounds of exile in the Arab psyche. Many Arab regimes were little better than Israel in their treatment of the Palestinian refugees. The disputes among Arab governments over the Palestinian refugee problem created a state of anger and prompted widespread self-examination and questioning in Arab countries. Arabs were disappointed because the new revolutionary regimes failed to achieve their dream of unity and prosperity. Instead of fighting the enemies of the nation, many Arab regimes established enormous police forces and a repressive apparatus to oppress their own citizens. The armies of these regimes were shamefully defeated in wars with Israel, and many Arabs realized that it was time for them to abandon what the Iraqi poet, Buland al-Haydari calls, "the long sleep of history" (al-Haydari 1987: 82). The Arab defeats in 1948 and 1967, as well as the rise of Arab dictatorial governments, left Arab people in a state of shock and they became sceptical about the validity of their socio-political systems.

With the new political realities, particularly the partition of Palestine, the creation of Israel, and the emergence of repressive Arab regimes, two main categories of Arab poets may be described as 'writing in exile'. The first category includes poets who were members of ethnic and religious minorities living in various Arab countries or representatives of political opposition groups. The second category constitutes Palestinian poets, both those living under Israeli occupation and those who have been compelled to leave their country. Among the former are poets such as Mahmud Darwish, Samih al Qasim, Tawfiq Zayyad, and Sadiq al-Saigh who have lived under Israeli occupation and who constitute the core of Palestinian poetry of exile and revolt. This group of poets has been dedicated to writing what is called the 'Palestinian poetry of resistance' since the 1960s. In spite of censorship, banning of books, jailing, torture, and assassination, the Palestinian resistance poets succeeded in continuing their poetic production, and their poems were smuggled into every Arab house. The Israeli regime inside Palestine, like the Arab regimes outside, has censored the rights of the Palestinian refugees to express their feelings about their plight. Even poetry of lamentation and elegies are considered forms of political and protest poetry.

The latter group includes Palestinian poets such as Kamal Nasir, Tawfiq Sayigh, Izz-al-Din-al-Manasira, Fadwa Tuqan, and others who left their country after the second exodus following the Arab-Israeli war in 1967, the defeat of the Arab armies, the occupation of Eastern Jerusalem, the West Bank, the Golan Heights, and the Sinai Desert. Nevertheless, Palestinian poets, whether living inside or outside their country, are able to participate in the modernist poetic tradition in the Arab world. They convey the angry voice of refugees living in exile through their haunting lyrics. The Palestinian poets in exile have suffered both physically and psychologically, and their poetry is coloured by feelings of death, tragedy, and defeat. However, they are not susceptible to despair or disappointment or frustration. These poets, living either in exile or in prisons, have never lost hope of having a homeland of their own. This dream recurs in their poetry as they talk about the pain and anguish of living in exile. They reflect this sense of anguish and use poetry as a means of facing their personal and national disasters. These poets, who belong to the community of the dispossessed, have a firm hope that they will one day achieve the dream of returning to their villages and cities after the resurrection of Palestine.

The dream of return which haunts these 'prisoners of fate' and these exiled poets is epitomised by the image of the reunion of families and lovers. In Palestinian poetry, the poet's own homeland, village, or city is personified as a fertile woman, a beautiful mistress, a beloved, a wife, or a mother. The metaphorical device which manipulates feminine personifications is integral to the Arabic poetic tradition. Mahmud Darwish, for example, in 'A Lover from Palestine', portrays his homeland, Palestine, as an innocent and beautiful beloved, and as a mother and a widow who has lost her husband in the battle for freedom and independence. Moreover, Palestinian poets, living in internal or external exiles, have struggled to affirm the Arab identity of their homeland and subvert the hostile image of the Palestinian as a terrorist. It is noteworthy that one of the most damaging ways in which Palestinians, living in exile and refugee camps, are presented in the West is through the image of terrorism, an image so pervasive that it seems to reflect "an almost platonic essence inherent in all Palestinians and Muslims" according to Edward Said's essay, 'Identity, Negation and Violence' (Said 1988: 52).

In addition to affirming the Arab identity of Palestine, these poets attempt to create some meaning out of a disintegrated world based on nationalistic illusions. They articulate their feelings of exile in poems which criticise Israeli policy and attack the passive attitudes of some Arab regimes toward the Palestinian-Israeli conflict. Like the radical black American poets of the 1960s, who replaced their points of reference in the American avant-garde with those of black revolution, Arab poets, such as Nizar Qabbani (a poet of sex and erotica) and others, turned into militant political poets due to the failure of the Arab dream. For example, Qabbani in "Marginal Notes on the Book of Defeat" criticizes a nation whose warfare consists of the "oriental cults of rhetoric and false heroism which never killed a black fly" (Qabbani 1987: 96). Like Qabbani, all the revolutionary Palestinian poets living in internal or external exile expressed their feelings of disappointment after they lost their country. As a result of the 1948 war, more than 1.5 million Palestinian citizens were scattered throughout the Arab world to live in permanent refugee camps. More than that number were forced to leave their cities and villages in Northern Palestine and live in refugee camps in Gaza and the West Bank. The remaining Palestinians were destined to live in exile outside the Arab world or as a minority inside the state of Israel. In their Israeli exile, Palestinians were cut off from their cultural roots and were dealt with as second-class citizens. In spite of having Israeli nationality, Palestinians, inside Israel, were poorly educated and were denied any right to have an identity or a culture of their own.

For Palestinians, exile has become a permanent condition in which they have attempted to express the wounds of a lost homeland and of a people transformed into a nation of refugees. In 'The View from No-Man's Land', Kamal Boullata recalls how Palestinians were forced to live in internal exile in their own land:

> I was less than ten years old when the meaning of no-man's land first found its way into my life. At the time, Jerusalem, the city in which I was born, had just been divided into two separate worlds. On one side, the city's Jews began to live in a state all their own. On the other side, Arabs, regardless of their religion, staggered together under the burdens of their newly-broken lives. Barbed wire marked the borders beyond which we were now forbidden to cross. Sites which grown-ups started referring to as no-man's land became the only terrain linking two segregated sides. Through the coils of barbed wire, we began to see what looked for a time like an irremediable wasteland

haunting our neighbourhoods. Trespassing through wild shrubs to
recover a ball that strayed into what only yesterday was a relative's
courtyard now meant risking stepping on a mine or being shot by a
sniper. (Boullata 1992: 579)

Boullata adds that, with the passage of time, Palestinians had to accept
exile as a basic reality in their lives:

Within a decade, the rest of Jerusalem fell to Israeli annexation. The
declaration that crowned the city 'the eternal capital of the Jewish
State' condemned all Palestinians like myself as outsiders in the city
of our birth. No-man's land was now hurriedly eradicated by Israeli
bulldozers. That former commons that had been turned into a bit of
nowhere had finally become the permanent site and symbol for the
state of exile in which I found myself. It is not in figurative terms,
however, that I primarily see the fusion of those two formative
experiences in my life. The sense of foreboding created by Jerusalem's
division and the daily predicaments of that experience confirmed the
inevitability of my actual exile. In time, the interrelatedness between
the two conditions became fused when on the very day that
Jerusalem's no-man's land was eradicated, exile became a central
reality in my life. (Boullata 1992: 580)

The Palestinian concept of living in exile (no-man's land) under
Israeli occupation recalls Le Roi Jones's comment on blacks living
under white racism in America. In *Home: Social Essays*, Jones points
out that black people live in "a no-man's land, a black country,
completely invisible to white America, but so essentially a part of it as
to stain its whole being into an ominous grey" (Jones 1966: 114).
Moreover, the Palestinian resistance against the Israeli occupation
during the 1960s was similar, in many ways, to the black revolution
against American racism in the same decade.

In his introduction to *Modern Black Poets*, Donald B. Gibson
argues that "the great social stress of the sixties has brought about the
creation for the first time of a significantly definable black poetry. It is
a poetry clearly distinguishable from that written by poets of the
majority culture and different, too, from poetry written by previous
generations of black writers" (Gibson 1973: 9). In fact, the 1960s was
a crucial time not only for blacks living in the American Diaspora but
for Palestinians living in exile, whether inside their occupied land or
outside their country. Both blacks and Palestinians not only voiced
protest on the streets but also screamed it in their poems. The
black/Palestinian exile poetry in the post-war era was a reflection of
what was happening in the socio-political arena. Poetry was used as an
agent, a weapon in the battle for freedom and independence. All the
frustrations and bitterness which had been suggested by earlier black

and Palestinian poets have erupted into an angry outspoken protest since the 1960s. Some poets, on both sides, were criticised for militancy and didacticism but the majority of black and Palestinian poets were not merely angry militants but creators of new techniques and forms. Proud of their identities, both black American and Palestinian poets wrote for their own people in their own language and in their own way, portraying the experience of nations that are forced to live in exile.

There has, indeed, grown up a dialogue between Palestinian and Afro-American poets. For example, the black American poet, Don L. Lee, in 'A Poem for a Poet', dedicated to the Palestinian poet Mahmud Darwish, establishes an analogy between the Palestinian tragedy and its black counterpart:

> Read yr exile
> I had a mother too & her death
> Will not be
> Talked of around the world.

Then, Lee compares the fate of Palestinians under Israeli occupation with the plight of blacks in America:

> Like you
> I live
> Walk a strange land
> My smiles are real but seldom.

Lee adds that both Palestinians and Afro-Americans are victims of the same colonising, hostile forces:

> Our enemies eat the same bread
> and the waste from their greed
> will darken your sun and hide your moon
> will dirty your grass and mis-use your water
> your people will talk with unchanging eyes
> and their speech will be slow & unsure & overquick

Finally, the Afro-American poet advises his Palestinian counterpart to avoid the crippling impact of the colonizer's culture:

> You must eat yr/own food
> Keep your realmen; yr/sculptors
> Yr/poets, yr/fathers, yr/musicians
> Yr/sons yr/warriors
> If you must send them, send them
> The way of the sun
> As to make them
>   Blacker

(Lee 1971: 167-168)

June Jordan is another Afro-American poet who sympathizes with the Palestinian people living in exile. In her poem 'Apologies to All People in Lebanon', dedicated to the Palestinian refugees who have been living in exile in Lebanon since 1948, she expresses her sympathy with exiled Palestinians. The poem, which was written after the Sabra and Shatila refugee camps' massacres, is a reflection of the pain and suffering of a nation of exiled refugees. Recalling the atrocities of the massacre which took place during the Israeli occupation of Lebanon, Jordan says with regret: "I didn't know and nobody told me and what / could I do or say anyway?" Lamenting the brutal mass murder of exiled Palestinians, Jordan dismisses the American and Israeli media reports about the Palestinian refugees in Lebanon. According to her, these false reports were used as a pretext to justify the Israeli invasion of Lebanon in 1982 which resulted in the death of thousands of Palestinian refugees living in exile:

> They said you shot the London Ambassador
> And when that wasn't true
> They said so
> What
> They said you shelled their northern villages
> And when U.N. forces reported that was not true
> Because your side of the cease-fire was holding
> Since more than a year before
> They said so / what
>
> (Jordan 1985: 104)

In her rage against the brutality of the Israeli war machine, June Jordan describes how the Palestinian refugee camps were subjected to devastation and ruin:

> They ravaged your
> Water supplies, your electricity, your
> Hospitals, your schools –
> They blew up your homes and demolished
> The grocery stores and blocked the
> Red Cross and took away doctors
> To jail and they cluster-bombed
> Girls and boys
> Whose bodies
> Swelled purple and black into twice
> The original size
>
> (Jordan 1985: 104)

The poet openly declares that the Israeli military machine is responsible for the massacre of innocent Palestinian citizens living in exile in Lebanon: "They tore the buttocks from a four month old baby and then / they said this was a brilliant / military accomplishment". Afterwards, the poet rejects the allegation that the Israeli attack against the refugee camps was a part of a military self-defence operation: "They said this was done in the name of self-defence, they said / that is the noblest concept / of mankind. Isn't that obvious?" According to Jordan, the Israeli military operation against the Palestinian refugee camps "made close to one million human beings / homeless / in less than three weeks and they killed or maimed / 40,000 of your men and your women and your children" . The poet also refers to the Zionist propaganda apparatus which seeks to beautify the face of the Israeli military machine and tarnish the Palestinian image:

> They said they were victims.
> They said you were Arabs.
> They called your apartments and gardens guerrilla
> strongholds.
> They called the screaming devastation
> That they created the rubble
> Then they told you to leave, didn't they?
>
> (Jordan 1985: 105)

By the end of the poem, Jordan visualizes an image of Palestinian refugees living in exile in Lebanon as they are being forced to leave their camps and move from one exile to another:

> Didn't you read the leaflets that they dropped
> from their hotshot fighter jets?
> they told you to go
> one hundred and thirty-five thousand
> Palestinian in Beirut and why
> didn't you take the hint?
> Go!
> There was the Mediterranean: you
> could walk into the water and stay
> there.
> What was the problem?
>
> (Jordan 1985: 105)

The black poet concludes her poem with an apology which reflects the collective attitude of honest American and Israeli citizens toward the Palestinian tragedy:

Yes I did know it was the money I earned as a poet that paid
for the bombs and the planes and the tanks
that they used to massacre your family
But I am not an evil person
The people of my country aren't so bad
you cannot expect but so much
from those of us who have to pay taxes and watch
American TV.
You see my point
I am sorry
I really am sorry

(Jordan 1985: 106)

Like Jordan, Palestinian poet Mahmud Darwish explores the massacres of Palestinian refugees. In his poetry, Darwish narrates the whole story of Palestinian suffering in Lebanon. The refugee camps of Palestinians living in Lebanon were brutally attacked by the Israeli army and its Lebanese allies — the right wing Christian militias. After the evacuation of the Palestine Liberation Organization troops from Lebanon, during the Israeli invasion of the country in 1982, the vulnerable refugee camps were attacked and thousands of unarmed women and children were slaughtered by Lebanese Christian militias supported by Israel. The same militias were responsible for the mass murder of Palestinian refugees during the Tel-Al-Zaatar massacre which took place during the Lebanese Civil War. The Palestinian refugee camps were also besieged for more than six months by the Shi'ite Muslim militias, supported by the Syrian army, during which hundreds of exiled refugees died of starvation. In 'Brief Reflections on an Ancient and Beautiful City on the Coast of the Mediterranean Sea', Darwish used the sea image as a symbol of the Palestinian exile. Displaced from their homeland, the Palestinian refuges have lived in exile in Lebanon since 1948. During the Israeli invasion of Lebanon in 1982, Palestinian refugees were forced to leave their camps in Lebanon and move to a new place of exile: "We have to sing for the sea's defeat within us / or for our dead lying by the sea / and wear salt and revolt to every port / before oblivion sucks us dry", writes Darwish (al-Udhari 1986:130). In this long poem, the poet describes the Palestinian refugees, who were evacuated by sea, as follows:

We are the leaves of tree
the words of a shattered time
we are the moon light sonata
we are the other river bank that lies between the voice and the
stone

> we are what we produced in the land that was ours
> we are what's left of us in exile
> we are what's left of us in exile
> we are the plants of broken vase
> we are what we are but who are we?
>
> (Al-Udhari 1986: 130)

Using the sea as an image of Palestinian exile, Darwish says:

> Greetings oh ancient sea
> you, sea that have saved us from the loneliness of the forests
> you, sea of all beginnings (the sea disappears) our blue body, our
> happiness, our soul tired of stretching from Jaffa to Carthage
> our broken pitcher, tablets of lost stories, we looked for the legends of
> civilizations but only could find the skull of man by the sea
>
> (Al-Udhari 1986: 134)

In the same poem, Darwish highlights the duration of Palestinian suffering. Palestinians were forced to leave their country twice, in 1948 and in 1967, after the occupation of all the Palestinian territories. In their third exodus in 1982, the Palestinian refugees in Lebanon were subjected to more suffering: "The sea cannot take another immigration / oh, the sea has no room for us". The remaining Palestinian refugees who survived the genocide of the camps and whom Darwish calls "the generation of the massacre" are doomed to move from one exile to another just to be killed: "Every land I long for as a bed / dangles as a gallows". Even in the Arab countries where Palestinians live in exile "a knight stabs his brother in the chest" and there "my dream leaves me only to make me laugh / or make people laugh at someone leading a dream like a camel in a market of whores". In their Arab places of exile, the Palestinian refugees have been slaughtered by Arabs such as the Lebanese, the Syrians and the Jordanians, just as they have been massacred by the Zionists in Israel: "We walk from one massacre to another massacre" (Al-Udhari 1986:138). Thus Darwish expresses his sympathy with the Palestinian people and he apologises to what he calls "the land / victim", for all the atrocities inflicted upon the Palestinians and their homeland:

> Whenever a prophet rises from our victims we slaughter him with
> our own hands
> I have the right to speak
> and the priest has the right to kill
> I have the right to dream
> and the executioner must listen to me or open the door to let my
> dream escape
>
> (Al-Udhari 1986: 138)

In 'Victim No. 48', Mahmud Darwish describes the experience of a Palestinian refugee living in exile in Lebanon who becomes a symbol of all Palestinian refugees in the Arab world. These refugees are not only subjected to the pains of exile and alienation but also to the danger of war and genocide: "He was lying dead on a stone / they found in his chest the moon and a rose lantern / They found in his pocket a few coins / A box of matches and a travel permit". As a Palestinian refugee, the victim, in the poem, is deprived of a national passport and is instead given a travel document by the host country. After his death, "his mother kissed him / and cried for a year". The poor mother, in the poem, like all Palestinian mothers, is destined to witness the death and agony of her sons and daughters, either at the hands of the Israeli soldiers or in Arab countries where Palestinian refugees are dealt with as aliens: "His brother grew up / And went to town looking for work / He was put in prison / Because he had no travel permit / He was carrying a dustbin / And boxes down the street" (al-Udhari 1986: 125). The victim's brother is arrested and sent to a Lebanese jail because his status as a refugee does not enable him to obtain a job outside the refugee camp. Even if the Palestinian refugee attempts to earn his living by working as a dustman, the laws of the host countries prevent him from practising this simple human right. The plight of the Palestinian refugees, in the poem, reflects the miserable and inhuman conditions of those who live in exile, particularly if this exile is a refugee camp, a ghetto where they are forced to stay for years. The title of the poem, 'Victim No. 48', refers to the 1948 Arab-Israeli war which resulted in the occupation of most of the Palestinian towns and villages and the dramatic exodus of half of the Palestinian people who were scattered in refugee camps in neighbouring Arab countries such as Lebanon, Jordan, Syria and Iraq. Darwish reminds us that the Palestinian refugee problem started in 1948 and, since that time, Palestinians have been subjected to massacres, suffering, alienation, exile and death: "Children of my country / that's how the moon died" (al-Udhari 1986: 125).

In addition to the pains of exile, Palestinians, in diaspora, and in the occupied territories, suffer from a loss of identity. The victim's brother, in the above-mentioned poem, is sent to prison because he has no Lebanese identity card which would enable him to find a suitable job. As a refugee and an exile, he is only allowed to look for work inside the boundaries of the poor refugee camps. When he was arrested by the police, in Beirut, he was "carrying a dustbin and boxes down the street". This indicates that the refugee is either a dustman or someone who looks for remains of food and clothes in the rich people's garbage. Being deprived of an independent homeland and a national passport, Palestinian people suffer not only from a deep identity crisis but also from humiliation and ridicule, particularly when they are forced to move from one place of exile to another. Darwish depicts this painful experience in 'The Passport': "They didn't recognize me / the passport's darkness / Erased the tones of my photographs / They put my wound on show / For tourists who love collecting pictures". Obviously, "the darkness of the passport" is due to the fact that it is not a genuine Palestinian passport but a travel document given to Palestinian refugees by the host countries. To be fair, it must be acknowledged that Israel is the only country in the region that gave Palestinians living inside Israel since 1948 passports and nationalities. Darwish himself has Israeli nationality and an Israeli passport, despite being an Arab. However, the poet indicates that his Israeli passport has eliminated his Palestinian identity and has become a reminder of a homeland which he has lost. This negation of identity leads to pain and trauma because the poet does not want strangers to identify him either as a refugee or an Israeli. Darwish takes pride in his Palestinian identity and it is sufficient for him that the Palestinian "boxthorn" and the Palestinian "rain songs recognize me" (al-Udhari 1986: 125). Further, in his journey of exile, the poet still remembers "all the dark eyes" of his own people, "all the wheat fields", "all the waving handkerchiefs", and all "the birds that followed my hand to the barriers of a distant airport". Being "deprived of a name, of an identity / in a land I tended with both hands", the Palestinian poet has to live in exile after the colonizers turned his homeland into "prisons" and "graves". In his exile, the Palestinian refugee/poet has become a symbol of suffering: "Today Job's voice rang throughout heaven". The Biblical/Quranic allusion to Job provides an insight into Palestinian suffering, linking the Palestinian ordeal to the human history of pain and to other persecuted people such as the Jews and the Afro-Americans. In these intense moments of misery, the speaker in the poem finds no need for his refugee passport or the nationality of a host country because "the hearts of people are my nationality / Take away my passport" (al-Udhari 1986: 126).

Thus, in 'Psalm 2', Darwish reveals his nostalgia for his homeland, Palestine, a "country, turning up in songs and massacres". He addresses his homeland: "Why do I smuggle you from airport to airport / like opium / invisible ink / a radio transmitter?". In his diaspora, the poet also takes great pains to recall the memories of a country "trapped between the dagger and the wind". He reflects his painful experience of exile as he addresses his homeland:

> I want to draw your shape
> you, scattered in files and surprises
> I want to draw your shape
> you, flying on shrapnel and birds' wings
> I want to draw your shape
> to find my shape in yours
> there isn't a name in Arab history
> I haven't borrowed
> to help me slip through your secret windows
> all the code-names are kept
> in air-conditioned recruiting offices
> will you accept my name — my only code name — Mahmud
> Darwish
>
>   (Al-Udhari 1986: 127)

Speaking about life in the diaspora, the poet in "Horses Neighing at the Foot of the Mountain" refers to an exilic experience which turns into a "journey in which a martyr kills a martyr" (al-Udhari 1986: 140). In this journey, the Palestinian refugees "travel like other people but we return to nowhere / we travel in the carriages of the psalms, sleep in the tents of the prophets and come out of speech of the gypsies" (142). The reference to "the tents" and the analogy between the Palestinians and the gypsies in Darwish's poem "We Travel Like Other People" signify the state of homelessness and alienation which characterizes the life of the Palestinian refugees: "We have a country of words speak, speak so I can put my road on the stone of a stone / speak so we may know the end of this travel" (al-Udhari 1986: 142). Moreover, in a poem entitled "Speech of the Red Indian", collected in his anthology *The Adam of Two Edens* (2000), Darwish draws an analogy between Palestinians and Native Americans, nations that were forced to live in diaspora in their own land. Darwish speaks to the colonizers of his land using some Quranic verses as an intertext: "you have your God / and we have ours / you have your religion and we have ours / Don't bury our God / in books that back up your claim of land over land". He continues: "you have come from beyond the seas, bent on war, / Don't cut down the tree of our names, / Don't gallop your flaming horses across/ the open plains" (al-Udhari 1986: 132). In the same historical context, the poet associates the loss of Palestine with the fall of Granada after the defeat of the Muslim/Arab invaders who stayed in Spain for more than seven centuries. Both catastrophes, according to the poet, led to suffering and Diaspora on the part of the Arab people. In spite of the Arab history of pain in ancient Spain, Darwish, who compares Palestine with Spain, identifies himself with the famous Spanish poet Federico Garcia Lorca: "the keys belong to me, / as well as the minarets and lamps. / I even belong to myself / I'm the Adam of Two Edens lost to me twice. / Expel me slowly. Kill me slowly / with Garcia Lorca / under my olive tree" (154).

The theme of exile is also explored in the works of Samih Al-Qasim, another prominent Palestinian poet. In 'The Will of Man Dying in Exile', he says: "light the fire so I can see my tears / on the night of the massacre / so I can see your sister's corpse / whose heart is a bird ripped up by foreign tongues / by foreign winds" (al-Udhari 1986: 108). In this poem, which was written after the 1967 Arab-Israeli war and the Israeli occupation of the rest of the Palestinian territories, Al-Qasim refers to the plight of exiled Palestinians who almost lost hope of returning to their homeland particularly after the appalling defeat of the Arab armies in war with Israel. The Palestinian, in the poem, who is both a refugee and an exile, is depicted as a 'scarecrow' without a name. Al-Qasim's refugee image is not only a reflection of Yeats' scarecrow in the 'Byzantium' poem, but it carries more pathetic overtones because the Palestinian refugee is a victim of both Israeli aggression and Arab indifference: "At the end of the road he stood / like a scarecrow in a vineyard / at the end of the road he stood / wearing an old coat / his name was the unknown man" (al-Udhari 1986: 108). The Palestinian refugee has no name and no identity because the Palestinian dream of having an independent homeland and returning to their own country has been frustrated. Even in exile, Palestinian refugees are brutally attacked by the Israeli army and hostile militias in host countries. In 'To Ariel Sharon', Al-Qasim speaks about the massacres of Palestinians by the Israeli army, not only inside Palestine but also in the refugee camps in Lebanon:

> The general's tank has five mouths
> under the tank a boy of five, a rose
> a boy and five stars adorn the general's shoulders
> under his tank five roses and five boys
> the tank has countless mouths
>
> (Al-Udhari 1986: 109)

The poet who is both black and American is similar, in many ways, to the Palestinian writer living in exile under Israeli occupation. Both of them create poetry in the context of a complex of factors which subtly affect the nature of their work. For example, the position of the black poet, living in the American diaspora, offers him/her a special insight into his/her social and political milieu. S/he views objectively what are called the antithetical black and white cultures of America. The result is a portrait of an ambiguous grey world in which irrational horrors and contradictory tensions are in operation. This poetry graphically describes the individual's place in an American social and cultural context which Le Roi Jones calls "the hopelessly interwoven fabric of American life" (Jones 1963: 111). Because black American or Palestinian poets are members of an oppressed group, defined by the majority culture to the latter's own advantage, the thrust of their creativity runs counter to the majority definition. That is to say, their work, if faithful to life, must challenge the superiority assumptions advocated by their oppressors (white Americans/Israelis). Black and Palestinian poetry will also reflect a cultural background that is fundamentally different, in many ways, from the dominant culture. It reflects the identity of oppressed and exiled nations that struggle for their dignity and honour. Further, black/Palestinian poets, in challenging the definitions of their oppressors and in choosing to correct these definitions/images, reclaim the historical right to self-determination and thus, their work is perceived, on some level, by the dominant group, as either revolutionary or propagandist.

In *Black Skins, White Masks*, Frantz Fanon points out that there is a moment at which "the colonialist reaches the point of no longer being able to imagine a time occurring without him. His eruption into the history of the colonized people is deified, transformed into absolute necessity" (Fanon 1969: 159). The attempt of the colonizers (white Americans/Israelis) to erase the history and culture of colonized peoples (blacks/Palestinians – not to mention Native Americans) by dismissing their poetry of exile as propagandist, is a part of what Edward Said calls "the moral epistemology of imperialism" (Said 1979: 18). In *The Question of Palestine*, Said argues that the approved history of colonialist nations such as America, Australia, South Africa, and Israel started with what he calls "a blotting out of knowledge" of the native people or the making of them into "people without history" (Said 1979: 23). In other words, the colonizer seeks to turn the colonized (blacks) or the native (Palestinians) into a non-entity, in order to erase their identity. Therefore, in both black and Palestinian poetry of exile, there is a focus on the issue of identity. In a poem entitled 'Palestinian', Harun Hashim Rashid affirms his own identity as a Palestinian, proud of his people, of his struggle, and of his just cause: "Palestinian / is my name

/ On all battlefields / I have inscribed my name / Palestinian / Such is my name, I know / It torments and grieves me / Their eyes hurt me / Pursue me, wound me / For my name is Palestinian" (Khouri 1975: 231). The Palestinian poet is not ashamed of his identity, regardless of all the prejudices against him: "Jails with their gates flung wide / summon me / And in all the airports of the world / Are found my names and titles" (233). He insists on showing the world the real identity of the Palestinian people who have been suffering in the attempt to gain their independence even after most of the Arab governments have abandoned them: "Palestinian I am / Though they betray me and my cause / Though they sell me in the market / Though to the flames they cast me" (233).

In *The Wretched of the Earth*, Frantz Fanon discusses the native writer's identity crisis as follows:

> In order to ensure his salvation and to escape from the supremacy of the white man's culture, the native intellectual feels the need to turn backwards towards his unknown roots. Because he feels he is becoming estranged, he decides to take all for granted and confirms everything even though he may lose body and soul. (Fanon 1967: 37)

Black American poets such as Le Roi Jones, Don Lee, Nikki Giovanni, and Sonia Sanchez, in search for their identity in the American diaspora in the 1960s, turned backward toward their roots in Africa. Don Lee, in 'The Primitive', acknowledges his African roots: "Taken from the / shores of Mother Africa / the savages they thought, we were - / they being real savages / to save us. (from what?) Our happiness, our love, each other?" (Lee 1971: 63). In 'Change is Not Always Progress', Lee cries: "Africa / don't let them steal / your face / Take your circles / and make them squares / don't let them / steal / your body" (Lee 1971: 169).

Likewise, the black poet Nikki Giovanni in 'Ego Tripping – There May Be a Reason Why', sticks to her racial roots in Africa: 'I was born in the Congo / I walked to the fertile crescent and built / the sphinx / I designed a pyramid / I sat on the throne / My oldest daughter is Nefertiti" (Giovanni 1970: 37). Furthermore, Sonia Sanchez, in her poetry, links blacks with their roots in Africa, recalling the sad memory of the journey of the African slaves to the new world:

> Come into black geography
> you seated like Manzu's cardinal
> Come up through tongues
> multiplying memories

and to avoid descent
among wounds
cruising like ships
climb into these sockets
golden with brine.

(Sanchez: 1974: 21)

Instead of going toward the west, the poet asks the ship carrying slaves to travel back through time and move toward the east, toward Africa.

Being displaced from their original homeland, the black people remain dispossessed, living in the American Diaspora. The feeling of being exiled in a white country coupled with the growing of black social and ethnic consciousness in the 1960s led to an identity crisis on the part of the black people in America. The black poet in America, like the Palestinian poet living in Israel, realizes that s/he is locked in a limbo between contradictory cultures: "I am inside someone / who hates me", says Le Roi Jones in *The Dead Lecturer* (Jones 1964: 15). In spite of being an American by birth, the black poet feels that he is lured into the tradition of an alien culture that cuts him off from his origin in Africa. But, the image of the homeland Africa to the black poet is different from the image of Palestine in the eyes of the Palestinian poets, in that, for the former, a permanent return to the land of his origins is not usually feasible.

Yusuf al-Khatib observes that

> by the end of the catastrophic year [1948] which brought about the most obnoxious defeat that could befall a nation, the concept of the land took two forms in the eyes of the Palestinian people: 'exile' and 'prison'. While 'exile' includes all lands where Palestinian refugees live whether inside Palestine or outside it, 'prison' involves the Palestinian land that came under the Israeli flag (cited in Sulaiman 1984: 118)

Some people wonder why Palestinians living in rich Arab countries have failed to be assimilated into these countries. In fact, Palestinians, whether living in refugee camps or in rich Arab countries or elsewhere, have deep and strong spiritual links with a country they believe is their rightful homeland. They long to return to their homeland simply because their relationship with Palestine is not based on material or political assumptions. This attitude toward their homeland is peculiar to the Palestinian people in exile.

Comparing contemporary Afro-American and Palestinian poetry, it becomes obvious that Africa, to the black American poet, is a fantasy, a dream world, a kind of Utopia. However, Palestine, to the

Palestinian poet, is a reality that exists; it is a land which has been usurped by a ruthless enemy, a mother, a sister, a wife raped by the colonizer, a refugee camp ravaged by Israeli tanks and American Apaches and F-16 bombers. To the black poet, "African blues / does not know me / does not feel what I am" (Jones 1964: 47). The black American poet is caught in a limbo between cultures and trapped in the language, fantasies and traditions of a people from whom s/he is alien by birth, thereby s/he feels that s/he is severed from his/her roots: "Africa is a foreign place / you are as any other sad man here — American" (Jones 1964: 47). Mahmud Darwish personifies Palestine as a refugee woman forced to live in exile. In "A Lover from Palestine" Darwish says: "yesterday I saw you at the harbour / travelling without relations or provisions" (Sulaiman 1984: 160). Palestine is also a mother:

> I ran to you like an orphan
> questioning the wisdom of our forefathers:
> "How can the green fruit grove
> after being dragged to a prison
> an exile and a harbour, remain green
> in spite of its travels
> and in spite of the scent of salt and longing?"

In the same poem, Darwish portrays Palestine as a Christ figure: "I saw you on the mountains covered / with thorny plants / a shepherdess without sheep / harried amidst the ruins". After the loss of Palestine Darwish's homeland and which is depicted as "the lungs in my chest/ the voice of my lips / the water and the fire for me", the poet is forced to live as an exile in alien countries: "I, who have been turned into a stranger". Thus, he weeps tears and blood after the loss of his homeland: "I saw you in rays of tears and wounds" (Sulaiman 1984: 160).

In Darwish's poem, Palestine also takes the shape of a widow who has lost her husband in the never-ending battle for freedom and independence: "I saw you at the mouth of the cave / hanging the rags of your orphans on a line". Darwish further portrays Palestine as an orphan who lost his/her father in the war with the colonizer: "I saw you in the songs of orphanhood and / misery". By the end of the poem, Palestine takes the identity of the poet's beautiful beloved: "I saw you in every drop of the sea / and in every grain of sand / beautiful as the earth / beautiful as children / beautiful as jasmine". In the final lines of the poem, Darwish promises his innocent and beautiful beloved to sacrifice himself for the sake of her eyes:

> I swear to you: I shall weave a scarf from my eyelashes
> embroidered with verses for your eyes
> and with your name on it
> A name when watered
> with the praises of my chanting heart
> will make the trees spread their branches again
> I shall write few words on the scarf
> more precious
> than kisses and the blood of the martyrs
>
>   (Sulaiman 1984: 160).

Darwish's magic words are a reminder that Palestine is an Arab country and will remain so: "Palestinian she was / and Palestinian she remains" (160).

Like Darwish, who insists on his identity as a Palestinian living in exile in the state of Israel, Le Roi Jones, in 'Kaba' affirms his black/African identity: "We have been captured brothers / and we labour to make our gateway into / the ancient image, into a new / correspondence with ourselves / and our black family" (Jones 1987: 146). Like Jones, Langston Hughes in 'Refugee in America' affirms his identity as a black poet, underlining the notion that blacks in America were deprived of human rights, particularly their freedom, which intensified their sense of alienation:

> There are words like freedom
> sweet and wonderful to say
> on my heart-strings freedom sings
> all day everyday
> There are words like liberty
> that almost make me cry
> If you had known what I knew
> you would know why
>
>   (Hughes 1974: 290)

Like Palestinians under Israeli occupation, blacks in America up to the 1960s were haunted with the dream of equality, but their dream was frustrated. However, Langston Hughes was confident that his dream would be realized: "In some lands / Dark night and cold steel / prevail / But the dream will come back / and the song breaks its jail" (Hughes 1967: 63). He insists on achieving his dream: "To fling my arms wide / In some place of the sun / to whirl and to dance / till the white day is done / Then rest at cool evening / Beneath a tall tree / while night comes on gently / dark like me" (14). Due to white racism and oppression, the black man's dream was delayed, thus he turned to Africa for a full realization of his dream. In Africa, the black poet seeks solace, consolation, and emotional support but, unlike the Palestinian poet, s/he discovers that Africa is so far away and s/he does not even have many African memories. The black American poets are infused with African blood, but the words that flow out of them are not in an African language but in a "strange un-Negro tongue" (Du Bois 1961: 16). Black American poets do not see Africa the same way the Palestinian poets sees their homeland, Palestine, because the Negro poet suffers from what W.E.B. DuBois calls, "double consciousness" (Du Bois 1961: 16).

DuBois, in his discussion of the notion of double consciousness points to

> this peculiar sensation, this double consciousness, this sense of always looking at one's soul by the type of the world that looks on in amused contempt and pity. In this merging, he [the black American] wishes neither of the older selves to be lost. The Negro would not Africanize America, for America has too much to teach the world and Africa. He (the black American) would not bleach his Negro soul in a flood of white Americanism, for he knows that Negro blood has a message for the world. He simply wishes to make it possible for a man to be both a Negro and an American without being cursed and spit upon by his fellows, without having the doors of opportunity closed roughly in his face. (DuBois 1961: 16-17)

Palestinians are more directly bound to their homeland than black Americans. Blacks living in the American exile have almost lost their connection with their African homeland; however, they cannot liberate their collective psyche from the feeling of being dispossessed. Sterling Plump argues that "the transporting of millions of Africans into the West was an environmental switch, but there was not a simultaneous cosmological or world view adjustment" (Plump 1972: 32). On the other hand, the transporting of millions of Zionists, and other immigrants whose connection to Judaism is tenuous, into the Promised Land has created many problems for both Israelis and Palestinians. Nevertheless, it can be argued that, regardless of the pains of exile that have characterized the lives of Palestinians, Afro-Americans and the Jewish nation, there is always a strong sense of hope for a better future of these oppressed peoples. The well-known Israeli poet, Yehuda Amichai expresses this hope for a new era of peace and love:

> An Arab shepherd searches for a lamb on Mount Zion,
> And on the hill across I search for my little son,
> An Arab shepherd and a Jewish father
> In their temporary failure.

Our voices meet above
the Sultan's pool in the middle of the valley.
We both want the son and the lamb
to never enter the process
of the terrible machine of 'Chad Gadya'.
Later we found them in the bushes,
and our voices returned to us crying and laughing inside.
The search for a lamb and for a son
was always
the beginning of a new religion in these hills.

(Coffin 1982: 341)

Bibliography

Al-Haydari, Buland. 1987. 'The Journey of the Yellow Letters' in Asfour, John
    Mikhail (tr. and ed.) *When the Words Burn: An Anthology of Modern Arabic
    Poetry* (1945-1987). Ontario: Cormorant Books: 81-82.
Al-Udhari, Abdullah (tr. and ed.). 1986. *Modern Poetry of the Arab World.* New
    York: Penguin Books.
Boullata, Kamal. 1992. 'The View From No-Man's Land' in *Michigan Quarterly
    Review* 31: 580-590.
Buruma, Ian. 2001. 'Real Wounds, Unreal Wounds: The Romance of Exile' in *New
    Republic* 224: 1-10.
Darwish, Mahmud. 2000. *The Adam of Two Edens: Poems.* Syracuse, New York:
    Syracuse University Press and Jusoor.
Coffin, Edna Amir. 1982. 'The Image of the Arab in Modern Hebrew Literature' in
    Michigan Quarterly Review 21: 319- 341.
Du Bois, W.E.B. 1961. *The Souls of Black Folk.* Greenwich, Connecticut: Fawcett
    Publications.
Fanon, Frantz. 1969. *Black Skins, White Masks* (tr. Charles Lam Markman). New
    York: Grove Press.
- - - . 1967. *The Wretched of the Earth* (tr. Constance Farrington). New York:
    Grove Press.
Gibson, Donald B (ed.). 1973. *Modern Black Poets: A Collection of Critical Essays.*
    Englewood Cliffs, New Jersey: Prentice-Hall.
Gohar, Saddik. 1998. *A Singer in the Ghetto: A Study of Le Roi Jones/Amiri Barak's
    Revolutionary Poetry.* Cairo: Anglo-Egyptian Book.
Giovanni, Nikki. 1970. *Re-Creation.* Detroit, Michigan: Broadside Press.
Hughes, Langston. 1974. *Selected Poems of Langston Hughes.* New York: Vintage.
- - - . 1967. *The Panther and the Lash.* New York: Knopf.
Jayyusi, Salma Khadra (ed.). 1987. *Modern Arabic Poetry: An Anthology.* New York:
    Columbia University Press.
Jones, Le Roi. 1969. *Black Magic: Collected Poetry (1961-1967).* Indianapolis:
    Bobbs-Merrill.
- - - . 1963. *Blues People.* New York: William Morrow.
- - - . 1966. *Home: Social Essays.* New York: William Morrow.
- - - . 1964. *The Dead Lecturer.* New York: Grove Press.
Jordan, June. 1985. *Living Room.* New York: Thunder's Mouth Press.
Khouri, Mounah and Hamid Algar (trs and eds). 1975. *An Anthology of Modern
    Arabic Poetry.* California: California University Press.

Lee, Don. 1971. *Directionscore: Selected and New Poems.* Michigan: Broadside Press.

Plump, Sterling. 1972. *Black Rituals.* Chicago: Third World Press.

Qabbani, Nizar, 1987. 'Marginal Notes on the Book of Defeat' in Asfour, John Mikhail (tr. and ed.) *When the Words Burn: An Anthology of Modern Arabic Poetry* (1945-1987). Ontario: Cormorant Books: 95-99.

Said, Edward. 1988. 'Identity, Negation and Violence' in *New Left Review* 171: 46-60.

- - - . 1979. *The Question of Palestine.* New York: Times Books.

Sanchez, Sonia. 1974. *Blues Book for Blue Black Magical Women.* Detroit: Broadside Press.

Sulaiman, Khalid A. 1984. *Palestine and Modern Arab Poetry.* London: Zed Books.

20

Annexing the Land of Exile: Language and History in the Work of Assia Djebar

Trudy Agar

Trudy Agar received her MA from the University of Waikato, New
Zealand, and her PhD conjointly from the University of Auckland and
the University of Paris 13. She has taught at the Université de la
Sorbonne, Paris, and then at the University of Auckland, before
joining the French department at the University of Canterbury, New
Zealand, as a lecturer in French. She has travelled in Europe and
North Africa. Her research interests are in the areas of Francophone
women's writing, violence in literature and postcolonial autobiography.

In this paper, she examines the many dimensions of exile in the
partially autobiographical novel *L'amour, la fantasia* (1985) of
Algerian writer Assia Djebar. One of very few indigenous Algerian
women to gain a formal education in the pre-Independence period,
including study at one of the most prestigious universities in France,
Djebar sees this experience as having, in one sense, cut her off from
the community of women she grew up with. While she does speak an
Arabic dialect and understands her maternal Berber, she has come to
use French, the language of 'yesterday's enemy', as the language of
her published writing. At the same time, she acknowledges that
speaking and writing French represents a liberation from some of the
most fundamental features of Algerian patriarchy. In *L'amour, la
fantasia* she recounts elements of both the French war of invasion in
the 1830s and the struggle for Independence in the 1960s,
interweaving official history, autobiographical material, and oral
accounts by illiterate Algerian women, who have themselves been cut
off from conventional written history. Her written French is enriched
with structures and expressions which derive from their speech. She
aims to recover her links with her Algerian sisters by giving voice to
their previously unrecorded stories. Sadly, with the targeting of
Algerian intellectuals by Islamic militants over the last decade, her
choice of residence in France and the United States has become
formal exile.

Assia Djebar is an Algerian woman writer whose work forms part of a
new literature that has its origins at the violent intersection of two
geographical spaces, two languages, religions, and cultures. Algerian

writing in French first appeared in the 1920s, but really came into its own in the 1950s just prior to Independence. Instead of declining with the French withdrawal from Algeria in 1962, this literature has continued to flourish, despite many writers' trepidation about expressing themselves in the French language, which Abdelkébir Khatibi called "*la belle et maléfique étrangère*" (Khatibi 1971: 12-13; 'the beautiful and maleficent stranger'[1]). Shortly after his country gained independence, Moroccan Abdellatif Laâbi warned that Maghribi writers should remain on their guard, aware of the danger of letting French become not simply an instrument of communication but an instrument of culture (Laâbi 1970: 36). Some, like the Algerian writers Kateb Yacine and Malek Haddad, ceased writing in French, preferring Arabic or even silence to the language of the former coloniser. Haddad referred to the French language as his "exile" and refused to live in this exile once independence was obtained (Déjeux 1975: 74-5). Yacine abandoned French-language fiction for theatre written in his native Arabic dialect. Yet other writers consider the French language to be "*le seul acquis positif de la colonisation*" ('the only positive legacy of colonisation'),[2] a position that is slowly beginning to find favour with the Algerian ruling class. Reversing a 40-year policy of official political hostility to the notion of *francophonie*, the incumbent president, Abdellaziz Bouteflika, has recently changed tack, pursuing a *rapprochement* with the international French-speaking community, a repositioning exemplified by his presence at the *Francophonie* Summit in 2002. Djebar's relationship to the language of her written expression is problematic and fraught with risk, tensions and conflicting desires. Her autobiographical novel, *L'amour, la fantasia* (1985; translated as *Fantasia: An Algerian Cavalcade*, 1993), reveals the ambiguous relationship this Algerian exile has with the languages of her homeland and with French, the language of yesterday's enemy.

Born in Cherchel, Algeria, in 1936, the daughter of a liberal-minded teacher and a housewife who taught herself French, Assia Djebar has led an extraordinary life. She was one of the few Algerian girls of the pre-independence period to receive a formal education. She wrote three novels prior to Independence, making her the first recognised Algerian woman novelist. In 1955, Djebar became the first Algerian woman to be admitted to the prestigious École normale supérieure in France. She then published novels, poetry, and drama before becoming the first Algerian woman to direct a film, *La nouba des femmes du mont Chenoua*. After Independence, and particularly since the assassination of writer and journalist Tahar Djaout in 1993, and the subsequent targeting of intellectuals by Islamic militants, Djebar, like many Algerian writers, chose to live in exile from her native country. Since leaving Algeria in the early 1980s, to live first in France then in the United States, she has continued writing to wide acclaim, returning occasionally to Algeria at great personal risk.[3] In 2002, she was awarded the German Peace Prize for her contribution to self-confidence among women in the Arab world and for bringing hope for peace to Algeria.

In *L'amour, la fantasia*, Djebar undertakes a vast project of rewriting the two wars between Algeria and France: from the first battle of the French invasion in 1830 to the end of the war of Independence, combining historical fact, autobiographical scenes, eye-witness accounts of events from the 1960s that she had recorded for the filming of *La nouba*, and the plural autobiography of her female compatriots, whom she calls her "sisters". Throughout the text, Djebar interrogates her own uneasy position as an exiled postcolonial writer telling the story of her illiterate countrywomen in the language of the former oppressor. The French language, which is, in Djebar's terms, the main character of *L'amour, la fantasia*, has become her "*idiome de l'exil*" (Djebar 2000: 1; "language of exile"). Through her rewriting of the linguistic war that was fought in the wake of the colonial invasion, Djebar tries to negotiate a new territory between the warring languages, one that will lead her back from exile.

The first two parts of *L'amour, la fantasia* consist of a rewriting of the colonial war of invasion, which Djebar imagines in terms of a troubling meeting of desire and violence, a coupling of terms announced in the title of the book - a fantasia being a demonstration performed by Arab horsemen, often as training for battle, which is accompanied by women's *youyous*, or ululations. The first battle is codified as a scene of seduction, where the French troops gaze upon the city of Algiers, which is stretched out before them like a veiled woman dressed in the traditional white *haik*. She unveils herself for the flotilla and allows herself to be seen by her future invaders. It is unclear, however, whether she allows herself to be gazed upon in order to be seen, or so that she might see. The desire is double: the female city, troubling to the soldiers as she is immobilised in her ghostly whiteness, dreams perhaps of a love affair. The first meeting of the two peoples takes place in silence, "*comme si les envahisseurs allaient être les amants!*" (Djebar 1995: 16; "as if the invaders were coming as lovers!", 1993: 8). The silence of the first encounter soon gives way to cries of pain and suffering from the Algerians, as the initial desire and reciprocal interest is transformed, for the French invaders, into rapine and a desire to subjugate the Oriental other.

The ambiguous enterprise of colonial conquest, according to Djebar's retelling of it, relies heavily on the power of language. Words are given a magical, mortal quality in Djebar's writing. Initial attempts between the two parties to communicate end, inevitably, in death. Any exchange of words is fatal. The elderly Algerian sent to receive Field Marshal de Bourmont's pseudo-pacific declarations is then murdered by his own when he returns with the written message. In a similar scene, the terms of dey Hussein's surrender are collected by a French interpreter. The dey abdicates, but the interpreter dies a few days later from a nervous illness. According to Djebar, all communication between the two sides, just like the initial mutual desire, is doomed to failure since the desire is tainted by violence.

For Djebar, language, with its mystical power, is the weapon *par excellence*. The imposition of French was used to stifle the voice of the colonised and to impose the cultural values of the coloniser. Djebar points to the unequal battle of words: of the thirty-seven published accounts of the July 1830 invasion, only three were written by Algerians. Algerian women were especially incapable of fighting the war of words on an equal footing because they were illiterate and their spoken languages, Berber and the Algerian Arabic dialect, had no written form. Most military accounts of the period attempted to silence Algerian suffering in order to sustain French support for the colonial enterprise. Djebar attempts to fill the gaps in the colonial accounts of this war through her own rewriting of it, and by sourcing her material not just from military accounts written by Frenchmen but also from oral stories told by illiterate Algerian women. Her account is at once deliberately historical and imaginative. Djebar, a former university lecturer in history, allows her imagination to fill in those aspects of history that have been silenced beyond recovery. This is a feminisation of history, a deliberate downplaying of the scientific, with an emphasis on the role of women as guardians and transmitters of history and an embracing of history as writing.[4]

To have one's suffering silenced or suppressed is, in the words of the text, to suffer "true death" (Djebar 1993: 92). This is why Djebar thanks Colonel Pélissier for having made an official report on his act of genocide, when he caused the death through asphyxiation of the Ouled Riah tribe, who were hiding in underground caves, without attempting to veil the suffering he had inflicted. Pélissier had the courage to order the bodies to be exhumed from the caves and laid out for counting. It is for this reason that Djebar calls him "*le premier écrivain de la première guerre d'Algérie!*" (Djebar 1995: 92; "the foremost chronicler of the first Algerian War!", 1993: 78). Pélissier's report, which caused a scandal in Paris for evoking Algerian suffering in too 'eloquent' and 'realistic' a way, exhumes the memory of the deaths by giving voice to them and prevents them from "*sécher au soleil*" (Djebar 1995: 89; "drying in the sun", 1993: 75).

The suppression of the voice of the colonised, in the past, has led to an exile from language, a condition Djebar terms "aphasia". Whereas French soldiers were gripped by "scribblomania" (1993: 44), the natives voiced only cries – both ululation and shouts of suffering. The aphasic Algerian woman, however, transformed her silence into a tool of resistance used to deny the vanquisher his victory; a victory unnamed, and therefore unrecognised, is no victory at all. Djebar attempts to counter the silence of female combatants in the war of Independence by basing her relation of this war on oral accounts given to her by women of her own tribe. She hands the autobiographical pronoun 'I' over to these women, transcribing and translating their stories into French while retaining some of the particularities of what she terms "subterranean" female language: understatement, religious formulae, enigma, and idiomatic expressions modelled on the Algerian Arabic dialect, such as 'to denude', meaning 'to remove one's veil'. The modelling of French on dialectal Arabic produces unsound sentences, such as "*Tout ce qui est passé sur moi ! Mon Dieu, tout ce qui est passé !*" (Djebar 1995: 171; "Everything that has happened to me! Oh Lord, everything that has happened", 1993: 150).[5] This mixing of the two languages, the only miscegenation Djebar's maternal culture will allow, is an instance of what Chantal Zabus has termed "relexification" (1991) and struggles against the standard, authoritative French language while at the same time making this language dynamic and heterogeneous. For the Moroccan writer Tahar Ben Jelloun, this mixing of two 'expressions' within Francophone texts serves to enrich and transform the French language, creating a French that is "*aimée, transfigurée, enrichie, remplie de nouvelles images, baignée dans des fleuves chauds et marinée dans des épices nouvelles, parfois piquantes, d'autres douces*" (Ben Jelloun, 2002; "loved, transfigured, enriched, charged with fresh images, bathed in warm rivers and marinated in new spices, sometimes piquant, sometimes mild").

Djebar's personal story is depicted as indissociable from the violent history of her country; a fact she insists on when she claims to have been born in 1842, the year French soldiers destroyed her family's *zaouia*, or religious monument. Her own development, both as a woman and as a writer, is presented in *L'amour, la fantasia* as the story of the meeting in violence and desire of these two cultures and languages.[6] Her entry into this encounter was a gift of love from her father, who wanted to give his daughter a formal education. Her ambiguous linguistic inheritance is illustrated in the first scene of *L'amour, la fantasia*: her father holds her hand as he takes her to school on her first day. He embodies the contradictions of the family's situation in colonial Algeria: he is dressed in a European suit, carries a satchel and wears a fez on his head. It is thus Djebar's father, the teacher, who introduces her to the French language, making it henceforth her father or stepmother tongue, as opposed to her mother tongue, the Algerian Arabic dialect with its strong Berber influences. Her schooling in French is presented in Djebar's autobiography as though it were an act of treason, a pact with the enemy. Like Kateb Yacine, she was sent into *"la gueule du loup"* (Yacine 1966: 181; "the jaws of the wolf"). The narrator imagines herself a prepubescent girl, offered by her father to the 'enemy camp', like girls in her town who are promised to other families at a young age. The narrator accuses her father of sacrificing his daughter but not in order to benefit from the union with the enemy camp. Rather, he sent her into the French camp out of love, out of a desire to protect her from confinement to the harem. Her audacious father, who wants to educate his daughter, is the object of neighbours' pity since, in their eyes, an educated girl represents a grave danger for her family in that her education may allow her to act outside the bounds of masculine control. In the text, the potential for emancipation lies largely in the power of words. Young girls who know how to write have a voice that may circulate beyond the confines of the harem, and the danger is that what they write will be words of female desire. Love written, says Djebar, is more dangerous than love sequestered.

Acculturation through her colonial French education first gives a voice to the Algerian girl; this voice will in turn liberate her body, allowing her to leave the harem and circulate unveiled, outside in the world of men. The French language, she says, blinds men who can no longer be her voyeurs. The words of the girl and her unveiled body separate her from other females in her milieu who must remain 'mute' and confined to the harem. The dominant language, that of Djebar's education, becomes for her the language of love, since it does not carry the weight of Algerian traditions in restraint and prudishness, and allows love to be spoken. Djebar's parents are the only Algerian couple she knows who address each other by name: to name one another is to love each other openly, a dramatic break with tradition. The narrator is quick to signal the contradictions inherent in this situation: the French language initiates her into love, while it was her father who gifted this language to her, the man who wants to protect her from desire. *"Cette langue"*, she writes, *"que m'a donnée le père me devient entremetteuse et mon initiation, dès lors, se place sous un signe double, contradictoire..."* (Djebar 1995: 12; "the language that my father had been at pains for me to learn, serves as a go-between, and from now on a double, contradictory sign reigns over my initiation...", 1993: 4).

Although French introduces Djebar to the language of desire, she is unable to speak these words due to the inherited prudishness of cultural traditions. She also wishes to avoid causing envy in her Algerian sisters to whom words of love will never be spoken. The impossibility of speaking love in her bilingual situation is a legacy of the violent past. No exchange of love is possible between the two enemy camps, states Djebar, because there has been violence – pillage, rape, and murder – in the French desire for Algeria. Djebar's amorous aphasia is a link to her feminine inheritance. Like her sisters, her stifled voice is bottled up inside her until released in a savage cry. Yet, exiled from the language of love, Djebar finds herself exiled too from the Algerian female community and the legacy of her maternal culture. Her body has been westernised by her French education. She finds it difficult to ululate; instead of bursting forth from her, the sound tears her throat. She acquires a taste for basketball and athletics, preferring these activities to trances at female meetings. Djebar says she has been exiled from her childhood by a war between the French and Arabic languages, fought within her. French, the stepmother tongue, necessitates the loss of the dominated culture in favour of the dominant French culture. Her bilingualism is a series of tactical, warlike, manoeuvres between the two camps; the foreign tongue, the language of exile, establishes a "proud *presidio*" within her, while the mother tongue "resists and attacks" (1993: 215). The gift of love from her father – education in the French system – has liberated Djebar into the world of men and of desire, just as it gave her parents the words to speak their love; but the violence of the colonial legacy means that this gift is also a taking-away. It robs the girl of the legacy left to her by her mother: her mother tongue and her place in the subterranean community of women. This double nature of her father's gift is presented in *L'amour, la fantasia* as a tunic of Nessus in which she must envelop herself when she writes, and whose equivocal nature means that the war between the two people can be heard in every sentence, as can the formulation of contradictory desire.

The ambiguities inherent in Djebar's linguistic exile undercut her project to rewrite the history of the Franco-Algerian conflicts. The project is a violent one: Djebar compares writing her autobiography to performing a live autopsy on herself. It is also a delicate undertaking; to translate the story of suffering into the 'adversary' language is to run the risk of unveiling too much, of robbing her sisters of the indomitability that lies in their refusal to name the vanquisher. Djebar's tactic, as we have seen, is to translate her sisters' subterranean language into her text, to speak from their point of view, modelling her French on their Arabic words.

Her autobiographical project is also a communal project, a plural autobiography. Djebar wonders why she, of all the women of her tribe, was the only one lucky enough to receive her freedom though a Western education. Though now cut off from her sisterly community, she still hears her sisters' voices, which have "besieged" her mind to force her to give them a voice in her writing (Djebar 1999: 29), thereby annexing for them the freedom she has acquired, the territory that lies between the two warring languages. The story of the Frenchwoman Pauline, recounted in *L'amour, la fantasia*, is a sign of hope that this autobiographical project of sisterly love might enact a *rapprochement* between the enemy camps. Pauline was a militant whose opposition to the French conquest of Algeria landed her in an Algerian prison, after which she lived out the rest of her life in poverty and exile. Drawn to the Algerian culture and people, Pauline wrote about Algerian women with tenderness, a desire for friendship to which violence was not a corollary. Djebar, in digging up the past of her sisters, with tenderness for them as well as for the French military officers, whose written accounts failed to disguise both their desire for the colonized and the latter's suffering, she suggests that love between these two peoples, cultures, and languages will not always be expressed through violence. By reviving her sisters, Djebar has awakened within herself the words of love of her mother tongue, paving a way for a return to the homeland of her Algerian sisterhood. Heeding Laâbi's warning, rather than using French as an instrument of culture, Djebar uses it as an instrument of "transformation" (Djebar

1999: 42), providing Algerian women with a public voice, as well as modifying the French language. In her acceptance speech for the German Peace Prize, Djebar stated that her role as a writer was to seize the French language that had entered her country with the 1830 invaders and shake from it *"toute sa poussière compromettante"* (Djebar 2000: 9; "all its compromising dust").

An image in the closing lines of the text, parallel to the first scene in which Djebar's father takes her by the hand to her French school, symbolizes the violent legacy of the French language in Algeria and Djebar's appropriation of it. Her father is replaced in this last scene by the writer and war painter Eugène Fromentin, and the image has become macabre. Djebar does not now receive a hand stretched out to her in love, and hope for emancipation, but the amputated hand of an Algerian woman that Fromentin had found and then thrown away. Djebar imagines that he passes to her this *"main inattendue, celle d'une inconnue qu'il n'a jamais pu dessiner"* (Djebar 1995: 255; "unexpected hand – the hand of an unknown woman he was never able to draw", 1993: 226). She then seizes this *"main vivante, main de la mutilation et du souvenir"* (Djebar 1995: 255; "living hand, hand of mutilation and of memory", 1993: 226), and tries to make it hold a *qalam* so that she may use it to write the story of her sisters, whose memory has been mutilated, exiled from history and into silence.

Notes

[1] This and all other translations with no source indicated are my own.

[2] Declaration by Mouloud Kassim Naït Belkacem, member of the Haut Conseil de la langue nationale, at the Algerian Cultural Centre in Paris, 10 October 1986 (Déjeux 1992: 4).

[3] Djebar evokes the risks of writing as an Algerian in *Le blanc de l'Algérie*, a narrative in which she relates the assassination of two close friends and her brother-in-law, the playwright Abdelkader Alloula, and of other Algerian intellectuals killed by Islamic fundamentalists.

[4] Djebar sees this approach to history as a legacy left by Polybius, for whom *"l'écriture de l'histoire est écriture d'abord : il instille dans la réalité mortifère dont il s'obstine à saisir trace un obscur germe de vie"* (Djebar 1995: 159; "the writing of history is writing first of all. Into the deadly reality that he describes he instils some obscure germ of life", 2002: 164).

[5] Blair's English translation fails to convey the grammatical unsoundness of the original French, which could be translated as 'Everything that happened on me!'.

[6] The linking of these two terms, violence and desire, is common in French-language literature of the Maghrib. The following line from Abdelkébir Khatibi's *La mémoire tatouée* is a well-known example: "*Quand je danse devant toi, Occident, sans me dessaisir de mon peuple, sache que cette danse est de désir mortel*" (Khatibi 1971: 188; 'When I dance before you, West, without renouncing my people, know that my dance is of mortal desire').

Bibliography

Ben Jelloun, Tahar. 2002. 'Éloge des langues françaises'. Editorial. *L'Orient Le Jour* Beirut (14 October 2002). On line at: www.lorient-lejour.com.lb/ aujourdhui/ tribune/tribunesujetw2.htm (consulted 14.10.2002).

Déjeux, Jean. 1975. *La littérature algérienne contemporaine*. Paris: Presses Universitaires de France.

- - - . 1992. *La littérature maghrébine d'expression française*. Paris: Presses Universitaires de France.

Djebar, Assia. 1999. *Ces voix qui m'assiègent... en marge de ma francophonie*. Paris: Albin Michel.

- - - . 1995. *L'amour, la fantasia*. Paris: Jean-Claude Lattès, 1985. Paris: Albin Michel. 1993, translated as *Fantasia, an Algerian Cavalcade* (tr. Dorothy S. Blair). Portsmouth, NH: Heinemann.

- - - . 1995. *Vaste est la prison*. Paris: Albin Michel. 2002, translated as *So Vast the Prison* (tr. Betsy Wing). Sydney: Duffy & Snellgrove.

- - - . 1995. *Le blanc de l'Algérie*. Paris: Albin Michel. 2000, translated as *Algerian White: A Narrative* (tr. David Kelley and Marjolijn de Jager). New York: Seven Stories Press.

- - - . 2000. 'Idiome de l'exil et langue de l'irréductibilité'. Acceptance speech for the German Peace Prize. 23 October 2000. On line at: www.remue.net/cont/ Djebar01.html (consulted 12.07.2003).

Khatibi, Abdelkébir. 1971. *La mémoire tatouée*. Paris: Denoël.

Laâbi, Abdellatif. 1970. 'Littérature maghrébine actuelle et francophonie' in *Souffles* 18 (March-April): 35-37.

Yacine, Kateb. 1966. *Le polygone étoilé*. Paris: Seuil.

Zabus, Chantal. 1991. *The African Palimpsest: Indigenization of Language in the West African Europhone Novel*. Cross Cultures 4. Amsterdam and Atlanta, GA: Rodopi.

21

Creating a Poetics in Exile: The Development of an Ethnic Palestinian-American Culture

Nir Yehudai

Nir Yehudai was born in Israel in 1947. After many years of working in agriculture, education, business & community management, and Arab-Jewish co-existence projects, he turned to academic study in the Department of Middle Eastern History at Haifa University, where he now teaches part-time. He gained his Master's degree with a thesis entitled 'Economic Cooperation Between Palestinian Arabs and Jews as a Possible Pattern For Relations Between Two National Communities in a State of Conflict, 1920-1930'. His PhD thesis is entitled 'The Palestinian Diaspora in the United States: Cultural, Political and Social Aspects, 1948-1995'.

In this paper, he explores the phenomenon of Palestinian-American culture. He argues that Palestinians in the United States, while they form part of the larger Arab-American community, possess a distinct consciousness and culture. Artistic creativity has been important in maintaining that consciousness and in expressing a range of emotions, including yearning, rage, frustration, and loss. He surveys artistic activities and centres that include: an exhibition of traditional Palestinian dresses and embroidery in New Jersey; poetry and prose alluding to such features of Palestinian everyday life as fig-trees, traditions of weaving and embroidery, and cooking; a Palestinian film project associated with Columbia University; an embroidered tent installation in an artist's studio in New York; and an internet site which brings together a wealth of Palestinian-related items. He emphasizes that these works serve not only to bring Palestinians in the US together, to reflect on their country and culture, but to communicate with a wider American audience. It lends support to the claim that immigration may lead not to the loss of ethnic cultural identity, but rather to its reappearance under a new guise and conditions. He employs a theoretical-methodological framework for immigration research which focuses on questions of ethnicity and culture, as well as social structures and institutions among immigrant groups, ethnic groups and communities, and the characterization of a diaspora. It deals with developments which have occurred in the immigrant's new country after s/he has made the geographical relocation (or was born as second or third generation), rather than analysing the circumstances and motivations for the immigration (although it is clear that, especially in the case of Palestinians, these motivations and circumstances are particularly important).

Let me begin with poems (or extracts from poems) by three contemporary Palestinian-American poets: Fawaz Turki, Naomi Shihab Nye, and Lisa Suhair Majaj:

Moments of Ridicule and Love

In moments of desperation
Palestinian poets wish
they had a government to assail,
politicians,
bureaucrats,
elected bodies
to ridicule.
We never realized
dragging such comic trivia
into a poem
could be,
like first love,
an exquisite thought […]

(Turki 1975: 4)

Kindness

Before you know what kindness really is
you must lose things,
feel the future dissolve in a moment
like salt in a weakened broth.
What you held in your hand,
what you counted and carefully saved,
all this must go so you know
how desolate the landscape can be
between the regions of kindness.

(Shihab Nye 1980: 42-43)

Departure

Some things
you take when
you go: light
no one can capture,
voices that sing
alone, the touch
of snow on air.

> Some things are lost
> in the leaving. Some
> remain. Some seeds
> planted in brine
> still grow.
>
> (Majaj 1999: 79-80)

The Palestinians who live in the United States are an inseparable part of the Arab-American community, and there are authors such as Elias Tuma, who do not even consider them as a unique and separate community in a sociological sense (Tuma 1981). However, the accumulated experience resulting from their history in the Middle East and their lives in a Diaspora, with its lack of a civil and political centre that can be identified as a homeland, as well as their being labelled suspect as a consequence of the stereotyping tendency of significant sectors of American society, has led to the formation of a unique shared consciousness as Palestinian-Americans. This consciousness has found interesting, and even poignant, expression in artistic creativity.

The turn to artistic activity is based on the perception that artists may often better express processes, sensations and conflicts, which the average person requires a "longer reaction time" to express (Rynearson 1996, 20). Using a few out of many possible examples, this paper seeks to demonstrate the emotional force which artistic creativity can give to simple objects from the homeland, including clothing, trees, foods. Feelings of yearning, rage, frustration, and loss – as well as empathy and identification with the fate of others – are expressed in these artistic works. The examples are presented with little analysis or elaboration, since I believe that the works speak for themselves. The poems were all written originally in English, even though they are clearly Middle Eastern and Palestinian in nature. This kind of creativity operates parallel to, and as a part of, everyday life, and as a component of the political agenda of Arabs and Palestinians in the United States. Although clear political and nationalist statements can be identified in the works of art, this does not detract from either the purely artistic value of the works or the emotional pleasure which they accord even to people who are not Palestinian.

Hanan Karaman Munayyer and Farah Munayyer, who have been living in West Caldwell, New Jersey since their immigration to the United States in the early 1970s, have developed an active exhibition of traditional Palestinian dresses and embroidery. In order to further this enterprise, they have set up an institute, located in their home, called the 'Palestinian Heritage Foundation' which organizes exhibitions and events throughout the United States and publishes on its website (http://www.palestineheritage.org/index.asp) a newsletter by the same name in English and Arabic.

In a recent article, Jane Friedman describes their collection and their enterprise with the words: "New Jersey Stops at the Munayyer Door". She writes:

> Their collection of embroidery and costumes, their sets of coffee utensils, the pillows and slipcovers, in fact, their entire living rooms leave you with the impression that you have entered an original Palestinian home. The collection and the fund which they have set up are dedicated to a mission: to preserve and revive a heritage which is being lost, and to inform and educate both Palestinians and Americans about a unique aspect of Palestinian culture. (Friedman 1997: 2)

In her own article about her family collection, Hanan Karaman Munayyer explains and analyzes the sources, roots, and historical contexts of textile art in the Middle East (1997: 5-8).

The Palestinian-American poet Lorene Zarou-Zouzounis has written a poem called 'Embroidered Memory' which includes reference to Palestinian dress. It reads, in part:

> Arabic tapestry embroidered
> Into my soul
> Is my memory
> Of home
> Red on black pyramids
> Octagons, lines and vines
> Each village distinct
> Bedouin purple and fuchsia
> Red poppies and tulips
> My mother, sixteen - creating
> Vibrant peacocks on linen
> Circle around
> Down, up
> Up, down
> A fine needle in and out
> An artist's tool piercing
> Fabric, weaving culture
> Women of this art
> Fill my heart with hues of
> Red and orange fruit orchards
> Filling the air with aroma
> Of a culture of olive,
> Almond and fig groves [...]

(Handal 2001: 317-8)

Fig trees are also invoked in the work of Naomi Shihab Nye, one of the best-known Palestinian creative figures in the United States, especially as a result of the wide-ranging variety of her poetry and prose which find readers in diverse audiences, and which deal with issues that go beyond the Palestinian experience. In the following story poem she examines the web of longing which links her father to the fig tree that once stood in the yard of his house, and stands for all those things which he could not take with him when he was exiled from his homeland:

My Father and the Figtree

For other fruits my father was indifferent.
He'd point at the cherry trees and say,
See those? I wish they were figs […]

The last time he moved, I had a phone call,
my father, in Arabic, chanting a song I'd never heard.
"What's that?"—"Wait till you see!"
He took me out to the new yard.
There, in the middle of Dallas, Texas,
a tree with the largest, fattest, sweetest figs in the world.
"It's a figtree song!" he said,
plucking his fruits like ripe tokens,
emblems, assurance
of a world that was always his own.

(Shihab Nye 1993: xiv-xvi)

Shihab Nye's father, 'Aziz Shihab, has published a small book of reminiscences which combines, for the most part, stories of his childhood in Jerusalem with recipes for traditional Palestinian dishes. The style and content of the book are primarily folkloric and, except for two chapters, does not include the political material which characterizes similar works written by Palestinians in the Diaspora. One of the 'political' chapters tells of 'Aziz Shihab's uncle who lived in the area of Beersheba and who became rich during the 1930s and 1940s by buying land cheaply from neighbouring Arabs and selling it secretly to a Jewish organization centred in London. Shihab describes a visit to this relative, 'the Sheik,' with his father when he was a boy. His father reprimanded the relative as a traitor who was becoming rich by betraying his nation and his homeland (Shihab 1993: 87-90). The second chapter, touching on politics, describes the burning insults, both personal and general, suffered by the author and the people around him from British soldiers and officers before 1948 (Shihab 1993: 32-34).

Sharif Elmusa, the co-editor of the anthology *Grape Leaves*, was born in 1947, in Abassia (today, Yahud, in the Jaffa district), to a family who earned their living by growing fruit trees. During the 1948 war, the family was uprooted to Nuʻaima, near Jericho, where they began to grow vegetables. In a poem inspired by a visit to Nablus, Elmusa writes:

> Summer. The figs are bruise pink,
> tomatoes luscious enough
> to stop a hurried man.
> Ignore the flies.
> At 9 a.m. peasants savour *shish-kebab*
> in puny, vaulted eateries.
> Ah, the roasting coffee's aroma,
> the folk-lore of each of the senses.
> This is a place for commerce.
> Everything here is for sale:
> children's toys, kitchen utensils,
> bananas, peanuts, pine nuts, posters,
> cassettes, straw mats, sponge mats, watches,
> Elvis' T-shirts, turkey breasts, shoes […].
>
> (Elmusa 1996: 361)

Annemarie Jacir is active in movie production, working in the Film Department of Columbia University in New York. Her parents were born in Bethlehem, where they still have family. In her work, Jacir deals extensively with the way in which the status and image of Arabs are presented in the American film industry. She states that she is caught in a cycle of discrimination and stereotypes against which she must struggle. In the past few years, she and a number of associates have set up a project called Palestine Films, under the auspices of Columbia University, which has produced a film called *Satellite Shooters*. The film is a kind of Western, centring on a Palestinian family in Texas. The hero is the teenage son of the family, played by an Arab American actor. The film deals with stereotypes, with the clash between 'Orientalism' and 'Occidentalism', with American foreign policy, and with criticism of traditional Arab society (Frayer 2000 and Annemarie Jacir website). Jacir has also produced a number of documentary films about the health system under the Palestinian Authority and about aspects of Israeli-Palestinian relations during the Oslo process. Jacir is also a published poet. 'Untitled Exile Poem' is a cry embodying the sense of loss of homeland and home, and the envy experienced by Palestinians towards their neighbours who were colonised by countries which ultimately gave up and left their colonies, while Palestine received the 'worst possible deal'. The following is a part of the poem:

> in america
> the coffee table arabs
> sip
> sip
> sip
> inventing words because there is
> no english translation
> demanding justice and freedom
> demanding to go home
> reading about turks in germany
> and wondering if they hear about us too
> the prophets of palestine
> now gather in cairo cafes
> stargazing
> dreaming
> old men inhale life from bubbling nargillas
> they talk and talk;
> who stole the past
> from our wrinkled palms?
> homeless, will we learn
> to carry out houses on our
> backs for our land is gone
> and we still carry it in our heads...

(Jacir 2001)

Emily Jacir is an artist involved with painting and the plastic arts. She has worked and exhibited in various places both within and outside the United States and, as I learned from a conversation with her on 8 February 2000, at a meeting at Columbia University, she is intensively active in Palestinian issues. She defines herself as a Palestinian artist and, in many cases, she answers questions about where she is from with the reply "from Bethlehem". Emily Jacir has been engaged in an additional undertaking, which is clearly Palestinian and artistic in nature: she has set up a large tent in her studio in New York to symbolize transience and the reality of being a refugee. On the walls of the tent she, along with friends and other volunteers, has embroidered in black thread the names of the Palestinian villages which were abandoned and destroyed in 1948. The list of villages is based on the book written by Walid Khalidi, *All That Remains*.

Artist Samia Halaby, who was born in Jerusalem in 1936, relates that she has always held pictures in her mind's eye of the beautiful

Jerusalem of her memories, of her family home, and of her grandmother. In addition to her art, Samia has, in recent years, set up an internet site where she presents her work, along with articles and essays, references to Palestinian artists, exhibitions of their work, and of views of the Palestinian homeland (http://www.art.net/~samia/ pal/olives/olives.html). As she explains: "In 1996 I wandered through the hills around Ramallah and did several little paintings. As I painted this little olive tree, it began to seem like a child. I began to pay attention to the different characters of olive trees as infants, toddlers, adolescents, powerful prime-of-life ones, elderly, and so on".

The artist writes of another painting:

> This is a fig tree with two little infant olives peeking in from the right side of the frame. Olive trunks have powerful shapes which grow as they resist the wind. The two infant olive trees are already bracing themselves diagonally against the attack of the wind. That is what makes them seem as though they are peeking in at me. Oh if it were possible for olive trees to know how to brace themselves against the Israeli settlers' bulldozers.

Suheir Hammad was born in Jordan, in 1973, to Palestinian refugee parents, who moved first to Beirut and later to Brooklyn, New York. Her poems and her prose speak of exile, of Palestinian suffering, and of urban America, as a Black woman in a racist society. She is one of a number of writers who have expressed penetrating criticism of the traditional role of the Palestinian woman. Her work is featured on the website of the The Poetry Center at Smith College, http://www.smith.edu/poetrycenter/bios.php?name= shammad, which says of her: "In addition to her work as a creative artist, Hammad has written and spoken out about issues such as the defence of Mumia Abu-Jamal, domestic violence, sexual abuse, racism, and homophobia." In an interview some years ago with Nathalie Handal, she said:

> In relation to Palestine, I am not sure. But I need to change so one day I may be writing so that people recognize Palestine, the next day I may be writing specifically for Palestinians, recognizing ourselves, treating ourselves better, especially our women... (Handal 1997)

In the poem 'There Are Many Usages for the Word Black' she identifies with those who are discriminated against and pursued in various places (Hammad 1996: 10). Hammad declares that her life has been transformed by the influence of the African-American poet and essayist June Jordan, and especially her work *Moving Towards Home*, a collection of political articles and poetry which appeared in 1989. In one of her poems, Hammad refers to her mother as "Mama Sweet Baklava":

> Everyone got a favourite
> sweet every woman got
> a recipe
> she is baklava
> back bone strong foundation
> layers thousand layers
> upon each other like
> refugees fleeing or cold
> children warming each other [...]

(www.cafearabica.com/culture/cultureold/articles/culsuh10x1.html)

Lisa Suhair Majaj, an important Palestinian-American researcher, poet, and author, has described the process of exposing Arab-American creative talents to a variety of readers as a process of negotiation between cultures which has placed many of these creators in a position of 'split-vision', as one eye looks at the American context while the other eye is always directed towards the Middle East. Her poem, 'Recognized Futures', is a good example for the poetic expression of that issue, and a suitable piece for concluding this paper:

> Turning to you, my name -
> this necklace of gold, these letters
> in script I cannot read
> this part of myself I long
> to recognize—falls forward
> into my mouth.
>
> You call my daily name, Lisa,
> the name I've finally declared
> my own, claiming a heritage
> half mine: corn fields silver
> in ripening haze, green music
> of crickets, summer light sloping
> to dusk on the Iowa farm.
>
> This other name fills my mouth,
> a taste faintly metallic,
> blunt edges around which my tongue
> moves tentatively: Suhair,
> an old-fashioned name,

little star in the night. The second girl,
small light on a distanced horizon.

Throughout childhood this rending split:
continents moving slowly apart,
rift widening beneath taut limbs.

(www.fas.harvard.edu/~gstudies/mideast/lessons/backgd.htm)

Bibliography

Elmusa, Sharif S. 1996. 'One Day in the Life of Nablus' in El-Zein, Amira and Munir Akash (eds) *Culture Creativity and Exile* special issue of *Jusoor: The Arab American Journal of Culture Exchange and Thought for the Future* 7/8: 361-364.

Frayer, Lauren. 2000. 'Annemarie Kattan Jacir: A Palestinian-American Filmmaker Trying to Make a Difference'. eStart.com, July 26, 2000, Washington, D.C. www3.estart.com/arab/women/annemarie.html (updated: 2001) (consulted 30.06.2004).

Friedman, Jane. 1997. 'These Stitches Speak' in *Aramco World* 48(2): 2-4.

Gonzalez, Nancie L, and Carolyn S. McCommon (eds). 1989. *Conflict, Migration, and the Expression of Ethnicity.* Boulder, CO: Westview Press.

Halaby, Samia. 'Olives of Palestine'. On line at: www.art.net/~samia/pal/olives/olives.html (consulted 20.07.2002).

Hammad, Suheir. 1996. *Born Palestinian, Born Black.* New York: Harlem River Press.

- - - . *Cafearabica: The Arab-American Online Community Center, Culture* 'Suheir Hammad: 2 poems excerpted from her upcoming book of Poetry, *Pariah*'. On line at: www.cafearabica.com/culture/cultureold/articles/culsuh10x1.html (consulted 14.04.2004)

Handal, Nathalie. 1997. 'Drops of Suheir Hammad: A Talk with a Palestinian Poet Born Black' in *Al Jadid* 3(20): s.pag.

- - - . (ed.). 2001. *The Poetry of Arab Women: A Contemporary Anthology.* New York: Interlink Books.

Jacir, Annemarie. 2001. 'Untitled Exile Poem' in *Mizna* 3(2): s.pag.

- - - . 'Funding Update' (for the Satellite Shooters). On line at: www.columbia.edu/~kdr7/funding.html (consulted 14.04.2004)

Khalidi, Walid (ed.). 1992. *All That Remains: The Palestinian Villages Occupied and Depopulated by Israel in 1948.* Washington D.C.: Institute for Palestine Studies.

Majaj, Lisa Suhair. 1999. 'New Directions: Arab-American Writing at Century's End' in Akash, Munir and Khalad Mattawa (eds) *Post-Gibran: Anthology of New Arab American Writing.* Jusoor: Syracuse University Press: 67-81.

- - - . www.fas.harvard.edu/~gstudies/mideast/lessons/backgd.htm (consulted 14.04.2004)

Munayyer, Hanan Karaman. 1997. 'New Images, Old Patterns: A Historical Glimpse' in *Aramco World* 48(2): 5-11.

Rynearson, Ann M. 1996. 'Living Within the Looking Glass: Refugee Artists and the Creation of Group Identity' in Rynearson, Ann M. and James Philips (eds)

Selected Papers on Refugee Issues. IV. Arlington, Virginia: American Anthropological Association: 20-44.

Shihab, 'Aziz. 1993. *A Taste of Palestine*. Introduction by Naomi Shihab Nye. San Antonio: Corona Publishing.

Shihab Nye, Naomi. 1995. *Words Under the Words: Selected Poems.* 1980. Portland, Oregon: A Far Corner Book.

Tuma, Elias. 1981. 'The Palestinians in America' in *The Link* 14(3): 1-14.

Turki, Fawaz. 1975. *Poems From Exile*. Washington D.C.: Free Palestine Press.

22

Poems: 'Do not live a day in a homeland's memory' and 'O fire be peaceful'

Emad Jabbar

Emad Jabbar was born in 1968 in Maysan, Southern Iraq. He has published two books of poetry in Arabic – *There Were Songs There* (1996) and *Tears On the Eyelids of Distant Windows* (1998) – and won a number of awards, including the Iraq Prize for Creativity, presented by the Ministry of Culture and Information in 2000. In March 2000 Emad travelled to the United Arab Emirates to receive a prize from the Al-Sada House for Journalism. He has not yet returned to Iraq. While he was living in Jordan as a political refugee with the UNHCR in 2001 his long poem 'O You Prayer Rug of Al-Aqsa' won the (American) Holy Land Institute for Relief and Development's Cultural Contest on the theme of 'The Suffering of the Palestinian Refugees'. In 2002, he won the Al-Sharjah Award for Arabic Creativity, presented by the Ministry of Information and Culture of the UAE, for the poetry collection *A Feather from Sorrow*. The material prize of the Al-Sharjah Award is the upcoming publication of *A Feather of Sorrow* (in Arabic) by the UAE government. Also in 2002, *A Feather of Sorrow* was translated into English by the Iraqi scholar Yaqoub Abouna. Emad has not yet sought publication of this work in translation. He migrated to New Zealand in 2002, and is currently living in Wellington where he is studying Religion at Victoria University, writing new pieces in both English and Arabic, and working with the International Writers' group (established 2002).

In a live performance recorded for the accompanying DVD, he reads two poems in Arabic which reflect his personal experience of exile. We are most grateful to Tarik Bary for providing the English subtitles.

See DVD

Do not live a day in a homeland's memory

Each time you pack up
      your things to travel
All the little stars flutter
      in you
All the bridge's lamps return
      you
All the house's eyes
The stubborn date palms
      return you
Their nascent clusters have landed
And the last squadrons are
      startled in your heart
And they shout: don't leave
You are a poet
You are he
Who gathers people's tears
In the dawn of registers
You are a witness
Live here between the
      twin rivers and persist
Live here and strew the
      years of sufferance
In the embers of the braziers
You weep every time a bullet
      hurts Baghdad
Every time the river's water
      returns a drowned babe
The voice of death's colour
      in its eyes wounds you

Leaves from the bushes' top
      falling
On the migrant's crown
And the green boughs almost
Grasping the garments
And the bitter orange
Throwing fragrance and questions
      in the way
Why do you pack the bags

today
If you leave, the door
    will weep
And the virgin footbridge
And your tired eyes mother
     will weep
And the wind shall fling her
     weeping lock
Upon the neighbours
Live here forever
And reproach whoever you wish
    to reproach

Who do you think will house
    you, who?
Who do you think will bring
    you close?
If the bird of songs
    cries in your ribs
Who will give you a hand's width
    of sympathy?
Do not live a day in a homeland's
    memory
You are this wind
    This cloud
       This water
You this remaining mountain
    across the ages
Do not live a day in a homeland's
    memory.

O fire be peaceful

O fire
O fire
O fire be peaceful
upon the river
    and love
       and the lovers

who are tired
        and broken
they tell their secrets
        to the water
and push their dreams
        like clouds in the evening
O fire be peaceful

clouds pass by my family's home
and forget a wisp
        and pass on
and I still farewell clouds
        in this cool
                and wait for clouds
O my family's cloud
I pray every day
to come
summoning night's tales
O fire be peaceful

there, mornings' greetings are a poem
there, children's quarrels are a poem
there, tears are a poem
and the *abaya*'s[1] night musk
is a poem of dew

so fire be peaceful
upon Al-Sayyaab's[2] face in the gloom
upon his hand wet with wavings
Benedictions of shrapnel from the Arab Gulf
        in his coat pocket
he kisses the children of his city
the children of Basra
        every morning
and casts greetings towards the poor
peace on people who fade
        before their time
peace on people who set like suns

---

[1] *Abaya* – a traditional woman's robe worn over clothes, it is almost always black in colour.
[2] Al-Sayyaab was a great Iraqi poet.

peace on people who are bleeding
on the Zakurah's[3] clay in
time's conscience
glory to you – the guardian of the poor
you will withstand horror
withstand warplanes
by what is in your words
    and in your heart
you will bleed in death much
more than life
and so lavender greens near to
    the verandas
salamun[4] when you scream
then songs come like boats
flapping with a wounded sail
and a lover's oath hits the waves

we smelt over the distance Iraq's breeze
and his boys' voices in the alley
we smelt over this distance, master…
and the tears poured on earth remain
salamun upon Iraq's mountains
How many exhausted among these stations
How many regretful beyond these oceans
with no bosom friends under
this darkness

so fire be peaceful
upon the rose and goodness
    and memories
upon the friends still noble
upon Youssif's[5] wound
when the wind leaves her children
in the reeds
upon his chest in the nights of exhaustion

---

[3] Zakurah (Ziggurat) – the sacred steps of ancient Sumarian temples.
[4] *Salamun, Salamaa* – are ways of saying the Islamic greeting *Salamun Alaikum* depending on the context.
[5] Youssif (Joseph) Al-Saiyigh is a great Iraqi poet who is dying of lung disease at the time of writing.

and say *salaamaa*

cough will go… and the poem remains
and the mountain grass will
wither… but the poem remains
and the singer's voice will
tire… but songs remain
and poets will be broken
          when their children starve
the poets will be broken when they
enter empty markets… but
the poem remains
the poem remains

23

Poem for Basim Furat, Emad Jabbar and Yilma Tafere Tasew: 'Exiles'

Nora Nadjarian

Cypriot writer Nora Nadjarian wrote this poem for three refugee writers who have settled in New Zealand, Iraqis Basim Furat and Emad Jabbar, and Ethiopian Yilma Tafere Tasew, after meeting them at the *Poetics of Exile* conference in Auckland in 2003. For her biographical details see the introduction to the DVD interview with her at number 14 above.

Exiles

We crossed the desert, leaving our hearts behind;
travelled through explosions of days and nights
to step onto the cold, wild shore of a new life.

We crossed the desert, blinding our memories,
pouring handfuls of sand to burn the sockets;
to fill the hole where a heart should beat.

On this cold, wild shore, a new life.

We sleep by the ocean, and listen
for voices from the past in the waves.

We sleep by the ocean, and wait
for salt surf to wash over the wounds.

We sleep by the ocean, and let
seagulls tear at the healing scars.

We sleep by the ocean, and dream
of the warmth of sweat and blood.

24

Exile and Memory: Re-membering Home After the Partition of Bengal

Urbashi Barat

Urbashi Barat was born and educated in Calcutta, India. She has experienced several kinds and modes of displacement: geographical, cultural, emotional. Since her marriage she has lived in Jabalpur, in the centre of India, where cultural and social traditions are distinctively different from what she knew in her birthplace in Bengal. If her own family belongs to East Bengal – now another country, Bangladesh, from which they have been effectively exiled as a result both of relocation and Partition – her husband's family migrated from their original home in West Bengal to Central India more than a century ago. She has been teaching English in Jabalpur for more than twenty years and is currently head of the Department of Postgraduate Studies & Research in English, at Rani Durgavati University, Jabalpur. She has published a book on Graham Greene and fifty research articles, mainly on women's writing, postcolonial fiction, and English language teaching. One of her areas of interest at present is the South Asian diaspora.

In this paper, she examines writing that derives from the partition of India and the brutality and degradation associated with the violent displacement of thousands of people following the imposition of invented borders. She focuses on two very different works, one in Bengali, the other in English, the first a factual recounting of the exilic experience, the other a fictionalised study of liminal lives, to discover the ways in which exiles from a partitioned Bengal attempted to make sense of what had happened to them by looking back at the past. The first work is an anthology of essays by sixty seven anonymous refugees from erstwhile East Pakistan (now Bangladesh) now living in India, *Chhere Asha Gram* (*The Abandoned Village*), written not only to enable them to recover for themselves, in memory, their lost village homes, but also to enable people living in Indian Bengal who had not personally experienced exile to understand something of their sufferings. This collection of (male) voices centres on the refugee's nostalgia, his inability to understand what has happened, and his yearning to re-establish himself without ever forgetting what he has left behind. The second text, Amitav Ghosh's novel in English, *The Shadow Lines*, builds on the traditional Bengali opposition of house and home to explore the different ways in which home is remembered, imagined, and re-created by those whose experiences of continuous dislocation, their own and their ancestors', have rendered them permanent exiles. As home and loss are narrativised, both fact and fiction suggest that the exilic memory, which Rushdie compares to shards of broken mirrors, does not simply recapture the past but creates a new reality which may have little in common with historical accounts. In both works, the remembered home ensures that the past continues into the present and loss is turned to gain, even as it also suggests that the condition of exile is permanent, irrevocable, and universal.

A Bengali nursery rhyme written just after India's Independence soon became a classic expression of the popular feeling about a newly achieved political freedom: not joy or relief, but, rather, an incomprehension and an anguish that this freedom was gained at the expense of home and homeland, which were now so broken up that they could never be put together again. The mocking question that the poem asks, using a domestic parallel, points out that those who should have known better were as complicit in this act of reckless and irresponsible violence as those whose careless scribbles across a map had erased the plural identity of Bengal: "*Teler shishi bhanglo bole khukur pore rag koro, / tomra je shob buro khoka, bangla bhenge bhag koro, / bharat bhenge bhag koro, / tar bela?*" ('when a little girl [accidentally] breaks a bottle of oil you're so angry, what about the way you adult little-boys [deliberately] broke up and divided Bengal, and India?', my translation). For Bengalis, Independence was also Partition, the invention of borders which permanently and irrevocably exiled entire communities. Even today, more than half a century after the event, the victims of Partition continue to explore the dimensions of their loss of home, to attempt to understand what it has done to their sense of identity and their social relationships.

Remembering, as Homi Bhabha points out in *The Location of Culture*, is "never a quiet act of introspection. It is a painful re-membering, a putting together of the dismembered past to make sense of the trauma of the present" (Bhabha 1994: 63). In this paper I use two very different works, one in Bengali, the other in English, as examples of some of the ways in which Hindu exiles from East Bengal attempted to make sense of what had happened to them through re-membering their lost home: like Derek Walcott's famous broken vase (Walcott 1992), the recovery through memory becomes a (re)discovery of love and longing. Leaving home is not, of course, a new experience for Bengalis, who have traditionally loved travelling: the popular stereotype of the indefatigably peripatetic Bengali is part of contemporary folklore in India. Since the mid-nineteenth century, moreover, the educated middle-class Bengali, especially from the East, has frequently left his village home in search of a livelihood; there are old-established communities of *probashi* Bengalis, Bengalis who live outside the homeland (Bengal), in most North Indian cities, and *adhibashi,* or diasporic, Bengalis, all over the world, particularly in the West.[1] But the exile of the *probashi* and the *adhibashi* is voluntary, self-imposed, and above all temporary; they have always been able to go back home, no matter how briefly or temporarily. The exiles who had to leave home after Partition, however, knew they could never return. Yearning for a past that can never be recovered, and desperately seeking for a present in which they can discover new roots, they continually attempt to remake their lost homes, albeit only in, and through, memory. This is what both these books reveal.

One of these volumes is a collection of Bengali periodical essays. The 67 anonymous essays it contains were originally written for a now defunct newspaper, *Jugantar*, around 1950, that is, almost immediately after Partition. These were later anthologized by Dakshinaranjan Basu into a single volume, *Chhere Asha Gram* (*The Abandoned Village*).[2] As the writers of these essays, apparently almost all male, describe the villages they had been forced to leave behind them, they (re)create their lost homes, to voice their own anguish and their incomprehension of what had happened; as they do so they also try to explain to their readers, their fellow-Bengalis in Indian Bengal who had never experienced exile, what this loss of home meant to them. The village home, especially in the fertile rural landscape of East Bengal, was, for the urban Bengali Hindu, their emotional centre and spiritual home, as well as a powerful pastoral image in Bengali literature and the Bengali imagination. Writers and readers alike always acknowledged the economic deprivations, social backwardness, and the meanness of spirit of rural society; but they also celebrated it as the source of all familial and social values, the place where the Bengali returned to celebrate his Hindu festivals. Cut off forever from this wellspring of the spirit, the essayists are devastated; striving to discover some kind of meaning in the fragmented and alienated lives they are now condemned to lead, they derive their resilience and their social identity through their memories of home.

The second text is Amitav Ghosh's *The Shadow Lines*, published on 1995. This is a novel that can be interpreted in several different ways, but, like the essays, its basis is the way (or ways) in which memory (re)constructs the past and the home/homeland. At the core of both, obviously, is the break-up of Bengal, and the consequent loss of home: a loss that in the novel represents and symbolizes all the dislocations in the lives of its characters as well as epitomising the contemporary human situation. Home here, however, is the city (Dhaka), not the village of the earlier volume. Perhaps that is one reason why, by contrast with the essays, the novel's focus is not so much on the exile's yearning but on the exilic memory; as the narrator explains, "for people like my grandmother, who have no home but in memory, learn to be very skilled in the art of recollection" (Ghosh 1995: 194). Its urban, middle-class characters are twice exiled: from their roots in the village, the 'real' home of all Bengalis (indeed, of all South Asians) – in Bengali the term *desh* is applied to both nation and village home – and the house in the city. Everyone in the novel travels all the time, over space and time and in the imagination, as though this will enable them to discover the lost home. Ila's paternal grandfather does go back once in a while to his Raibajar house, deep in the (West) Bengal countryside, but the family's ties to the ancestral village home are only tenuous; consequently, they never find or make a home anywhere else, try as hard as they may. The sense of unbelonging that the narrator's Tha'mma (*Tha'mma* is a popular diminutive of the Bengali word for grandmother) feels after the loss of her Dhaka home leads her to locate 'home' in the idea of a nation created from blood; her values and principles, her dreams and her actions, all derive from a driving need to compensate for her loss in one way or the other. The redoubtable grandmother's strident nationalism is thus a sublimation of her longing for home: a nation for her is a "a family born of the same pool of blood" sharing a home(land), no matter what religious community or region its members belong to, for which they can sacrifice everything (Ghosh 1995: 78). Her idea of the nation is like her family home in Dhaka, "a very old house" that had "evolved slowly, growing like a honeycomb, with every generation of Boses adding layers and extensions, until it was like a huge, lop-sided step-pyramid, inhabited by so many branches of the family that even the most knowledgeable amongst them had become a little confused about their relationships" (1995: 121). Ila's experience of constant dislocation, on the other hand, has uprooted her from 'home'. Rejecting as stifling the bourgeois world of Calcutta, where she observes her stay-at-home relatives leading their petty humdrum lives, she chooses to live in London, where she has spent a part of her childhood, believing that it will give her the personal freedom she longs for. In the end, however, she realizes that she can never really be free of the past, for "the squalor of the genteel little lives she had so much despised" is very much a part of "the free world she had tried to build for herself" (1995: 188). Ila's failure to reconstruct home is due to her inability to use her imagination, as the narrator points out early in the novel (1995: 21). Indeed, Tha'mma declares that Ila had no right to a home in Britain; her ancestors had not given their blood for it, and so it could never be her nation/*desh* (1995: 78). By trying to grab something that could never be hers by right, and thereby refusing to acknowledge the burden of responsibilities towards 'home' that real freedom means (1995: 89), her great-niece has become "a greedy little slut" (1995: 79). It is only Tridib, Ila's uncle and the narrator's mentor, and the narrator himself who recognize that 'home' exists outside a specific geographical space; it is an emotional and imaginative construct that, as Tridib puts it, is born out of "a pure, painful and primitive desire, a longing for everything that was not in oneself, a torment of the flesh, that carried one beyond the limits of one's mind" (1995: 29).

The novel thus explores the different ways in which home is remembered, imagined, and re-created by those whose experiences of continuous displacement, their own and their ancestors', have rendered them permanent exiles. The exilic voice here is a female one, by contrast with the male voice of the essays; it is the voice of Tha'mma, echoed, eerily distorted, in Ila's. But both these voices are heard in and through the memory of the anonymous narrator, who is male, like the novelist himself (who, it might be interesting to recall, is the son of a migrant, *probashi*, Bengali family and who has become an *adhibashi* in the U.S. He is thus as much a dislocated person as his characters.) The contesting notions of what 'home' means grow out of the different responses of individuals, of males and females, to the physical act of exile from home/homeland, and identify with differing notions of nationhood. Not surprisingly, the recurrent, and perhaps central, trope of the novel is the house, just as that of the essays is the village as idyll/ideal.

There is, then, a continuous tension between male and female notions of home and nation in the novel. The matter of gender is of some significance: home/homeland for the Bengali is traditionally seen in feminine terms, as a maternal figure, with *janani*, mother, she who gives birth, and *janmabhoomi,* birthplace, usually conflated and described as being even loftier than heaven. Home, then, is a sacral site, the one space that the colonized male could preserve from the depredations of the colonial influence: in a patriarchal society, therefore, it is inevitably the location of femininity/femaleness. In Bengali writing, the woman is frequently seen as the (sole or primary) upholder of the community's history and identity; her body is the sign through which are conducted the interactions and contests between rival patriarchal concepts and groups.[3] In conventional Bengali literature, therefore, the male might be seen abandoning the female; never, however, does a mother reject her son. Hence the unnaturalness of Partition: the mother and the son have been forcibly parted. If the first essay in *The Abandoned Village* refers to the soil of the writer's village home as his mother (Basu 1975: 1), a later one has the despairing cry, "Won't it ever be possible to go back to the lap of the mother we have left behind? Mother - my motherland - does she really belong to somebody else now?" (Basu 1975: 257). In Ghosh's novel, the violence of Tha'mma's beliefs about the sanctity of the nation and the bleakness of Ila's domestic arrangements in London alike underscore the reversal of social values that the loss of home involves; both are women, the perversity of whose ideas, hopes and convictions mark them out as unfeminine and unnatural. The men, however, from the narrator, or Tridib, to Shaheb, Tridib's father, the narrator's father, or even Nick, the Englishman Ila marries and in whose house in London she lived as a little girl, are more passive figures, for whom what has been lost can be regained only through imaginative reconstruction, through narrativisation of memory. Any other way will lead ultimately to death and disaster, as becomes obvious when Tha'mma tries to bring her uncle 'home' from his 'home' in Dhaka and both he and Tridib are killed.

'Home' is always an emotive word, but in Bengal it has certain special associations. Constantly exposed to travel and migration, the Bengali traditionally distinguishes between where one lives, one's house, *basha*, and where one belongs to, one's home, *bari. Bari*, then, is one's permanent home, where one's patrilineal (ironical, perhaps, in the context of the convention of the maternalisation of home!) ancestors belonged, the source of one's identity and family. As someone from Dhaka remarked in his essay in *The Abandoned Village*, "The sacred memory of my ancestors is mixed with [the] soil [from the village *bari*]" (Basu 1975: 1). One might live in a *basha* of one's own choosing anywhere, but to be forcibly cut off from one's *bari*, one's family home, is a much more devastating experience than to lose one's *basha*: it is to lose one's ties to the past and to the basis of one's being. A lamp must be lit every evening in the family/ancestral village *bari* (almost invariably by the women of the family) to signify continuity of family line and of self; not to do so is to invite the extinction of both. This is why it is so important to the Bengali that home must constantly be recalled and re-membered; this is why Partition, destroying as it did one's ties to the land to which one belongs, became an act of violation and defilement.

In both *The Abandoned Village* and *The Shadow Lines*, memory is much more than simply a function by which information stored in the brain is later recalled to consciousness. The experience of exile brings about in its victims a kind of paramnesia, a conjoining of what Lacan called *Verdrängung*, repression, and *Verwerfung*, repudiation, a distortion of recall that Salman Rushdie was famously to compare with the shards of a mirror. This frequently means a retrospective falsification (when the memory becomes unintentionally or unconsciously distorted by being filtered through the narrator's present emotional, cognitive, and experiential state), a confabulation (the unconscious filling of gaps in the memory by imagined or untrue experiences that the narrator believes in), and a recovered memory, when a repressed experience is brought back to consciousness. Memory and paramnesia in both *The Abandoned Village* and *The Shadow Lines* work together to empower the exiles to (re)create their lost spaces, the heterotopias (as Foucault might have called them) of and from the past that help them to deal with their present. These 'other spaces' are at once real places and locations that exist beyond them; exile engenders a shift in perspective that, as it registers change, also renders the familiar unfamiliar, the real unreal. Home is the site of nostalgia as well as of a terror of the unknown; the borders between the spaces are 'shadow' ones, achieving presence only when they are crossed.

The narrative structure of the exilic memory is very different, then, from that of history. History recovers events by chronological narration, by explaining why certain things happened and why they did so at that particular moment in time. But for both these exilic narratives, Partition and the loss of home are things that can never be explained. They can only be experienced as monstrous, and embody the breakdown of all social values. In essay after essay these refugees from East Bengal agonize over the loss of innocence and the collapse of certainties that their forcible departure from home has brought about. They ask themselves and their readers why it is that they were forced to leave their villages, why neighbour turned against neighbour after so many centuries of living harmoniously, even lovingly, together: "Was our feeling of kinship based on quicksand?" (Basu

1975: 156). "Why did the structure of the human mind change so suddenly?" (1975: 101). "What happened is something ordinary human beings can never comprehend" (1975: 91). Above all, "[j]ust one line drawn on a map, and my own home becomes a foreign country?" (1975: 66).

This is the question that haunts Tha'mma, too, in *The Shadow Lines*. She is determined to bring her old uncle, her Jethamoshai, 'home' to India when she hears he is still alive in Dhaka: "Imagine what it must be to die *in another country*, abandoned and alone in your old age" (Ghosh 1995: 136; emphasis added). Yet Jethamoshai knows very well he is in his own home, his own homeland: "As for me, I was born here, and I'll die here" (1995: 215). As Tha'mma applies for an Indian passport, the anomalousness of her own situation strikes her. She finds it hard to mention Dhaka as her place of birth in her application, for what was once home to her is now the capital of East Pakistan, a foreign country. Separated from her home by the forces of history, Tha'mma finds it difficult to explain "how her place of birth had come to be so messily at odds with her nationality" (Ghosh 1995: 152). Before flying to Dhaka she even wonders whether she will be able to see the border between the two Bengals from the aircraft, and this apparent ignorance causes much amusement in the family. Yet Tha'mma is no fool; she is an educated woman, a former schoolteacher and school principal, who has always been very much aware of social and political events in the world outside the house. Her bewilderment, then, sums up the confusion that the conflicting notions of home and homeland cause: "But if there aren't any trenches or anything, how are people to know? I mean, what's the difference then? And if there's no difference, both sides will be the same; it will be just like it used to be before [...]. What was it all for then - Partition and all the killing and everything - if there isn't something in between?" (1995: 151).

Eschewing the straightforward narrative mode of the essays, the novel loops back and forth in time, linking past to the present, the partition of Bengal in 1947 to the exilic lives of the present. Like all Bengali women Tha'mma lost her first home, her paternal home or *baaper bari*, when she left it after marriage. Nor did she have the support of her *shoshur bari*, father-in-law's home, which was expected to fulfil that role for married women and widows. Her husband worked far away from their native Bengal, in Burma, and he died too early to provide her with the security of a home of her own. Partition meant that she could never revisit her *baaper bari*, and would have to make do in a one-room tenement in Bhowanipore (a middle-class Calcutta neighbourhood) until her son grew up and married, at which time they found other places to live which were more suitable to her son's growing professional success. But for all their apparent comforts these houses are simply *bashas* that her son rents; they are very different from her memories of her Dhaka house and her notions of home. That is why, as she grows older, she progressively loses interest in her Calcutta locations. She comes back to her old self only when her obsessive desire to bring her uncle away from the Dhaka home to India, and the Calcutta house that was still not home, seems about to be fulfilled. Now she is caught between memory and belonging, on the one hand, and reality and nationality, on the other, and loses her sense of place and time: instead of saying that she would 'go' to Dhaka, she says that she would 'come home' to Dhaka. Her young grandson finds her slip very funny, but the adult narrator realizes that the confusion in his grandmother's mind between coming and going, which he had laughed at as a young boy, was not really her fault: "Every language assumes a centrality, and fixed and settled point to go away from and come back to, and what my grandmother was looking for was a word for a journey which was not a coming or going at all: a journey that was a search for precisely that fixed point which permits the proper use of verbs of movement" (1995: 153) – the centrality and fixed point of home.

This is why Jethamoshai refuses to leave his Dhaka home. All his family, his children and their families have left for India, his house has been turned into a makeshift motor-cycle-repair shop, and he is looked after by Muslim squatters who have taken possession of the house; but, as he has told his sons, he will never leave his home for an imaginary one in an imaginary India: "I don't believe in this India-Shindia. Once you start moving you never stop, he said. It's all very well, you're going away now, but suppose when you get there they decide to draw another line somewhere? What will you do then? Where will you move to? No one will have you anywhere" (Ghosh 1995: 215). When Tha'mma tries to remove him from home by force, he dies on the way from one 'home' to another. For the essayists of *The Abandoned Village* home was the last and ultimate refuge of all that they have held sacred: "The village, mingled with the memories of my forefathers, was a place of pilgrimage for me" (Basu 1975: 241). But now that they have lost it, they have also lost, like the characters in *Shadow Lines*, the sense of fixity and certainty that 'home', 'birthplace' and 'country/nation' traditionally have. No wonder, then, that they are bewildered. A writer originally from a village in Chittagong asks sadly, "The village where my ancestors had lived for seven generations [a conventional Bengali expression], a village which is more precious than gold to me, where is it today?" (Basu 1975: 197). Another person, from Mymensingh, points out the irony of his situation: "My home is in a country I have no connection with any more. The house is there, the village is there, the property is there, but I am homeless" (Basu 1975: 88). A refugee from Kushtia relates his present condition to that of the goat he had loved as a child but which he had quite cheerfully given up to be slaughtered as a sacrifice to the goddess Kali; it sums up for him what has happened to human relationships in the carnage of Partition (Basu 1975: 239).

Indeed, writer after writer in *The Abandoned Village* recalls with nostalgia their emotional bonds with their lost homes. A man from Barisal recalls how whenever he used to return home for his holidays it was like going back to his mother's embrace, which had helped him to "forget all the insults, suffering and the weariness I had suffered" in the stifling and depressing atmosphere of his city house (Basu 1975: 111-2). The essays in *The Abandoned Village* rewrite, in fact, the *basha/bari* opposition into the more conventional one between town and country: "We are educated; we have tasted the intoxication of the city. We have lost our caste". Perhaps that is why they have been punished today: they can never return home; "The doors of our return to the village have been shut for ever" (Basu 1975: 68-9). For Tha'mma, too, Ila is a gold-digging whore because she has consciously rejected home in the margins, for self-exile in the metropolis, abandoned a world of belonging for one of cultural dislocation and deracination. Certainly the home that Ila tries to create for herself with Nick in London gives her only unhappiness and uncertainty. Because the narrator, like Tridib, does not look for home outside the imagination he is freer than all the other characters; he knows that homelessness and dislocation are an integral part of human experience everywhere.

What is especially interesting is how the Hindu essayists and the Hindu characters in the novel reconstruct the role of Muslims in their memories of home; for East Bengal has always been predominantly Muslim. There is, perhaps surprisingly, less anger than incomprehension. Tha'mma, for one, knows how much Muslims were a part of the freedom movement; she remembers with admiration the silent young Muslim classmate in college who was later discovered to be actively involved in the violent activities of militant freedom-fighters. She does not, as she could well have, object to the narrator's close friendship with a Muslim boy. But when she thinks of her uncle and her Dhaka home being looked after by Muslims she cannot accept it. The underlying distrust between the two communities surfaces in Dhaka itself, especially when Tridib is killed by a mob there. When the essayists in *The Abandoned Village* look back at their Muslim neighbours, with whom they, too, shared so much through the generations, there is much affection, but more bewilderment. "We have lived together for generations, sharing each other's joys and sorrows, but did they [their Muslim friends] feel the least regret when we left? Did it take only one blow of the scimitar of politics to cut off the ties that had existed from the beginning of time?" (Basu 1975: 235). The writers remember Muslims in their villages as very much a part of the daily lives of the Bengali Hindu community: "For so long we Hindus and Muslims have lived together like brothers – we have always felt a close relationship with everybody [....]. But today?" (Basu 1975: 258). Living together as brothers, however, means, for the Hindu, the way in which their Muslim friends and neighbours participated in Hindu festivals; no-one ever mentions Hindus doing the same with Muslim celebrations. It is as though the Muslim way of life had never existed in the Bengali Hindu consciousness. In their constructions of the lost homeland, the harmony between the two communities is a given, but the home is fundamentally a Hindu one, in which the Bengali Muslim might be a respected guest while his Islamic way of life is treated as irrelevant. Not surprisingly, therefore, the Bengali Hindu in the essays tends to see the Muslims' hatred of them at the time of Partition as inexplicable, fundamentally alien to the Bengali temperament, and engendered by forces outside Bengal.

Where factual memory is baffled by changes that the essayists failed to notice were inevitable, Ghosh's fiction juxtaposes them against the stories people create about their own lives and by stories from the individual memory that do not necessarily coincide with received history. By doing so, he interrogates the meaning of home, nation and history themselves. For Tha'mma, who lived in Burma and Calcutta for longer than she lived in Dhaka, it is not Calcutta, but Dhaka, that was 'home'. But when she goes home to a city and a house that is no longer home, she discovers that Partition changed everything, and asks in anguish, "Where's Dhaka? I can't see Dhaka" (Ghosh 1995: 193). She is more of a foreigner at home than May, the English girl who did not need a visa to visit Dhaka as she did (1995: 195). When she and Mayadebi, her sister, finally visit their old house they realize that it is no longer home, their home, but an automobile workshop and a home for numerous Muslim refugees from India. Indeed, the story of the Partition is a retelling of the story of the partition of her family home many years ago: just as the traditional joint family in Bengal was disintegrating under the force of growing urbanization and individualism, and brother rose against brother in bitter family strife, so did the two communities who had lived together so long as brothers, the sons of the same Mother(land). Like warring brothers in notoriously litigious Bengal, they decided to divide their parental/family property, the home and the homeland. When Tha'mma's ancestral house was partitioned, the two brothers, Tha'mma's father and Jethamoshai, insisted on an exact division of the property, even if it meant that the dividing line went through doors and an old bathroom commode, just as during the Partition of the homeland the newly-drawn lines on the map of Bengal literally ran through homes, dividing them between the two nations, and houses on the border frequently had their bedroom in one country and their kitchen in another. As a child Tha'mma saw both the bitterness of the separation and its strangeness, especially the way the old loyalties to the family continued when it came to matters of family honour and pride, such as arranging marriages. She made up stories then for her little sister about the other side of the house, stories of an upside-down world, which provided a source of endless fascination and amusement for the two little girls, even as she knew she belonged there just as it continued to belong to her part of the house in spite of the division. The recurring metaphor of the mirror in the novel, reflecting and distorting experience of past and present, of people and places, underscores the skewed relationship between memory and fact.

Thus, during the 1964 Hindu-Muslim riots in Calcutta, following the theft of the Prophet's hair from the Hazratbal Mosque in Srinagar, the schoolboy narrator suddenly finds his best friend Mantu (Mansur) transformed into an enemy, the Governments of India and Pakistan trading symmetrical accusations, and the people on both sides of the border reacting with an identical sense of horror and outrage. Many Muslims in East Pakistan gave shelter to Hindus, just as many Hindus in India helped their Muslim neighbours. As a college student, however, the narrator finds the day's violence in Calcutta forgotten in histories and archives. When, at last, he discovers a mention of the riots in Bengal in the old newspapers, it is of one in Khulna (erstwhile East Pakistan), not in Calcutta; he finds out then how Tridib, whose mirror-image he was supposed to be, was killed by a mob in Dhaka in the same riots that engulfed Calcutta, and realizes that there is always something that will connect Calcutta to Dhaka, Bengali to Bengali. Even in their self-destructive violence the people of East and West Bengal exhibit their common inheritance and kinship, just as the families of Tha'mma's father and Jethamoshai had always done. As Foucault remarks of the heterotopia, which he describes as a mirror: "The space in which we live, which draws us out of ourselves, in which the erosion of our lives, our time and our history occurs, the space that claws and gnaws at us, is also, in itself, a heterogeneous space. In other words, we do not live in a kind of void, inside of which we could place individuals and things. We do not live inside a void that could be coloured with diverse shades of light, we live inside a set of relations that delineates sites which are irreducible to one another and absolutely not superimposable on one another" (Foucault 1986: 23).

These remarks are equally applicable to the stories about home by the anonymous essayists of the earlier volume: 'home' is in the imagination as a constant symbol of loss. The heterotopic mirror, moreover, enables both the essayists and Ghosh's narrator to see themselves where they are absent, in the memory and the imagination, even as it removes them from where they are and puts them inside their reflections. In Ghosh's novel, of course, it is not only the narrator or his mentor who do so: the characters image each other through their imaginations and their shared pasts: the narrator and Ila, Tridib and Nick, the families of the Basus, the Datta-Chaudhuris, the Tresawsens and the Prices, Tha'mma and Mayadebi, Tha'mma and Ila, Tha'mma and the narrator's mother, and so on. As they construct stories and histories about each other they constantly go back to their conceptions of 'home' and to Tha'mma's memories of the upside-down house in Dhaka, for that is where it all starts: the removal from place. The ferocity with which the grandmother defends her home and its values is clearly a part of the alienation and the disorientation that are themselves the products of exile; the fluidity of borders that Tridib and the narrator experience are also born of their dislocation from home. For the essayists, too, what remains of their 'home' is nostalgia and yearning, a sense of loss that can be overcome only through narration. As in *The Shadow Lines*, the narrative of the exilic memory helps to rebuild what has been temporally and spatially destroyed, not simply by recapturing the past but also by creating a new one, whether or not that has anything in common with historical accounts. After all, as the narrator himself points out, "a place does not merely exist, [but] has to be invented in one's imagination" (Ghosh 1995: 21). In both *The Abandoned Village* and *The Shadow Lines* the re-membered home ensures that the past continues into the present, making the condition of exile permanent, irrevocable, and universal.

Notes

[1] The original term for the Bengali migrant was *probashi*, one who lives outside his home(land); as 'homeland' now encompasses more than Bengal, and includes the whole of India (or Bangladesh for Bengalis from East Bengal), Bengalis settled 'outside' India/Bangladesh are called *adhibashis*.

[2] All quotations from the text are my own translations. I am indebted to Dipesh Chakrabarty's article, 'Remembered Villages: Representations of Hindu-Bengali Memories in the Aftermath of the Partition' in Mushirul Hasan (ed.) *Inventing Boundaries: Gender, Politics and the Partition of India* (N. Delhi: Oxford University Press, 2002), for an introduction to this book, which now appears to be out of print.

[3] See Partha Chatterjee, *The Nation and its Fragments: Colonial and Postcolonial Histories* (New Delhi: Oxford University Press, 1999), and Veena Das, *Critical Events: An Anthropological Perspective on Contemporary India* (New Delhi: Oxford University Press, 1995).

Bibliography

Basu, Dakshinaranjan (ed.). 1975. *Chhere Asha Gram.* Calcutta: Ananda Publishers.
Bhabha, Homi J. 1994. *The Location of Culture.* London: Routledge.
Foucault, Michel. 1986. 'Text/Context of Other Space' in *Diacritics* 16(1): 22-27.
Ghosh, Amitav. 1995. *The Shadow Lines.* New. Delhi: Oxford University Press.
Walcott, Derek. 1992. 'The Antilles: Fragments of Epic Memory'. Nobel Prize
        Lecture. December 7, 1992. On line at: www.nobel.se/literature/ laureates/
        1992/walcott-lecture.html (consulted 05.05.2002).

25

Film Excerpts: *A Taste of Place: Stories of Food and Longing*

Shuchi Kothari and Sarina Pearson

Shuchi Kothari was born in Ahmedabad, India. She studied and lived in Austin, Texas for seven years, before moving to New Zealand in 1997. She writes film scripts for the film industries in India, New Zealand, and the United States. She is a lecturer in the Department of Film, Television & Media Studies at the University of Auckland.

Sarina Pearson was born in Honolulu, Hawaii, and has lived in Canada, the United States, and New Zealand. She has produced films and currently lectures in the Department of Film, Television & Media Studies at the University of Auckland. Sarina and Shuchi run *Nomadz Unlimited*, a small production company committed to fostering new talent and producing provocative work.

The brief excerpts presented on the accompanying DVD are taken from the film *A Taste of Place: Stories of Food and Longing* (2001), directed by Susan Pointon, written and presented by Shuchi Kothari and produced by Sarina Pearson. In this film, Kothari talks to immigrants to New Zealand from the Pacific nation of Niue, from former Yugoslavia, from India, from China, and from Ethiopia about what it means to them to prepare the food typical of their mother countries in their adopted country, using ingredients which often only approximate the original materials. As she watches (and helps) them cook, she reflects on the complex psychological and social processes at work. Preparing traditional foods is one of the most powerful means for migrants to maintain their collective identity and links with the homeland, especially when the food is consumed in a communal setting. Primal emotions of longing, and sorrow over what has been lost, are tempered by a range of other feelings, including pride at having adapted to a new environment. While, in most cases, the people Kothari meets prefer not to discuss the trials they have experienced on camera, their stories reveal instances of discrimination or exclusion related specifically to their food. In particular, they meet official prohibitions on the importing of certain ingredients and on methods of outdoor cooking, as well as dislike among neighbours for alien cooking smells. Nevertheless, as Kothari comments, many locals enjoy eating at 'ethnic' restaurants, even if they show little interest in the welfare or culture of the migrants whose dishes are served there. The excerpts presented on the DVD show Eyerusalem Atalay, a recent Ethiopian immigrant, roasting coffee in the traditional way over a small coal brazier and preparing meat and pancake dishes for an Ethiopian community celebration. A war-widow, who speaks little English, she came to New Zealand with her two small daughters via exile in Sudan, where she ran a successful restaurant, while her sons remain in Ethiopia.

See DVD

26

Food and the Exile

Hilary Funnell

Hilary Funnell was born in New Zealand and lives in Auckland where she is completing her Masters in English Literature. A life-long passion for food and cooking, coupled with her foreign travel experiences, and the fact that she lives in a particularly migrant-rich area, have resulted in a fascination with the cultural function of food as a marker of identity.

In this paper she examines the ways in which food bridges the old and new lives of exiles, enabling them to remain connected to their past while also constituting a language with which to negotiate their presence in the host country, and ultimately choose to what degree they become a part of their new culture.

From the moment of arriving in a new country, exiles are forced to think of themselves in a different light. In a new land one suddenly becomes 'Other' and things previously taken for granted assume a fresh significance. As the exiled Iranian writer Mahnaz Afkhami observes: "through the disruption of the given and the accepted, the exile experience brings into focus the sources on which the self is composed and structured" (Afkhami 2003). Everyday practices such as dress, language, manners, and food become points of difference and visibility and, sometimes, sites of discrimination; they may become redundant or unacceptable or merely, in the case of food, unavailable. What was once simply 'home' is now 'Home'; rituals take on more significance, meals become an expression and affirmation of culture and a celebration of group ties rather than just an opportunity for sustenance.

Whether exiled voluntarily or by force, exiles share a common sense of loss which is often reiterated most acutely through food. Margaret Morse writes that "food is often considered 'a lived metaphor of culture itself'" (quoted in Khoo 2002: 204); in exile it also becomes a symbol of the exilic struggle to adapt to a new life. It is impossible to overestimate the importance of food, both physically and culturally – in the words of anthropologists Counihan and Van

Esterik: "food touches everything" (1997: 1). Through it we experience and express hardship, estrangement, loss, comfort, love, creativity, power, nostalgia, and, of course, exile. This paper focuses on the ways in which food, for exiles, functions as a bridge between their old culture and their new life; allowing exiles to remain connected – as much as possible – to their old life, through the relationships sustained by shared meals and the memories invoked by smells and tastes. It also examines the way food constitutes a language with which to negotiate one's presence in the host culture, allowing exiles to choose between identifying solely with their original culture, and reinventing themselves in the new one.

*

> [T]he sense of ourselves has always been located [...] in the idea of roots, the idea of coming from a place, the idea of inhabiting a kind of language which you have in common and the kind of social convention within which you live. And then what happens to the migrant is that they lose all three [...] and they find themselves in a new place, a new language. And so they have to reinvent a sense of self [...]. (Rushdie 1987: 63)

Rushdie's words refer to language as it is conventionally understood, however, the 'language' he refers to could equally be that of food. Not only does food have its own language of preparation but, as we have seen, it can articulate a multitude of meanings. Roland Barthes terms food an "alimentary language" which he describes, after Saussure, as subject to the rules regulating any signifying system, and which he breaks down into the abstract, non-specific "food" and its performative aspect (Barthes 1964: s.p.).

The abstract 'food' is the *langue* in Saussurean terms, "the system or totality of language shared by the 'collective consciousness'" (Cuddon 1999: 449); it comprises the rules (or 'grammar') governing its use. This grammar consists of "rules of exclusion", operated by taboos such as kosher or halal laws, "signifying oppositions", such as savoury and sweet or raw and cooked , "rules of association", which operate at dish level or at menu level, and "rituals of use" which function as "alimentary rhetoric" (Barthes 1964: s.p.). All of these function at a social level, "the individual cannot by himself either create or modify [the *langue*]; it is essentially a collective contract which one must accept in its entirety if one wishes to communicate" (Barthes 1964: s.p.).

Where food is concerned, this means exiles must choose between living within their customary *langue* and reinventing themselves within the new. As Andrew Buckser writes, "while culturally constructed, food must be consumed physically by individuals; thus eating always involves an individual choice about connection with a group" (1999: 192). On the one hand exiles can maintain their connection to the *langue* of their cultural community, thus emphasising their otherness in the host culture and resisting assimilation; on the other hand they can adopt the *langue* of the host culture in order to communicate within that society and reduce their otherness. Obviously, there are degrees of integration, the two *langues* are not completely exclusive although one will naturally dominate; however, where diet is concerned it is not always possible to be 'bilingual'. Put very simply, exiles whose food preferences are very different from those of their host country, or those who observe strict dietary laws, for example orthodox Jews, cannot easily be invited to dinner where these laws or tastes are not followed, thereby excluding them from a great deal of social interaction within the host culture.

Buckser describes the Jewish community of Denmark which is so fully integrated that, despite seeing dietary laws as "one of the few symbolic systems […] through which [they] can express their Jewish identity" (1999: 195), many Jews choose not to keep kosher outside their homes, recognizing that "being simply a Dane among other Danes, cannot coexist with a forthright observance of Jewish dietary rules" (1999: 197). Clearly this is no longer a community in exile; however, the dilemma confronting Danish Jews is similar to that faced by other exiles intent on merging with their host culture; the question it poses is "which comes first, the imperatives of conviviality implicit in one's Danishness, or the food taboos implicit in one's Jewishness? How far is one willing to transgress one identity in order to keep step with the other?" (1999: 197). The solution for many of these Jews is to regard kosher laws as non-applicable outside their home, minimizing their difference in the wider community and making their "Jewishness a private identity" (1999: 197).

The compromise devised by the Danish Jews is motivated by the desire to avoid disrupting the dual identities they enjoy. Other exiles who are more visible and less accepted by the host culture are compelled to deny their own foodways in an effort to communicate their desire to belong. For this reason, children of exiles will very often demand the food that their peers eat as a way of blending in. As

Bell and Valentine point out, consuming western food, particularly for young people, is "a way of exhibiting some control over their own bodies and of articulating their hybrid identities" (1997: 43).

André Aciman asks "how do you – indeed can you ever – rebuild a home? What kinds of shifts must take place for a person to acquire, let alone accept, a new identity, a new language?" (1999: 14). By choosing to make the fundamental shift in their dietary habits that eating the host food often requires, exiles are attempting to anchor themselves to their new home and regain the sense of place and identity which is lost in the process of exile. The sense of 'rootedness' that they seek is what Simone Weil described as "perhaps the most important and least recognised need of the human soul" (quoted in Said 1994: 146); by inhabiting a new language of food the exile can recover a sense of home.

However, diet is not always a matter of choice for exiles, and has often been inflicted on societies by colonising powers, or on people exiled as slaves. When Goa, in India, was colonised by the Portuguese in the sixteenth century, the Goans were forcibly converted to Christianity; consequently their diet changed from Hindu vegetarianism to a meat-based diet which permitted alcohol. Slaves in the Southern American states and in the Caribbean were given the foods which their oppressors rejected; in the American South these were pig parts such as intestines, tripe, trotters, and so on, which are described by African-American writer Donnell Alexander as "massa's garbage" (2003). In each situation, the only recourse available to the exiles, apart from starving, was to embrace the food forced upon them and make it distinctly their own. As a result, descendants of these exiles inherit an alimentary language which speaks of their ancestors' oppression, whilst also expressing home and comfort. However, like any colonised population forced to speak their coloniser's language, this language becomes part of who they are and how they express themselves; to reject it is to lose part of themselves. This dilemma is expressed by Jennifer Iré, writing of her Trinidadian origins:

> I found out that some of the favourite foods of my people came from the creation of the 'slave diet' by Europeans and are therefore an artifice of slavery. [...]. My ancestors were fed denatured food, salted meat and fish and condensed milk, and we came to treasure these foods as our heritage. On first learning this history of the foods I loved [...] I had a dilemma. I could not stomach the food and yet I craved the food. (1997: 255-256)

Iré goes on to explain how, unable to bear losing part of her heritage, she instead learned to celebrate the food of her ancestors as a symbol of her foremothers' creativity and wisdom and of their ability to create an identity, through food, that endures.

The essential, sustaining nature of food is repeatedly invoked in the imagery used to describe the exilic experience. Amy Kaminsky describes Cortázar as an "expatriate who was always nourished by the language and presence of his Argentina" (1999: 10); Mary McCarthy writes of exiles "wasting away" and being "deprived of sustenance" without news from home, "hungry for scraps of rumour" or "thirsting for news" (1994: 50). Other exiles write of overcoming exile as a process of being "melted down in the common pot" (Avakian 1997: 229). The fact that these metaphors are universally recognisable ensures their effectiveness. References to a food commonly associated with their culture are often employed as pejorative labels for the exile, reducing them to a universally understood concept (food) and presumably reducing their perceived threat; Indians become 'curry-munchers', Pacific Islanders become 'coconuts', Hispanics are referred to with variations on 'burrito-brain/head'. Exiles themselves have food-related labels for their assimilated compatriots, such as 'banana – yellow on the outside, white on the inside'.

*

> Many migrant groups maintain their previous cultures and lifestyles in their countries of adoption, often insisting that their children do the same. But this is by way of acclimatising to their new situation, creating a bridge between the past and the present they had opted for [...]. My parents did not choose to leave Palestine and they never willingly acquiesced in its loss. They [...] [saw] England as [...] a staging post on a route that only pointed back [...]. My father's finest achievements [...] were in fact the bridges he built to connect him to the past, to Palestine'. (Karmi 1999: 60)

Some exiles, such as Ghada Karmi's family, maintain their traditions in an attempt to repair this rupture and resist the new culture, living as if nothing has changed and as if their presence there is temporary. Other exiles use food as a bridge between their old culture and their new life – looking both ways, as it were. Some use food as a means of survival in the host culture and a bridge beyond exile.

Ghada Karmi's family were exiled from Palestine to London in 1949. Karmi's article describes how her mother maintained her family's cultural identity at all costs, interacting only with other

Arabs, speaking no English and, despite the difficulty and expense of obtaining ingredients, cooking only traditional food. Her determination not to become part of British society extended to her refusal to have heating or a fridge, as Karmi writes, "succumbing to the refrigerator would for her have symbolized her acceptance of the European way of life" (1999: 56). In the film *A Taste of Place* (see number 25 above) the Ethiopian woman Eyerusalem exhibits a similar resistance to her new life in New Zealand, due in part, no doubt, to having left children behind in Africa. Eyerusalem speaks no English and keeps the link to her old life alive by cooking traditional foods and by making her (Ethiopian) coffee the traditional way, on a small charcoal burner in her living room. The round-bottomed, metal coffee pot that she uses is an evocative symbol of her attitude to her new life – by not using her treasured earthenware pot, which is from Ethiopia, and which she fears will get broken, she ensures that the coffee she makes here is never quite the same or as good as the coffee made at 'home'.

The most poignant instances of food being used as a bridge to the past occur in extreme circumstances during which food becomes a means to resist oppression. David Sutton writes of exiles in brutal situations such as concentration camps, using memories of food to "defy dehumanisation and to dream of the past and of the future" (2001: 167). During the Second World War, Jewish women in the Terezin Concentration Camp surreptitiously compiled a book of their favourite recipes in an attempt to resist the despair of being in the camps and to keep alive the memory of what they had to live for. Cara De Silva, editor of the now-published book (*In Memory's Kitchen*, 1996), explains: "food is such a powerful identity marker [...], a central part of who we are" (De Silva 1996); by remembering special meals and the celebrations they are associated with, she says, "you are reinforcing who you are in the face of those who want to annihilate you and your culture and your traditions, and everything about you [...]" (1996). Sutton also writes of concentration camp internees who elected to fast for religious reasons, or who formed bread into chess pieces rather than eating it, and in so doing preserved their dignity and, ironically, unwittingly gave themselves a better chance of survival than those who were totally subjugated by their need for food (Sutton 2001: 167).

*

[…] in der heym   at home
where she does everything to keep
yidishkayt   alive

yidishkayt   a way of being
Jewish   always arguable
in mark   where she buys
di kartofl un khalah
(yes, potatoes and challah)

di kartofl   the physical counterpart of yidishkayt

.mit tsibeles   with onions
that bring trern tsu di oygn
tears to her eyes   when she sees
how little it all is
veyniker un veyniker
less and less […]
                    (Irena Klepfisz in Keenan and Lloyd 1990: 29 -30)

The food writer Claudia Roden, herself a one-time exile, writes in her *Book of Jewish Food* that "dishes are important because they are a link with the past, a celebration of roots, a symbol of continuity. They are a part of immigrant culture which survives the longest" (1996: 11). The dishes that Roden refers to represent the Jewish way of life; they have been maintained in many Jewish communities as a link to the past. As the extract from Irena Klepfisz's poem suggests, even in times of hardship, food has been the physical manifestation of the Jewish way of life. Many Jewish recipes symbolise events in Jewish history or reflect the mobility of Jewish populations. Even in integrated communities, like that of the Danish Jews, they constitute an important acknowledgement of history and group bonds and are a feature of celebrations. Eva Hoffman writes that "for Jews, in their long Diaspora, the need to preserve the symbolic centre in an indifferent world…often led them to insulate themselves from their surroundings, to retreat to their community as a place of refuge and spiritual fortress" (Hoffman 1999: 53). In communities which are more vulnerable and which do not enjoy the same long and peaceful residence as the Danes,[1] holding on to the past through food and dietary laws represents "culinary conservatism" (Gabaccia 1998: 9), which offers a way of maintaining control over one's life as an exile and of strengthening group bonds and, as Sneja Gunew writes, resisting being "overwhelmed and assimilated" (Gunew 2000: 228).

*

> [...] when you mourn a loved one, you wish more than anything to be [...] with others who share your sense of loss. I sought mostly the company of other exiled Iranians [...].We remembered tastes, smells, sounds. We knew that no fruit would ever have the pungent aroma and the luscious sweetness of the fruit in Iran that the sun would never shine so bright [...]. (Afkhami 1994: 6)

> Meals were elaborate affairs to which much care and attention were given [...]. Long white cloths were spread on the lush carpets. Huge round trays were carried from the kitchen [...]. Numerous dishes of saffron rice, meat and vegetable stews, fresh herbs and cheese and bread were placed in the middle of the *sofreh* [...]. (Azar Salamat in Afkhami 1994: 80)

> I wish for the night
> Dark as a pith of date;
> I wish for the night
> Ripe as a pith of date;
> I wish for the night
> Sweet as a pith of date.
>
> (Mishra 2002: 15)

Reading the work of exiled writers (particularly that of women), one is struck by the presence of food, either in nostalgic memories of lavish meals, as in the extract from Azar Salamat, or used as metaphors for the motherland, as in Sudesh Mishra's description of Palestine. The hyperbole that thrives in these works, as the extract from Mahnaz Afkhami demonstrates, is a feature of nostalgia's reconstruction of the past as an ideal place. As Suzanne Vromen describes it, nostalgia recalls "a world from which pain has been removed" (qtd. in Spitzer 1998: 378); food nostalgia typically recalls meals associated with the freedom and innocence of childhood or the abundance of celebration; it also recreates a time of unity before the community or family bonds were ruptured by exile, and before identity was blurred by hybridity.

*

> [...] inside that moment
> which comes to be, when we remember,
> at the only centre where it has always been,
> an aproned figure stands kneading, ripe

with yeast, her children at her skirts.
                    (Pattiann Rogers in Keenan and Lloyd 1990: 75)

What is clear from exilic writing is that food, whether actual or remembered, represents home and safety for the exile. Hamid Naficy writes that "a smell, a sound, or a taste suddenly and directly sutures one to a former house or home and to cherished memories of childhood" (1999: 6); Amy Kaminsky describes "all the familiar landmarks of home – food smells, [...] the sounds of a familiar language [...] the kinetic knowledge of a place that is your home, *where* you can feel safe[...]" (Kaminsky 1999: 11), that are the first casualties of exile. This safe place is often associated with the hearth, the centre of the house, symbolising the mother who is the traditional source of food and comfort; this is illustrated by Pattiann Roger's poem, and Diana Der Hovanessian's poem 'Without You I Am', the middle lines of which read: "home without hearth/ hearth without fire/ fire without fuel" (Keenan and Lloyd 1990: 47). This imagery is amplified by the use of metaphors of nurturing to refer to the exile's native land such as 'motherland', and 'provider of plenty', the construction of the motherland "as a warm, cornucopian breast from which people selectively seek nourishment" (De Souza 2004) and the figuring of language as 'the mother-tongue'. Kaminsky points out that 'mother' in Lacanian theory is "figured as place", and "rootedness" constitutes the "integration of self and place" (1999: 59). "This", says Kaminsky, "echoes the position of the child before separation from the mother and before entry into language" (1999: 59). Therefore, the attempt to reconnect with the motherland by cooking or remembering the food from one's past, has at its heart a desire to mend our first 'exile' from the body of the mother.

                                   *

The exile, as Edward Said has written, is someone who exists

> in a median state, neither completely at one with the new setting nor fully disencumbered of the old, beset with half involvements, half detachments, nostalgic and sentimental on one level, an adept mimic or a secret outcast on another. (Said 1994: 36)

As a bridge between cultures, food becomes a blend of the old and the new, a reflection of the exile's evolving identity in what Said terms the 'median state' of exile. In this state the 'speech' or *parole* of the exile's alimentary language becomes a tool for adaptation to the new culture. While *langue* is the 'grammar' of language, *parole* is its performative aspect; it encompasses recipes and cooking methods which are subject to endless variation by both groups and individuals. Menus represent the coincidence of *langue* and performance. It is the *parole* of food that allows exiles 'play' in the production of meals – and it is their presence in a foreign culture that demands it.

One of the first hurdles the exile faces on arrival in a new country is obtaining familiar ingredients. They may be difficult or impossible to find or they may be over-priced, forcing the exile to use substitutes where available, or to go without. Eyerusalem, the Ethiopian woman in the film *A Taste of Place*, is shown making traditional pancakes for which she has had to use a replacement flour, with the result that they are 'not as good' as the 'real' ones. Every time Eyerusalem makes these pancakes she is reminded of where she is – 'not home' – and of where she is from – 'not here'. However, as Panikos Panayi points out, it is not just the lack of familiar foods, but the presence of unfamiliar and unpalatable foods that symbolise absence from the exile's homeland (Panayi 2002: 47). The Niuean family in the same film sometimes use canned peaches instead of papaya in their special celebratory *taro* dish; they also have to cook the dish in an electric oven rather than an *umu,* or earth oven*,* as is traditional.[2] Despite this, these substitutions serve to make the resultant dish more significant – it is both a symbol of their readiness to adapt and of the difficulties they have had to overcome. It is worth noting that changes to the diet of exiles in their host country are not always negative. Exiles who have come from refugee camps or impoverished or war torn areas very often find the selection and availability of food in the host culture a huge improvement. Foods that were previously out of reach can now be consumed regularly; David Simpson writes of migrants in this situation developing meat-heavy diets based on their social aspirations in their home country (1999: 161).

The expatriate Bulgarian writer Kapka Kassabova states that she "writes English with an accent".[3] This comment is an apposite analogy for the cooking of exiles as, once they have adapted their recipes to local conditions, they are, indeed, cooking with an accent of their new culture. Exiles who eat local food frequently use the condiments of their own cooking to make the food more palatable, in this case, cooking with their own accent. The presence of exiled populations will very often make itself felt, eventually, through its influence on the local food: through restaurants, imported ingredients and so on. This may be as simple as a brief fashion for using the spice *sumac* or as pervasive as the adoption of stir-frying techniques; whichever it is, the exile's food could be said to have 'contaminated' the local cuisine. In much the same way that (in the words of Trudy Agar, this volume: 187) a language can be 'contaminated' by another and be made "dynamic and heterogeneous", so the local cuisine becomes "enriched, charged with fresh images, bathed in warm rivers and marinated in new spices, sometimes piquant, sometimes mild" (Agar, this volume: 187). This influence on local food can ease acceptance of the exile in the host culture; as Sneja Gunew writes: "the notion of multiculturalism as food" is usually the most readily acceptable form of cultural difference (Gunew 2000: 227). Interestingly, while the host language and food eventually replace or alter the language *and* food of the exile, it is generally only the host food that is similarly affected.

*

> "I wish they liked us as much as they like our curries" "[actually], they like *their* version of our curry" (words of a Pakistani taxi-driver in the film *A Taste of Place*, an excerpt of which is included in the accompanying DVD – see number 25, this volume)

As a bridge beyond exile, food represents a means of survival and the opportunity for many exiles to prosper and become part of the community. However, I question whether the exile and the exile's food don't lose both something vital in the process, becoming a hybrid of their two cultures which is never free of a sense of otherness.

To return to the analogy of food as a language, the performance, or 'text' of food, like any other language, can be deconstructed, after Derrida, in order to demonstrate that it says "something quite different from what it appears to be saying and …may be read as carrying a plurality of significance… at variance with… a single stable meaning" (Cuddon 1999: 210). Exiles who operate restaurants in their host country (as very many do) produce food which speaks of authenticity and exoticism to their customers but which, in reality, tells a tale of hardship and adaptation and, very likely, inauthenticity.

Some critics describe this inauthenticity as a deliberate holding back which allows ethnic restaurateurs some agency in the marketing of their national cuisine, while preserving at least some part of it for themselves. Others describe it as a bastardisation forced on the producer by the demands of the host culture for cheap, fast meals that come in a choice of 'mild, medium or hot'. Bell and Valentine write of the process of "acculturation and hybridisation" (1997: 116) by which ethnic food is "water[ed] down" through its exposure to the host cuisine, until the food available in ethnic restaurants is very often "removed from its original form and meaning"(1997: 116). According to Kaminsky, some see this hybridisation as "reprehensible and transgressive" (1999: 96); others, such as Gunew, see it as a "form of internalized subjugation which characterizes power relations in diaspora" (2000: 228). Sau-ling Wong writes of "food pornographers" who make "a living by exploiting the 'exotic' aspects of [their] ethnic foodways" (quoted in Khoo 2000: 204), a process which Samir Gandesha describes as reducing "the Other to the status of the 'other', as what is simply the antithesis of Western identity" (quoted in Gunew 2000: 228). The result of this is a blurring of cuisines and ethnic identities to meet the misconceptions of the host consumer; Anne Kershen writes of Pakistani-run restaurants purporting to be Indian because that is the assumed origin of 'curry', and of non-traditional dishes, like Chicken *Tikka Masala*, which have become a feature of Indian menus around the Western world (2002: 5); in addition, traditionally regional cuisines like those of China and India are presented as homogenous entities. *A Taste of Place* highlighted the prevalence of 'fusion cuisine' in Auckland restaurants – an often meaningless and fashion-driven amalgamation of different cuisines which Gabaccia aptly labels "*ciao mein*" (1998: 216).

The sale and consumption of ethnic food has its own set of power relations. Not only does it provide an opportunity for the western diner to symbolically 'consume the other', on a societal level as well as individually, but it allows the provider of the food to subvert the host/guest relationship to which he/she is subject as an exile. This is particularly true of restaurants which cater chiefly for their own cultural group where a westerner might be confronted with unfamiliar food and a language barrier and briefly experience what it is to be foreign. However, Kershen suggests that, in some ethnic restaurants, the newly configured host/guest opposition becomes one of master/servant and asks if western diners "experience any empathy with those who are cooking and serving their food or are their xenophobic sentiments heightened by being *served* by members of an ethnic minority?" (2002: 6).

*

'An accent marks the lag between two cultures, two languages, the space where you let go of one identity, invent another, and end up being more than one person though never quite two'. (Aciman 1999: 10)

I have examined food as a language that bridges the different stages of the exile's adaptation (or resistance) to a new culture and to the state of exile. Food serves as both a route back to the old culture and a means of reinventing oneself in the new. Although it offers the promise of a bridge beyond the state of exile, I question whether exiles can ever really liberate themselves from this state, or whether they simply swap one form of exile for another. Eventually exiles and their food assume a hybrid identity that is both more exotic than the host culture and less 'authentic' than the original: witness the ubiquitous spring roll for sale in non-Asian cafés. Aciman claims that the exile can never be completely one thing or another; each aspect of the exile's identity is accented by the other, as with his/her cooking. Exiles may lose their sense of loss for their homeland, but they never completely lose their otherness in the host culture. As Rina Ferrarelli's poem below suggests, exiles are always outside the 'interior', forever exiled to the 'border town' of their aspiration to belong.

Emigrant/Immigrant II

A slight accent.
    Forming
each phrase before
delivery
and never a slur.

Checking
    every move,
prepared
for all contingencies.
        Close,
yet not quite.

    Insisting
on a knife and fork
when your fingers
would do as well.

Almost there.
The place sighted,
But out of reach.
Destined never to cross

Into the interior.
A bridge, a border town.

(Keenan and Lloyd 1990: 62)

Notes

[1] According to Buckser, practically the entire Jewish population of Denmark was saved from the Nazis by a spontaneous effort on the part of the Danes.
[2] They do have an *umu,* but it is big enough to cook for 250-300 people, clearly too large for their family Sunday lunch.
[3] Kapka Kassabova, e-mail to the author, 02 February 2004.

Bibliography

Aciman, André. 1999. 'Foreword: Permanent Transients' in his *Letters of Transit: Reflections on Exile, Identity, Language, and Loss.* New York: The New Press: 7-14.
Afkhami, Mahnaz. 1994. *Women in Exile.* Charlottesville and London: University of Virginia.
- - - . 2003. 'Women in Exile: Searching for the Sources of the Self'. *The Scholar and Feminist Online* 1(1). On line at: www.barnard.columbia.edu/ sfonline/ wth/afkhami.htm (consulted 05.08.2003).
Agar, Trudy. 2004. 'Annexing the Land of Exile: Language and History in the Work of Assia Djebar', present volume: 183-192.
Alexander, Donnell. 2001. 'Are Black People Cooler than White People?' *UTNE Reader Online,* 06 Feb. 2001. On line at: www.oakland.edu/~kitchens /150d/ 150d/Alexander/ (consulted 08.11.2003).
Avakian, Arlene Voski (ed.). 1997. *Through the Kitchen Window: Women Explore the Intimate Meanings of Food and Cooking.* Boston: Beacon Press.
Barthes, Roland. 1964. *Elements of Semiology.* On line at: www.marxists.org/ reference/subject /philosophy/works/fr/barthes.htm (consulted 26.08.2003).
Bell, David and Gill Valentine. 1997. *Consuming Geographies: We Are Where We Eat.* London and New York: Routledge.
Buckser, Andrew. 1999. 'Keeping Kosher: Eating and Social Identity Among the Jews of Denmark' in *Ethnology* 38(3): 191-209.
Counihan, Carole and Penny Van Esterik (eds). 1997. *Food and Culture: A Reader,* New York and London: Routledge.
Cuddon, J.A. 1999. *The Penguin Dictionary of Literary Terms and Literary Theory* (rev. C.E.Preston). London and New York: Penguin Books.
De Silva, Cara. 1996. Interview with Elizabeth Farnsworth, *Online NewsHour,* PBS, 17 Dec. 1996, transcript on line at: www.pbs.org/newshour/bb/europe/ december96/cook_12-17.html (consulted 01.11.2003).
De Souza, Ruth. 2003. 'A Mirage of Stability and Continuity: How Goan Women Maintain Culture Despite Inter-generational Exile'. Unpublished paper presented at *Poetics of Exile* conference (University of Auckland, 17-19 July 2003).

Gabaccia, Donna R. 1998. *We Are What We Eat: Ethnic Food and the Making of Americans*. Cambridge, Mass: Harvard University Press.

Gunew, Sneja. 2000. 'Introduction: Multicultural Translations of Food, Bodies, Language' in *Journal of Intercultural Studies* 21(3): 227 - 241.

Hoffman, Eva. 1999 'The New Nomads' in Aciman (1999): 35-63.

Iré, Jennifer. 1997. 'The Power of the Pepper: From Slave Food to Spirit Food' in Avakian (1997): 255-258.

Kaminsky, Amy. 1999. *After Exile: Writing the Latin American Diaspora*. Minneapolis and London: University of Minnesota Press.

Karmi, Ghada. 1999. 'After the Nakba: An Experience of Exile in England' in *Journal of Palestine Studies* 111: 52 – 63.

Keenan, Deborah and Roseann Lloyd (eds). 1990. *Looking for Home: Women Writing about Exile*. Minneapolis: Milkweed Editions.

Kershen, Anne J. (ed.). 2002. *Food in the Migrant Experience*. Hampshire and Burlington VT: Ashgate.

Khoo, Olivia. 2000. 'Folding Chinese Boxes: Asian Exoticism in Australia', *Journal of Australian Studies* June: 200 – 210.

McCarthy, Mary. 1994. 'A Guide to Exiles, Expatriates, and Internal *Émigrés*' in Robinson, Marc (ed.) *Altogether Elsewhere: Writers on Exile*. San Diego, New York and London: Harcourt Brace and Company: 49-58.

Mishra, Sudesh. 2002. *Diaspora and the Difficult Art of Dying*. Dunedin: Otago University Press.

Naficy, Hamid. 1999. 'Introduction: Framing Exile from Homeland to Homepage' in his *Home, Exile, Homeland: Film, Media, and the Politics of Place*. New York and London: Routledge: 1-13.

Panayi, Panikos. 2002. 'The Spicing up of English Provincial Life: The History of Curry in Leicester' in Kershen (2002): 42-76.

Roden, Claudia. 1996. *The Book of Jewish Food: An Odyssey from Samarkand and Vilna to the Present Day*. London and New York: Penguin Books.

Rushdie, Salman. 1987. in Bourne, Bill, Udi Eichler and David Herman (eds) *Voices: Writers and Politics*. Nottingham, NY: Spokesman: 60-63.

Said, Edward. 1994. 'Reflections on Exile' in Robinson, Marc (ed.) *Altogether Elsewhere: Writers on Exile*. San Diego, New York and London: Harcourt Brace and Company: 137-149.

- - - . 1994. *Representations of the Intellectual*. London: Vintage.

Simpson, David. 1999. *A Distant Feast: The Origins of New Zealand's Cuisine*. Auckland: Godwit.

Spitzer, Leo. 1998. 'Persistent Memory: Central European Refugees in an Andean Land' in Suleiman, Susan Rubin (ed.) *Exile and Creativity*, Durham and London: Duke University Press: 373-396.

Sutton, David. 2001 *Remembrance of Repasts: An Anthropology of Food and Memory*. Oxford and New York: Berg.

A Taste of Place: Stories of Food and Longing, 2001. Dir. Susy Pointon, writ. Shuchi Kothari, prod. Sarina Pearson. Auckland: Nomadz Unlimited (see number 25, this volume).

27

The Other Side of Exile: Malaysian Writers Who Stayed Behind

Zawiah Yahya

Zawiah Yahya was, until her retirement in 2004, a professor of postcolonial studies and critical theory at the School of Language Studies and Linguistics, Universiti Kebangsaan Malaysia where she also served as Head of Department and Dean. Her early education at home in Malaysia was largely based on the British system, a tradition which continued through her BA and MA in English literature at Victoria University of Wellington, New Zealand. Her sense of academic displacement began on her return home to a changing postcolonial landscape in which English was marginalized by the education policies of the day. Later, it was her doctoral research in postcolonial studies at the University of Nottingham that provided her with an academic mission which finally gave her professional relevance in her own country. Since then, she has published books and papers that reflect this struggle. Her *Resisting Colonialist Discourse* (1994) signals an important intellectual departure from the English tradition of her early formative years.

In this paper she examines the contribution of Malaysian writers in English who stayed behind at a time when others went into self-exile. Post-independence conditions in Malaysia after 1957 and, in particular, government policies on language and education drove many writers in English to migrate to English-speaking countries such as Canada, Australia, and the USA. But those who chose to stay behind continued to practise their craft in English, in an environment that was far from ideal, and yet were able to produce powerful narratives and poetry out of their engagement with the tensions of their time. This paper assesses their contributions to a postcolonial nation in the process of becoming, as well as the role they can play today, 45 years on, at a time when a change in policy is bringing about the re-entry of literature in English into the national curriculum.

This paper is concerned with the poetics of survival, for writers who chose to stay when others went into self-exile. Malaysia's post-Independence policies on language and education drove a few writers in English to English-speaking countries. Other writers such as Lloyd Fernando, K.S. Maniam, Wong Phui Nam, and Lee Kok Liang chose to stay to continue to practise their craft under circumstances that were far from ideal; yet they were able to produce powerful narratives and poetry out of their engagement with the tensions of their time. In the process, they gave literature in English a local habitation and a name.

Much that happened in Malaysia after Independence in 1957 made English-language writers feel alienated and marginalised. The language policy that made Malay the national language, the concept of national literature as literature written in the national language, and the state patronage it enjoyed by virtue of this status, gave some English-language writers life-long grievances. Some left the country and became extra-territorial and diasporic. Some stayed behind to work out their angst. Some aligned themselves with the state agenda for nation-building while others remained, "unaccommodated, discontented, internal exiles" (Quayum and Wicks 2001: 155).

What happened in Malaysia also happened elsewhere in the postcolonial countries of Africa, the Caribbean, and the Indian subcontinent. Since Independence in 1957, language policies in Malaysia have become nationalist in orientation. The Malaysian government began the process of displacing English from its pedestal and replacing it with the Malay language as the national medium. The process had actually been initiated earlier, in the twilight of British rule in 1951, with the Barnes Committee Report which recommended the institution of a national school system, with Malay as the main medium of instruction.

This was followed in 1956 by the Abdul Razak Report and the National Language Act of 1967 requiring the full conversion of all English primary and secondary schools to the national medium by 1978, and tertiary education by 1983. The establishment in 1970 of Universiti Kebangsaan Malaysia (UKM) as Malaysia's first fully Malay-medium university was the climax of the nationalist dream. English was relegated to the position of second language, although all public universities have always provided English proficiency courses and made a pass in English compulsory for getting a degree.

The development of language policy is a significant dimension of the postcolonial condition, which is characterized by a desire to chart a common destiny and define a common identity. This has become necessary because, somewhere in our colonial past, when Great Britain launched her civilizing mission, her empire-builders created the image of their own language, culture, and literature as features of a superior civilization. Now, after Independence, excolonised people like us have to begin the process of reclaiming and reconstructing their own linguistic, cultural and literary identities.

The about-turn in language policy, however, upset the westernised English-educated middle-class that was created in the first instance by the colonial administration. It is easy to understand why English-language writers viewed this linguistic and literary development with resentment. What was so objectionable about the state ideology as they perceived it, was that it had chosen the language, literature, and culture of the Malays as the basis for national identity and unity. Writers in English and other languages thus felt that they were denied "an active engagement in nation building and the formation of national culture" (Quayum and Wicks 2001: x). They also felt they had been denied official recognition and sponsorship because of their use of a language that had fallen out of favour. The issue is complicated by competing linguistic and ethnic identities, the warring existence of two literary traditions in Malay and English, and the clash between national and communal ideologies.

To understand the complexity of this issue we need to go back to where it started, with the British education policy that implemented a dual system of Malay vernacular and English education. Malay-medium education was for the Malay rural masses, English was for the immigrant non-Malay community in the urban centres. Unlike the English-medium and Christian missionary schools, Malay vernacular education suffered extreme government neglect, characterized by an intellectually deprived content, virtually non-existent instructional material, poorly paid and badly trained staff, and dilapidated, makeshift premises. Later, faced with growing Malay demands, the British established a teacher-training college – the Sultan Idris Training College (SITC), in 1922 – to train sons of fishermen and padi-planters so that they could return to their villages to educate their own people. Among the subjects for the three-year course was Malay literature. It was these non-elite, mostly Malay-educated teachers-turned-writers and journalists who were said to have initiated the birth of modern Malay literature and preserved its umbilical links to the tradition of the peasantry from which it sprang.

Through the medium of newspapers and magazines they played their dual role as champion and critic of their society, making it aware of, and shaping its responses to, the threatening changes taking place in its environment. Because their social and political consciousness was then raised, they first became aware, and then resentful of, their disadvantaged position in their own country, ruled and drained of its resources by a foreign power, invaded by an endless influx of immigrants, run by a money-based economy they had no access to, and infiltrated by western values alien to them. Rather than 'high' western literature, journalism, with its interest in current affairs and its tendency towards social criticism, gave the indigenous literature of this period its social orientation. In fact, Malay writers have always seen themselves as playing a role in national development. "Art for society" was the slogan for ASAS 50 (Generation 50 Writers), a literary organization in the 1950s whose central agenda was the promotion of Malay language and literature and resistance to colonial rule and to English as the official language.

We need to know these historical details in order to understand the thinking of Malay nationalists and their antagonistic relationship with their English-medium counterparts, who they thought did not share their social commitment and ideals. These details also give an insight into the deep rift that writers on either side of 'The Great Divide' have not been able to cross to this day.

Unlike Malay literature, early English-language writings by Malaysians did not have their roots in Malaysian soil. The small group that began writing in the 1950s consisted of budding writers from the ivory tower who were taught to bend westwards in search of light. The literature syllabus, like that in other colonies, was centred on the study of the English literary tradition from Shakespeare to Milton, from *Beowulf* to Virginia Woolf, and the great humanist tradition of European culture, taught as if its only concern was with the universal themes of love, fear, birth, and death. Literary criticism revolved around Matthew Arnold's quest for the enlightenment of a Hellenised English middle class, T.S. Eliot's high culture of an Anglo-Catholic feudal tradition, F.R. Leavis's sermons on the moral significance of the Great Tradition and I.A. Richards's *im*practical criticism on the Equator. Although there was then in existence a Malay literary tradition, which had a history that went back some five hundred years, the colonial perception was that it was inferior, and had not risen above its peasant beginnings.

It is ironical that, at the time when the English-language writers, who belonged to the non-Malay University educated elite, were busy internalizing the codes, diction, images, and rhythm of the English masters, Malay-educated writers of the newly formed ASAS 50 were busy promoting the use of Malay language and literature for the attainment of nationalism, independence, and social equity, and resisting the domination of colonial rule and of English as the official language (Zawiah 1994: 55).

English-medium writers who stayed while others left had to come to terms with this politics of emergent nationalism. They have often been accused of being the carriers of colonialist attitudes, of obstructing the full expression of national sentiments, and of not being as committed to the literary and political activism as indigenous writers. They have been made to feel a sense of alienation from the mainstream national agenda, a sense of estrangement that comes with writing against the grain of the national language and the national canon. Their westernised education was thought to have drawn them into an unthinking, self-centred individualism. Some of those who stayed dealt with their alienation by withdrawing from the domain of the State to the exclusive domain of their art, to the "more immediate and personal problems of craftsmanship [...]. To concentrate on the business of writing and so produce poems, not manifestoes or commemorative stamps" because "[p]oet and nation do not always speak the same language" and because "the poet [...] is responsible only for his art and to himself" (Ee 1979: 72-73).

Apart from this English-Malay dichotomy, English-language writers have a real problem of not having their own tradition to fall back on. Although their immigrant forefathers had come from other countries that had long histories and literary traditions, they had been uprooted by the British as indentured labour from under-privileged socio-economic margins where only hard labour, not philosophy or poetry or the ancient classics, could fill up their rice-bowls. As a result, there was very little that they could pass down to the next generation in the new land. This is what Wong Phui Nam, one of the stayers, refers to when he says a Malaysian writer in English will bring to his work "a naked and orphaned psyche" (Wong 1991: 169), by which he means an absence of cultural and spiritual resources carried over from a 'mother' culture. The vacuum was to be filled by Anglo-European cultural constructs, by the best that had been thought and said in works published in Oxford, Cambridge, London, New York. Many poets who suffered from 'orphaned psyches' modelled their works on T.S. Eliot's *Wasteland*; Edwin Thumboo claimed W.B. Yeats as a major influence and Arthur Yap, Larkin.

Writers in Malay do not have the problem of double exile that constantly plagues writers in English. The language the English-language writers use to describe their world is culturally rooted in the Anglo-European tradition and locates them as outsiders looking in. At the same time, there is always the pressure to prove their worth against an external, cosmopolitan standard, yet their self-conscious use of the language does not quite produce the kind of authenticity that makes them heirs to the tradition of Shakespeare and Milton.

These are some of the problems that English-language writers in Malaysia face, from both within and without. Yet, it is precisely in the process of negotiating the problematics of linguistic exile, literary isolation, and political marginalisation that their real contribution to the nation is to be found. What has resulted is a corpus of writings that reflects, in essence and in details, the postcolonial realities of the country.

To start with, it helps a great deal that Malaysian writers, especially fiction writers, choose to focus on the specific socio-political issues that beset the society of their time. K.S. Maniam, in *The Return*, writes about the problems experienced by an Indian immigrant family in their attempts to adapt to the new country. In another novel, *In a Far Country,* he explores the question of identity for succeeding generations of Indians faced with the problem of displacement and loss of home. Lloyd Fernando, in *Scorpion Orchid,* explores the superficiality and fragility of race relations, as exemplified by four multiracial university graduates, beneath the tensions of the race riots of the 60s. His second novel, *Green Is the Colour*, set in the period following the riots between Malays and Chinese on 13 May 1969, unravels the uneasy, disturbing phase of national history that ensued and asks the pertinent question: Is unity in diversity possible?

K.S. Maniam and Lloyd Fernando are examples of writers who have successfully interfaced forms, techniques, and style with specific realities of national and political events, social changes, state policies, and cultural ideologies. Their novels are really about a nation in the process of becoming.

The most daunting task for English-language writers is of finding their real ethnocentric voices in a colonial language with 'built-in' historical, cultural, and aesthetic assumptions, and associations with the imperial centre, and of transforming this language "to bear the burden of their experience" (Achebe 1975: 62). Some have to find recourse in their own cultural and spiritual heritage which is often, ironically, older than the European tradition. Many create their own imagery, symbols, and myths.

This process of transformation is called 'domesticating' or 'Malaysianising' the English language to "convey in a language that is not one's own, the spirit that is one's own" (Rao 1938: vii). It is, as Wong Phui Nam puts it, "the wiping away of 'the sweet incense that hangs upon the boughs' on a summer night or the colour and movement of daffodils from the word 'flower' and putting in their place the rude, odourless, and pendulous beauty of the hibiscus" (Wong 1991: 175). The act of emptying a sign of its cultural content is, in itself, an awesome but commendable task; although, to have "full many a hibiscus born to blush unseen and waste its sweetness in the desert air" can be quite tiresome if not handled with care.

To overcome an over-dependence on the English tradition, writers like K.S. Maniam, Lloyd Fernando, and Lee Kok Liang either return to the spirituality of their own pre-colonial cultures or create and develop their own symbols and myths. In *The Return,* for example, K.S. Maniam draws his imagery and symbolism from Indian philosophy and Hinduism. The Indian immigrant's struggle to adapt to a new life is cumulatively expressed in the symbolism of a grafted culture and rituals, as the following passage demonstrates:

> He fashioned his own urns, lamps, jars, and statues with many arms and faces, out of the clay he brought from the river. Sitting on the map he had woven from lallang and wild reeds that grew near the river, he began to chant in a garbled language. It embarrassed me to hear him recite a rhythm mounted on Tamil, Malay and even Chinese words [...]. (Maniam 1981: 100)

By contrast, Lloyd Fernando, in *Scorpion Orchid,* develops his own religious symbolism. He creates the enigmatic figure of Tok Said who appears differently to different people: as Indian/Hindu priest, Malay/Muslim medicine man, Chinese/Buddhist medium, and as Christian/Eurasian. Tok Said, as a racial fusion, is used to project a need for multiracial Malaysian society to be united at a deeper spiritual level than the fragile and shallow camaraderie of the four multi-racial protagonists in the novel. As a symbol or a myth of common Malaysian identity, Tok Said is Fernando's argument against racial loyalties that seem to obstruct integration.

What is also interesting about *Scorpion Orchid* is Fernando's attempt to integrate local Malay folklore into his fiction. This can be seen in the meaningful juxtaposition of a passage from *Sejarah Melayu* (*Malay Annals*), written in the sixteenth century, with contemporary discourse, to show parallel incidents that both demand an answer to the question "Do you want to join the new society or not?"

If mythic power is lacking in Malaysian literature in English, it is not because a local indigenous tradition or history does not exist. Fernando asked, in a paper delivered in 1969, why local writers of literature in English shouldn't re-examine this deep and varied past and put it to fresh purposes. Part of *Scorpion Orchid's* freshness is the use of indigenous history to remind us that there was, and could be, a history independent of, and outside, European history, whether or not the telling of it follows the conventions of Western historiography. It is writers like Fernando and Maniam who, both despite and because of their misgivings and problems, have developed, enriched, and charted the direction of Malaysian Literature in English. It is an act of commitment to the new society that is multiracial and multilingual, and "to one's cultural roots and the past without also or necessarily, committing oneself to the ancestral homelands of one's origin" (Quayum and Wicks 2001:164).

Some problems, especially on a national scale, take a long time to work themselves out. On Malaysia's long-distance run as a nation, circumstances and priorities change and we must brace ourselves to confront each reality and absorb its effect as it comes, with faith and commitment. Perhaps what will redefine our society is not the destination, but the journey. We have experienced ambushes in the past, such as that of 13 May 1969, that changed the course of our history. We will no doubt experience other surprises along the way. Right now, we are grappling with the imperatives of globalization that are fast making English-proficiency a matter of necessity. Public statements about it are made by policy-makers every other day, in the same breath as they claim the ills of globalization. The winds of change are a-blowing and official language policies are shifting, yet again, to take the blows. For example, the Private Higher Educational Institutions Act 1996 now allows for courses to be taught in the English language in the private institutions, to the consternation of nationalists who see it as a betrayal of the spirit of the National Language Act of 1967. They say that the 1996 Act has created a dual system of tertiary education, one in the national language, the other in English, as represented by eleven Malay-medium public universities on the one hand and, on the other, the more than six hundred English-medium private university colleges. In a way, the English language has come full circle. It looks as if history has repeated itself, only this time the British can no longer be blamed.

Other indicators from the Ministry of Education, of the 'second coming', include the introduction of the Malaysian University English

Test (MUET) as a prerequisite for entering local universities; the inclusion of literature in English as a compulsory component in the English language papers for the secondary school curriculum, the inclusion of literary passages in English in the SPM English paper 1119 and, more recently, the change of medium of instruction from Malay to English for mathematics and science in schools.

What this means to literature written in English is that a potential pool of English-speaking readers is now in the making. This is in addition to the large number of young Malaysians who, since the early 1990s, have been returning home from universities in English-speaking countries like Australia, New Zealand, Britain, Canada, and the USA. Some of them, including the beneficiaries of the post-May 13th New Economic Policy, are now actively engaged in the writing and publication of creative writings in English. This multi-ethnic mix of writers is now taking over where the older generation left off, replacing earlier issues of immigrant consciousness with a wider spread of contemporary problems associated with modernity. English-language theatre is now, for instance, the in-thing in cosmopolitan areas like Kuala Lumpur and Penang, for the yuppies of middle and upper-middle class background. The old elitism is, of course, still there although contemporary Malaysian writing in English is certainly more cross-cultural and inter-communal than that of the preceding generation.

As a result of all these changes, English-language writings are now finding their legitimate places in the school and university curricula. Both Maniam and Fernando are now part of the staple diet for students at 'O' and 'A' Levels. Malaysian literature in English as a course or even as a programme has been running in public universities for some years now.

For the contribution of English-language writers who have walked the mile with us, we are indeed very grateful that they did not leave us.

Bibliography

Achebe, Chinua. 1975. *Morning Yet On Creation Day*. New York: Doubleday.
Ee, Tiang Hong. 1979. 'Malaysian Poetry In English: Influence and "Independence"' in *Pacific Quarterly* 1(4): 69-73.
Fernando, Lloyd. 1976. *Scorpion Orchid*. Kuala Lumpur: Heinemann.
- - -. 1993. *Green is the Colour*. Singapore: Landmark Books.
Maniam, K.S. 1981. *The Return*. Kuala Lumpur: Heinemann.
- - -. 1993. *In a Far Country*. Kuala Lumpur: Skoob Books.

Quayum, Mohammad A. and Peter C Wicks. 2001. *Malaysian Literature in English: A Critical Reader*. Malaysia: Longman/Pearson Education.
Rao, Raja. 1938. *Kanthapura*. New York: New Directions.
Wong Phui Nam. 1991. 'Out of the Stony .... A Personal Perspective of the Writing of Verse in English in Malaysia' in Edwin Thumboo (ed.), *Perceiving Other Worlds*. Singapore: Times Academic Press: 169-178.
Zawiah Yahya. 1994. *Resisting Colonialist Discourse*. Bangi: Penerbitan UKM.

28

The Cultivation of Exile: Qi Biaojia and his Allegory Mountain

Duncan Campbell

Duncan Campbell was born in New Zealand but spent his childhood in West Africa and the West Indies before being sent 'home' to boarding school. He began his study of Chinese in Malaysia in the 1970s and spent the years 1976-78 in China. Since that time he has taught Chinese language and literature at both the University of Auckland and Victoria University of Wellington, but returns to China as often as he can.

His paper examines the remarkable exile of Qi Biaojia, a senior Chinese official of the mid-seventeenth century. During the late Ming dynasty (1368-1644), as at earlier times in the history of China, exile for members of the literati was often more a matter of self-imposed return to their native place than enforced removal from it, in the hope that estrangement from the power and privileges of office-holding could be compensated for by the opportunity exile provided to read and write. In 1635, with the imperial bureaucracy paralysed by factionalism and the empire itself threatened by internal rebellion and foreign invasion, Qi Biaojia (1602-45) took leave from court and returned to his birthplace of Shanyin in Zhejiang Province. For the next few years he devoted his time and energy to the creation of a garden wherein he housed his immense book collection. A decade later, the Ming dynasty having collapsed and been replaced by the Qing, he chose to commit suicide in the lake within his garden rather than face pressure to take up office again under the new and 'foreign' political order. Making use of both Qi Biaojia's celebrated account of the construction of his garden ('Footnotes to Allegory Mountain') and his diaries covering this period of his life, this paper discusses the uses to which he put his self-imposed exile and the twinned joy and pain that it afforded him.

「子曰：『君子之道或出或處或默或語』」《易．繫辭》¹

Allegory Garden

A scene of desolation now this garden of old,
My sense of loss redoubled as I visit it again.
Throughout the garden, *prunus* buds burst into whiteness,
Along both banks the willows unfurl their greenness.
In clumps the fragrant grasses grow anew,
And here and there gushing springs begin to sing.
When the nightjar's call hastens on the fall of day,
I linger still beside the bright moon's rays.

Shang Jinglan 商景蘭 (1604-ca. 1680) (Qi Biaojia 1960: 268)

Exile and its representation, in China's literary and artistic traditions, are freighted, both traditionally and still to this day, with a special resonance. In keeping with both the longevity and the sophistication of China's political culture, the possibility of exile has spanned a broad but well-defined spectrum ranging from reclusion (both major and minor) ² to enforced or self-imposed exile to permanent banishment beyond the pale of the civilised Chinese world but, traditionally, always within the borders of the Chinese political order.³ Each choice – if choice there were – obviously had its own terrible price to pay, its own particular burden to bear. At the same time, removal, whether from the court or from one's native place, whether by volition or by imperial sanction, often presented China's literary elite with a range of possibilities and alternative paths towards immortality.

"The things of this world sing out only when in a state of disequilibrium", claimed the great Tang dynasty intellectual Han Yu 韓愈(768-824), a man who knew a thing or two about exile (Han Yu 1986: 233). Indeed, if, in the words of David Hawkes, Qu Yuan's 屈原 (c. 340-278 BCE) "despairing cry" from exile signals "the birth of literature" in China (Hawkes 1985: 68), then the received poetic traditions of ancient China, in particular, would be all but inconceivable without reference to the exilic conditions which occasioned much of its bulk.

It was not just the Chinese poetic voice that flowed from such terrible circumstances; in an example that is more directly germane to the protagonist of my paper, that protean figure Su Shi 蘇軾 (1037-1101) claims that it was during his two periods of exile (to Huangzhou between 1080-84 and to Lingnan between 1094 and 1100) that he completed his commentaries on the *Book of Changes*, the *Book of Documents*, and the *Analects* of Confucius. In a letter written during the last year of his life, Su Shi states that only when he thinks of these three commentaries, the last of which, sadly, is no longer extant, does he "feel this life has not been lived in vain. Nothing else is worth mentioning" (Bol 1992: 282).

If it was to the classics that Chinese men of letters such as Su Shi turned for guidance in times of personal or political crisis, it is not always in written texts alone that we find evidence of their solutions to the dilemmas they faced. Such meditations on disequilibrium could also be embodied in particular designed landscapes, inscribed with mountains and rivers, rocks and trees.

In the confused and often dangerous late-Ming dynasty political order, if the choices before the fall of the dynasty in 1644, described as the most cataclysmic dynastic transition in Chinese history, [4] seemed complex, then the choices afterwards, depending on those made earlier, were often stark: suicide or lasting infamy.

Qi Biaojia 祁彪佳 (1602-45)[5] was one such man born into this disordered age, in his case to one of the wealthiest and most socially prestigious families of one of the wealthiest and most prestigious regions of Southern China. For a while, during the late despairing years of the Ming dynasty, he held some of the most important posts at the Court in Peking. In 1634, tiring of the factionalism that had crippled the bureaucracy, he retired to his hometown of Shanyin 山陰 (present day Shaoxing 紹興) in Zhejiang Province, to care for his aged mother, he claimed, and to study under the philosopher Liu Zongzhou 劉宗周 (1578-1645), [6] one of the most thoroughgoing Confucian moralists of the age. Whilst thus in self-imposed exile, however, Qi Biaojia also indulged his self-confessed obsession for the mountains and the rivers (*shanshuipi* 山水癖)[7] by building himself a large and most elaborate garden wherein to house his family's enormous book collection, [8] expending much of his family's fortunes in the process. This garden was named Allegory Mountain, and Qi wrote a wonderful account, entitled 'Footnotes to Allegory Mountain' (hereafter, 'Footnotes'), of both the design of the garden and the process of its construction (Qi Biaojia 1960: 150-70). [9] Just as his garden was a complex one, so is his representation of it multi-layered and susceptible to a variety of readings. With reference to the theme of this volume, and on the basis of a translation of this text that I produced some years ago (Campbell 1999: 243-71), I want to suggest one particular understanding of both Qi Biaojia's garden and his representation of it.

On a certain level, I suppose, all gardens, especially once they become more than simply economic units perhaps, acquire levels of metaphoric meaning. Most frequently, these meanings relate to a desired and perfected world; the etymology of the English word 'paradise', after all, is an Old Persian word (*pairidaeza*) meaning an enclosed park or orchard. For Qi Biaojia, Allegory Mountain provided, in part at least, a simulacrum of the perfect order that he had sought so long and hard, albeit unsuccessfully, to bring about through his efforts at Court. As such, his representation of it, if not entirely the garden itself, makes explicit reference to the text that had been so crucial to Su Shi during his first period of exile, the *Book of Changes*.[10] For one thing, although we know from his diaries that the garden contained more vistas than those Qi Biaojia chose to take us to in his 'Footnotes', he includes accounts of only forty-nine such vistas. As the *Book of Changes* states, in reference to the number of yarrow stalks employed in the process of divination: "The number of the total is fifty. Of these, forty-nine are used. They are divided into two portions, to represent the three powers" (Wilhelm 1968: 310).[11] The garden, in Qi Biaojia's representation of it, is to this extent best understood therefore as an embodiment in miniature of the entirety of the cosmos and its normative moral order.[12] Secondly, it is to his Abode for the Study of the *Book of Changes* that Qi Biaojia conducts us first on our tour of the garden, once we have passed through the main gate and made our way along Water Bright Gallery. Here is his account of this site:

Abode for the Study of the *Book of Changes*

Of the many fine features of Allegory Garden it is the rocks that prove most excellent, but it is not the rocks alone that embody the excellence of the garden. Once a rock is placed in the midst of water, even the most recalcitrant of them seems to acquire a divine intelligence.[13] And it is only from my Abode for the Study of the *Book of Changes* that this perfect marriage between rock and water can be observed to full advantage.[14] The abode overlooks the eastern corner of Asymmetrical Pond and stands across the water from the Hall of My Four Unfulfilled Obligations. As one raises one's eyes upwards or stares downwards, the sky and the pond present a seamless flow of purity and one feels a profound affinity for the birds and fishes.[15] When along the bank the lamps are lit, their inverted reflections dance enticingly upon the surface of the water, and when the strings and flutes strike up their tunes seem driven across the surface of the pond like waves of snow. It is at times such as this that I feel the scene before me to have been Heaven sent. And when the Master of the garden becomes wearied of the sights of his garden he spends his days with a copy of the *Book of Changes* in hand; painstakingly he works his way through the text, achieving in the process a sense of release from the vexations of life. Although my family has specialised in the exegesis of this classic for generations, I am as yet incapable of fully understanding its principles of change. I have managed to develop an inkling of the Way of waxing and waning, however, of the ebb and flow of the cosmos. This mountain has existed for as long as Heaven and Earth themselves. Before the present moment, it was no more than a tiny mound of earth. How can one guarantee that, sometime in the future, these arrayed pavilions and storied studios will stand tall yet upon these sheer cliffs and here within this secluded valley? Nothing is spared Heaven and Earth's determination of its fate. How silly of Li Deyu of the Tang dynasty who, when demoted and in exile at Red Cliff in Canton, wrote to his sons so assiduously, instructing them to seek to preserve every stone and every leaf of his Peaceful Springs Garden. Had he forgotten the fate of the Golden Valley and Flowery Grove gardens?[16] Where are they today? And thus does the Master have an inkling of the truth, taking joy in those pleasures afforded us in this present life and caring not a jot for what might become of this garden in the future. (Campbell 1999: 248; Qi Biaojia 1960: 152)

This level of philosophic distance from the world around him proved a short-lived consolation for Qi Biaojia, however, and just across Asymmetrical Pond stood a structure that perhaps better embodies the anxieties that characterise Qi's attempt to exile himself from that world; the Hall of My Four Unfulfilled Obligations, the forty-eighth site that he leads us to:

Hall of My Four Unfulfilled Obligations:

Within my Farm of Abundance stands a three-columned hall, overlooking the flowing water, as if its wings outspread. Here the Master of the Garden raises his silkworms and stores his grain. Here, occasionally, too he entertains his guests with wine served in finest rhinoceros-shaped goblets. I happened at the time to have taken as my teacher Master Wang Chaoshi. [17] He took grave issue with my obsession with the construction of my garden and upbraided me in a letter, in the following manner:

Recently I took a look at your garden and found that it embodied four unfulfilled obligations, three of which are failings on your part, and one on mine.

Great has been the favour bestowed upon you by the state. You ought to be considering how you can show yourself worthy of such favour. Even though you have retired to the countryside, you ought nonetheless to be discussing the Way and thinking about the great profession, each day deliberating how you may restore to their glory the gods of the grains and the soil, and confer benefits to the common folk. But for the past two years that you have been here, far from concerning yourself with such matters, you have simply devoted yourself to the construction of your garden, with carving and engraving, with flowers and rocks. In order to display your mastery of such petty skills, you have neglected the Grand Scheme of things as far as your state goes. If everyone were to be like you, what then could the state rely upon? This then can be said to be the manner in which you have failed to fulfil your obligation to the sovereign.

Your revered father long cleaved true to the Way, and was also conversant with the Buddhist scriptures. He purchased more than 10,000 books and entrusted them to the care of his sons and grandsons. To bring glory to the illustrious example of one's parents is a matter for the progeny of such parents. You are today approaching your fortieth year, the age at which you should be without doubt,[18] and you have served in the past in the post of censor. The requirement to establish yourself and implement the Way does not change with the circumstances of the times. But of such a determination I can observe no evidence and all you seem capable of is following the precedent set by your forebears, but with even greater flourish than they. How can such behaviour be regarded as an expression of the filial piety expected of you? In this way, you can be said to have failed to fulfil your obligation to your father.

You are blessed with heaven given talents and a quick intelligence, by nature you are loyal and upright. Your attributes are such that you could have become a mentor who benefits the age, an effective vessel of the Way. At the same time, your fortunate destiny is such that you enjoy the pleasures of friends and teachers and without having to quit your home you could have followed in the footsteps of the sages of old, if only you had devoted yourself to such an effort. On the contrary, however, far from cherishing your considerable abilities, you have associated with vulgar types and have pursued this particular task. Word of your efforts has spread to all four quarters, earning you the awe of mere boys and girls everywhere. You pay no heed to the frowns of those intent upon the Way, casting your pearls amongst the worthless potsherds and allowing your fine fields to become overgrown with weeds. In this respect you can be said to have failed to fulfil your obligation to yourself.

If you are guilty of having not fulfilled these three obligations, then I for my part should have repaid the affection you have shown me with some straight talking in order to nip your enterprise off in its bud. This I have failed to

> do, vainly hoping now to remedy the situation with my present remonstrance, once the deed has already been done. I regret that I have been remiss in my effort to rectify myself, and I am ashamed that nor have I been able to provide you with an appropriate role model. In this way I may be said to have failed to fulfil my obligation of friendship.[19]

Alas! What excellent counsel this is! How very fortunate I am to have been the recipient of such excellent counsel. Of all the criticism of the error of my ways I have received since I embarked upon the construction of my garden, only these words have served to cut to the quick. Having been counselled in this manner, I have nonetheless been unable to act like Wang Jian who destroyed his Studio of the Long Beams as soon as his uncle criticised it for its lavishness, and this exacerbates my failing. The Master has accused me of failing to fulfil three obligations. This accusation I readily accept. Having heard his counsel and having proven incapable of changing my ways, this may be said to be a failure to fulfil the obligation of friendship on my part, not his. I have named this place the Hall of My Four Unfulfilled Obligations in order to record my remorse and my intention to reform myself. (Campbell 1999: 262-63; Qi Biaojia 1960: 168-69)

For a brief moment, then, Qi Biaojia's garden served both to embody the dilemma he faced and to offer him, through a process of self-cultivation and contemplation – the traditional alternative to taking office – a resolution of the crisis he faced. But of course, just as the walls of his garden had failed to keep out the stream of unwanted guests that distracted him from his books, so too did they prove ineffectual in the face of events elsewhere. As the "halfway house on [his] pilgrimage [...] [as] the setting for [his] dreams [...] [the garden became] also the site of ruin and desolation" (Minford 1998: 260).[20] Regular reports of the collapse of the Ming political order continued to reach him, seeping through the porous walls of his enclosed garden and breaching its symbolic order.[21] When the death of his mother in 1644 finally released him from his filial obligations, Qi Biaojia took up office again, and after the fall of Beijing and the suicide of the Chongzhen Emperor, news of which reached Qi as he made his way to the Southern Capital, he was appointed Governor of Suzhou.[22] Factional infighting in the court of the Prince of Lu soon enforced his retirement once more, however, and he returned to Shanyin. Facing increasing pressure to accept office under the new dynasty, Qi Biaojia appears to have believed that he had little alternative but to end his life a martyr. The official history of the period records his demise in the following manner:

In the 5th month of the next year [1645] the Southern Capital was lost, and by the 6th month, Hangzhou too, in turn, had fallen. [Qi] Biaojia thereupon began his fast. On the 4th day of the succeeding intercalary month, having told his family that he was going to repair early to his bedchamber, he proceeded to his lake wherein he sat bolt upright and awaited his death. He was 44 years old. (Zhang Tingyu et al. 1974: 7054)

There is a record of his last conversation with one of his sons. A relaxed smile on his lips, he turned to him and said: "Although your father did not fail in his family duties, I was however somewhat too addicted to the springs and the rocks. I was lavish in constructing my garden and this was my failing" (Qi Biaojia 1960: 252). He was buried within his garden, in a coffin that he had already prepared for himself. In his will, written shortly before he made his way from Jar Hideaway toward Asymmetrical Lake, he asked that Allegory Mountain be made over to the care of the local temple to provide, he says, the living for a number of Chanist monks. A final annotation to his diary reads: "My grandfather's diary ends on this day. During the 5th watch of the 6th day, he died a martyr" (Qi Biaojia 1991: 1447).

Notes

[1] A literal translation of this, the "Attached Verbalisation" to Hexagram # 13 ("Tongren" 同人 [Fellowship with Men]), might read: "The Master said: 'Such is the Way of the Superior Man that he either goes out [and takes office] or he remains at home [and does not], that he remains silent or that he speaks up'". *The I Ching or Book of Changes*, tr. Richard Wilhelm, rendered into English by Cary F. Baynes (London: Routledge & Kegan Paul, 1968) 305-06, provides this suggestive reading: "The Master said:/ Life leads the thoughtful man on a path of many windings./ Now the course is checked, now it runs straight again./ Here winged thoughts may pour freely forth in words,/ There the heavy burden of knowledge must be shut away in silence".

[2] The secondary literature on reclusion is extensive; for recent studies, see Aat Vervoon, 1990. *Men of the Cliffs and Caves: The Development of the Chinese Eremitic Traditions to the End of the Han Dynasty* (Hong Kong: The Chinese University of Hong Kong); and both Alan Berkowitz, 'Topos and Entelechy in the Ethos of Reclusion in China', *Journal of the American Oriental Society* (1994), 114(4): 632-38 and his *The Practice and Portrayal of Reclusion in Early Medieval China* (Stanford: Stanford University Press, 2000). On that most iconic of poetic recluses, Tao Qian (365-427), see A.R. Davis, 'The Narrow Lane: Some Observations on the Recluse in Traditional Chinese Society', *East Asian History* (1996), 11: 33-44.

[3] Interestingly, the modern Chinese poet and historian Wen Yiduo 聞一多 (1899-1946), a man steeped in China's classical poetic traditions, highlights what can be understood as a disjunctive moment in China's exilic traditions in a letter addressed to his friend Liang Shiqiu written shortly before returning to China from his studies in Chicago:

"Living abroad is like being exiled to a frontier region", for which see Wang-chi Wong, "'I am a Prisoner in Exile'": Wen Yiduo in the United States', in Gregory B. Lee, (ed.), *Chinese Writing and Exile,* Select Papers Vol. 7, The Centre for East Asian Studies (Chicago: The University of Chicago Press, 1993) 19, 34. Here, Wen Yiduo seems to be picking up on a connection made by late Qing dynasty officials dispatched on embassies abroad between exile and travel beyond the borders of the Chinese political order, for which see Qian Zhongshu 錢鍾書, 'Han yi diyishou yingyu shi "Renshengsong" ji youguan er san shi' 漢譯第一首英語詩《人生頌》及有關二三事 [Longfellow's 'A Psalm of Life' – The First English Poem Translated into Chinese – and Several Other Related Matters], *Qizhui ji* 七綴集 (Shanghai: Guji chubanshe, 1985) 130-31. The post-1989 growth of mainland diasporic Chinese communities throughout the world, with the consequent expansion of the Chinese linguistic world and the partial resinification of the historic overseas Chinese communities, represents perhaps another disjunctive moment in this tradition of reclusion and exile.

[4] Ho Koon-piu, for example, argues that the Ming-Qing transition, which he dates as between 1628-1722, "was marked by the greatest number of scholar-officials dying as martyrs for their dynasty", for which see his 'Should We Die as Martyrs to the Ming Cause? Scholar-Officials' Views on Martyrdom During the Ming-Qing Transition', *Oriens Extremus* (1994), 37(2): 123.

[5] For short English-language biographies of Qi Biaojia, see the note on him appended to the biography of his father Qi Chenghan (1568-1628) in L. Carrington Goodrich & Chaoying Fang, (eds) (1970), *Dictionary of Ming Biography, 1368-1644* (New York & London: Columbia University Press) 1: 216-20; and A.W. Hummel, (ed.) (1943), *Eminent Chinese of the Ch'ing Period, 1644-1912* (Washington: Government Printing Office) 126. More recently, on Qi Biaojia's philanthropic activities, see Joanna F. Handlin Smith, 'Opening and Closing a Dispensary in Shan-yin County: Some Thoughts about Charitable Associations, Organizations, and Institutions in Late Ming China', *Journal of the Economic and Social History of the Orient* (1995), 38(3): 371-92; on his garden, see Joanna F. Handlin Smith, 'Gardens in Ch'i Piao-chia's Social World: Wealth and Values in Late-Ming Kiangnan', *The Journal of Asian Studies* (1992), 51(2): 55-81; for a translation of his celebrated account of the construction of this garden, see Duncan Campbell, tr., 'Footnotes to Allegory Mountain', *Studies in the History of Gardens and Designed Landscapes* (1999), 19(3/4): 243-71; Dorothy Ko, *Teachers of the Inner Chambers: Women and Culture in Seventeenth-Century China* (Stanford, California: Stanford University Press, 1994) 226-32, has a discussion of Qi Biaojia's wife Shang Jinglan. This paper is based in part on a reading of Qi Biaojia's fourteen diaries covering the period from the 29th day of the 7th month of the 4th year of the reign of the Chongzhen Emperor (1631) to the 4th day of the 6th month of the *Yiyou* year (1645) (listed in the Bibliography), the manuscripts of which are photomechanically reproduced in *Qi Biaojia wengao* 祁彪佳文稿 (Beijing: Shumu wenxian chubanshe, 1991) 2: 921-1447.

[6] For a short biography of this man, see A.W. Hummel, ed., *Eminent Chinese of the Ch'ing Period, 1644-1912*, 532-33. For discussions of his philosophic contributions, see Tang Chun-i, 'Liu Tsung-chou's Doctrine of Moral Mind and Practice and His Critique of Wang Yangming', in Wm. Theodore De Bary, ed. (1975), *The Unfolding of Neo-Confucianism* (New York & London: Columbia University Press) 305-31.

[7] On the concept of 'obsession' in Chinese culture, and its intensification during the late Ming period, see Judith T. Zeitlin, 'The Petrified Heart: Obsession in Chinese

Literature, Art, and Medicine', *Late Imperial China* (1991), 12(1): 1-26; and the
chapter dealing with this topic in her subsequent book *Historian of the Strange: Pu
Songling and the Chinese Classical Tale* (Stanford, California: Stanford University
Press, 1993). For a more recent treatment, see Wai-yee Li, 'The Collector, the
Connoisseur, and Late-Ming Sensibility', *T'oung Pao* (1995), 81(4-5): 269-302.

[8] After Qi Biaojia's death, the break up of his library and the disposition of the books
that it had once contained was to occasion one of the most notorious disputes of the
early Qing period, that between the two Ming loyalist scholars Huang Zongxi 黃宗羲
(1610-95) and Lü Liuliang 呂留良 (1629-83), for which see Tom Fisher, 'Loyalist
Alternatives in the Early Ch'ing', *Harvard Journal of Asiatic Studies* (1984), 44 (1):
83-122.

[9] Qi Biaojia seems to have begun his account of his garden late in the 9th year of the
reign of the Chongzhen Emperor (1636) ('Linju shibi', *Qi Biaojia wengao*, 2: 1062).
His diaries show that he worked intensively upon it during the 4th and 5th months of
the next year, at the same time that he was reading both Wang Shizhen's (1526-1590)
'Record of My Mount Yan Garden' and Li Daoyuan's (d. 527) *Footnotes to the
Classic of the Waterways*, finishing it on the 21st day of the 5th month ('Shanju
zhuolu', *Qi Biaojia wengao*, 2: 1085-87). Having circulated the manuscript among
friends, Qi made some changes before having it copied and sent for printing ('Shanju
zhuolu', *Qi Biaojia wengao*, 2: 1095). By this time the text had acquired its present
title. Construction of the garden continued of course, and in his diaries Qi Biaojia
speaks of having a friend put the finishing touches to a text entitled 'More Footnotes
to Allegory Mountain' ('Zijian lu', *Qi Biaojia wengao*, 2: 1127). It appears that this
text is no longer extant.

[10] Peter Bol argues that Su Shi's commentary on the *Book of Changes*, as well as
providing a means to "correct the mistakes of past and present" and to "bring benefit
to the age", was also intended as his "account of himself", a way for others to know
him, for which see his 'Su Shi and Culture', in Kidder Smith, Jr., Peter K. Bol, Joseph
A. Adler & Don J. Wyatt, eds., *Sung Dynasty Uses of the I Ching* (Princeton, New
Jersey: Princeton University Press, 1990), 56.

[11] On this aspect of Qi Biaojia's garden, see Cao Shujuan 曹淑娟, 'Meng jue jie yu –
"Yushan zhu" de yuanlin quanshi xitong' 夢覺皆寓 -《寓山注》的園林詮釋係統, *Taida
zhongwen xuebao* 臺大中文學報 (2001), 15: 193-240. I am indebted to Alison Hardie
for bringing this article to my attention.

[12] On this tradition, see Edward H. Schafer, 'Cosmos in Miniature: The Tradition of
the Chinese Garden', *Landscape* (1963), 12 (3): 24-26.

[13] For a discussion of these two categories of rock, see Jing Wang, *The Story of Stone:
Intertextuality, Ancient Chinese Stone Lore, and the Stone Symbolism of* Dream of the
Red Chamber, Water Margin, *and* The Journey to the West (Durham & London: Duke
University Press, 1992), especially 193-98. More generally, see John Hay, *Kernels of
Energy, Bones of Earth: The Rock in Chinese Art* (New York: China House Gallery,
China Institute in America, 1985); and Edward Schafer, *Tu Wan's Stone Catalogue of
Cloudy Forest* (Berkeley & Los Angeles: University of California Press, 1961).

[14] This alludes to a passage from the *Shishuo xinyu* 世說新語 which, in Richard
Mather's translation (*Shih-shuo Hsin-yü: A New Account of Tales of the World*
(Minneopolis: University of Minnesota Press, 1976), 402; romanisation altered), goes:
"When Sun Chu was young he wanted to become a recluse. Speaking of it once to
Wang Ji, he intended to say, 'I'll pillow my head on the rocks and rinse my mouth in

the streams'. Instead, he said by mistake, 'I'll rinse my mouth with rocks and pillow my head on the streams'. Wang asked, 'Are streams something you can pillow on, and rocks something you can rinse with?' Sun replied, 'My reason for pillowing on streams is to 'wash my ears', and my reason for rinsing with rocks is to 'sharpen my teeth''''..

[15] This appears to be a conflation of two allusions; the first to that passage from the 'The Great Treatise' attached to the *Yi jing* that goes: "Looking upward, we contemplate with its [the *Yi jing*] help the signs in the heavens; looking down, we examine the lines of the earth. Thus we come to know the circumstances of the dark and the light. Going back to the beginnings of things and pursuing them to the end, we come to know the lessons of birth and of death…". (*The I Ching or Book of Changes*, 294); the second from the 'Autumn Floods' chapter of the *Zhuangzi* which goes: "Zhuangzi and Huizi were strolling along the dam of the Hao River when Zhuangzi said, 'See how the minnows come out and dart around where they please! That's what fish really enjoy!' Huizi said, 'You're not a fish - how do you know what fish enjoy?' Zhuangzi said, 'You're not I, so how do you know I don't know what fish enjoy?' Huizi said, 'I'm not you, so I certainly don't know what you know. On the other hand, you're certainly not a fish - so that still proves you don't know what fish enjoy!' Zhuangzi said, 'Let's go back to your original question, please. You asked me *how* I know what fish enjoy - so you already knew I knew it when you asked the question. I know it by standing here beside the Hao'". (See Burton Watson, tr., *Chuang Tzu: Basic Writings* (New York & London: Columbia University Press, 1964), 110; romanisation altered).

[16] Two famous gardens of old, the first built by Shi Chong of the Jin dynasty, and the latter an imperial garden sited in Luoyang and given this name during the Three Kingdoms period.

[17] On Wang Chaoshi 王朝式 (1603-40), another disciple of Liu Zongzhou, see He Guanbiao (Ho Koon Piu) 何冠彪, 'Wan Ming lixuejia san kao' 晚明理學家三考, *Ming Qing renwu yu zhushu* 明清人物與著述 [Personages and Writings in Ming-Qing China], Asian Studies Series # 6 (Hong Kong: Hong Kong Educational Publishing, 1996), 39-43.

[18] A reference to *Lunyu*, II.iv: "The Master said: 'At fifteen, I set my mind upon learning. At thirty, I took my stand. At forty, I had no doubts. At fifty, I knew the will of Heaven. At sixty, my ear was attuned. At seventy, I follow all the desires of my heart without breaking any rule'". (See Simon Leys, tr., *The Analects of Confucius* (New York & London: W.W. Norton, 1997, 6).

[19] In his diary, Qi Biaojia records receiving this letter on the 20th day of the 2nd month of the 10th year of the reign of the Chongzhen Emperor (1637), see 'Shanju zhuolu', *Qi Biaojia wengao*, 2: 1076. "His letter put me in quite a funk for the rest of the day", he tells us. On a visit to the garden the next day, Qi Biaojia decides to build a hall within his Farm of Abundance and to give it this name, in order, he says, "to record the error of my ways".

[20] Minford is here speaking about Prospect Garden, the focus of so much of the action of the novel *The Story of the Stone*.

[21] On this most dramatic of dynastic transitions from Ming to Qing, see Lynn A. Struve, *The Southern Ming, 1644-1662* (New Haven & London: Yale University Press, 1984); and her similarly entitled chapter in Frederick W. Mote & Denis Twitchett, eds., *The Cambridge History of China: Volume 7, The Ming Dynasty, 1368-1644, Part 1* (Cambridge: Cambridge University Press, 1988), 641-725.

[22] On the important role that Qi Biaojia played in attempting to pacify the countryside around the Southern Capital, see Jerry Dennerline, 'Hsü Tu and the Lesson of Nanking: Political Integration and the Local Defense in Chiang-nan, 1634-1645', in Jonathan D. Spence & John E. Wills, Jr., (eds), *From Ming to Ch'ing: Conquest, Region, and Continuity in Seventeenth-Century China* (New Haven & London: Yale University Press, 1979), 89-132.

Bibliography

Bol, Peter K. 1992. *"This Culture of Ours": Intellectual Transitions in T'ang and Sung China.* Stanford: Stanford University Press.
Campbell, Duncan. 1999. 'Qi Biaojia's "Footnotes to Allegory Mountain": Introduction and Translation' in *Studies in the History of Gardens & Designed Landscapes.* 19 (3/4): 243-71.
Han Yu. 1986. 'Song Meng Dongye xu' 送孟東野序 [Preface Sent to Meng Jiao] in *Han Changli wenji jiaozhu* 韓昌黎文集校注 (Shanghai: Guji chubanshe).
Hawkes, David, (ed. and tr.).1985. *The Songs of the South: An Ancient Chinese Anthology of Poems by Qu Yuan and Other Poets.* Harmondsworth: Penguin.
Minford, John. 1998. 'The Chinese Garden: Death of a Symbol' in *Studies in the History of Gardens & Designed Landscapes* 18 (3): 257-68
Qi Biaojia. 1960. *Qi Biaojia ji* 祁彪佳集. Beijing: Zhonghua shuju.
- - - . 1991. 'Qi Zhongmin gong riji' 祁忠敏公日記 in *Qi Biaojia wengao* 祁彪佳文稿 Beijing: Shumu wenxian chubanshe 2, containing:

1. 'She bei chengyan' 涉北程言 [Chronological Report of My Excursion North] [Chongzhen 4 (1631): 29th day 7th month – 30th day 12th month]: 921-39.

2. 'Xi bei rongyan (shang)' 棲北冗言（上）[Miscellaneous Report of My Stay in the North: Part One]
[Chongzhen 5 (1632): 1st day 1st month – 30th day 6th month]: 940-64.
'Xi bei rongyan (xia)' 棲北冗言（下）[Miscellaneous Report of My Stay in the North: Part Two]
[Chongzhen 5 (1632): 1st day 7th month – 29th day 12th month]: 965-91.

3. 'Yi nan suoji' 役南瑣記 [Occasional Record of My Service in the South]
[Chongzhen 6 (1633): 1st day 5th month – 4th day 6th month]: 992-1010.
[Supplement: 'Xun Wu sheng lu' 巡吳省錄 [A Brief Record of My Tour of Wu]
[Chongzhen 7 (1634): 11th day 6th month – 16th day 6th month]: 1010-11.

4. 'Gui nan kuailu' 歸南快錄 [A Joyous Account of My Return to the South]
[Chongzhen 8 (1635): 9th day 4th month – 30th day 12th month]: 1012-1038.

5. 'Linju shibi' 林居適筆 [Occasional Jottings from My Sojourn in the Woods]
[Chongzhen 9 (1636): 1st day 1st month – 30th day 12th month]: 1039-70.

6. 'Shanju zhuolu' 山居拙錄 [A Clumsy Account of My Sojourn on the Mountain]
[Chongzhen 10 (1637): 1st day 1st month – 30th day 12th month]: 1071-1108.

7. 'Zijian lu' 自鑒錄 [An Account of My Self-Admonition]

[Chongzhen 11 (1638): 1ˢᵗ day 1ˢᵗ month – 30ᵗʰ day 12ᵗʰ month]: 1109-1142.

8. 'Qi lu' 棄錄 [An Account of My Dissolution]
   [Chongzhen 12 (1639): 1ˢᵗ day 1ˢᵗ month – 30ᵗʰ day 12ᵗʰ month]: 1143-1176.

9. 'Ganmu lu' 感慕錄 [An Account of My Gratitude for Kindness Granted Me]
   [Chongzhen 13 (1640): 1ˢᵗ day 1ˢᵗ month – 30ᵗʰ day 12ᵗʰ month]: 1177-1214.

10. 'Xiaojiu lu' 小捄錄 [An Account of My Small Efforts at Famine Relief]
    [Chongzhen 14 (1641): 1ˢᵗ day 1ˢᵗ month – 29ᵗʰ day 12ᵗʰ month]: 1215-1280.

11. 'Renwu rili' 壬午日曆 [Diary of the Renwu Year]
    [Chongzhen 15 (1642): 1ˢᵗ day 1ˢᵗ month – 30ᵗʰ day 12ᵗʰ month]: 1281-1317.

12. 'Guiwei rili' 癸未日曆 [Diary of the Guiwei Year]
    [Chongzhen 16 (1643): 1ˢᵗ day 1ˢᵗ month – 29ᵗʰ day 12ᵗʰ month]: 1318-1362.

13. 'Jiashen rili' 甲申日曆 [Diary of the Jiashen Year]
    [Chongzhen 17 (1644): 1ˢᵗ day 1ˢᵗ month – 30ᵗʰ day 12ᵗʰ month]: 1363-1423.

14. 'Yiyou rili' 乙酉日曆 [Diary of the Yiyou Year]
    [Yiyou(1645): 1ˢᵗ day 1ˢᵗ month – 4ᵗʰ day 6ᵗʰ month (inter.)]: 1424-1447.

Wilhelm, Richard (ed. and tr.). 1968. *The I Ching or Book of Changes*, rendered into English by Cary F. Baynes. London: Routledge & Kegan Paul.

29

A Sense of Place: Colombian Artists on Violence and Exile

Marta Jimena Cabrera

Marta Jimena Cabrera was born in Bogotá, Colombia. She moved to Australia to undertake a PhD in Cultural Studies at the University of Wollongong. She has returned to live in Bogotá. Her work deals mostly with memory and identity in the field of the visual arts.

In this paper, she examines the response of the latest generation of Colombian artists to the grave socio-political situation of their country. In the past few years around one million Colombians have become internal refugees, fleeing violence and poverty. Such displacement is not entirely new and has, in the past, been addressed by such notable painters as Alejandro Obregon and Fernando Botero. Currently, as the situation has worsened, issues surrounding the disruption of everyday life, brought about by the loss of place, have come to the attention of a new generation of Colombian artists working in other media, including performance artists Maria Teresa Hincapié, sculptor Doris Salcedo, video artist José Alejandro Restrepo, and installation artist Oscar Muñoz. This paper explores the strategies by which contemporary Colombian visual artists address issues of loss, memory, and displacement, bringing these issues into the public sphere and seeking to inscribe them in collective memory.

The displacement of civilians in Colombia as a consequence of violence has a long and convoluted history. My father's family, for instance, was displaced from its province in the 1950s, a period known, appropriately, as *La Violencia*. The family was lucky, not only because they fled before a potential massacre, but also because they were able to go back to their land. Today, however, my father, now retired, is again unable to live on the land he inherited from his father because to do so is still dangerous.

The dynamics of terror have, in fact, shifted since the time of the bipartisan violence of my father's childhood. Besides the army and the guerrillas, the paramilitary and drug traffickers have come to make Colombia's violence an extremely complex phenomenon of decentred repression (with many forces involved), occurring at the intersection of territorial and economic interests, neoliberalism, corruption, and state weakness. The civilian population is forced to flee, not as a mere by-product of armed confrontations between these factions, but rather as the result of direct intimidation, terror, and extortion, as parties to the conflict settle scores by attacking civilians suspected of sympathising with the adversary. Hence, displacement in Colombia must now be seen as a strategy of war aimed at different objectives: the establishment of control over territories, expanded cultivation of illicit crops, or to the seizure of land and private property. In order to save their lives, around three million people have undergone displacement within the country in the last fifteen years, most of them fleeing to the impoverished shantytowns encircling many cities, where they are often even more exposed to crime and violence. As a result of the high level of violence against them, both during and after flight, displaced people are often reluctant to register with authorities or even seek humanitarian assistance. Around half of these are women and children and a disproportionate number of displaced persons are members of minority groups. Although Afro-Colombians make up only sixteen percent of the Colombian population and indigenous people two percent, together they account for more than one-third of all displaced people.

The anger and aspirations of displaced people have been expressed in numerous statements and in testimonies appearing in academic studies on displacement:

> After the killing of several relatives we did not want to leave, so we were threatened again; they returned several times and sprayed the house with bullets, we had to remain under the bed all day. (Alvarez-Correa 1998: 37)

> I don't want to return to my land because of violence. I don't want to remember what happened. (51)

> I'd like to live like I did before, having food, clothes and housing, so as not to feel displaced. (79)

> I'd like to make myself up once in a while, like before, and not remain like I am now [...] without makeup, to put on a good pair of shoes. Like that [...]. (79)

Within this context of ongoing turmoil, violence seems so pervasive that it appears as a mythical force that engulfs everything, as Michael Taussig argues in an essay on Colombia, appropriately entitled 'Terror as Usual':

> Forces become disembodied from social contexts as one enters a world in which things become animated paralleling the impossibly contradictory need to both establish and disestablish a centre, a motive force, or a reason explaining everything. (Taussig 1992: 19)

According to this widespread view, itself a symptom of cultural anaesthesia, Colombia is 'a culture of violence', fated to an endless, inescapable cycle of collective guilt and individual impunity. Such perception has definitely been heightened by the pervasiveness of violence in the media (particularly on television), eroding public sensitivity in the face of extreme acts of violence. In consequence, the visual arts, which actively treated the topic through the 1990s, sought to address violence in fresh ways, that is, by trying to create a mental space for violence to register, a strategy which may or may not involve the use of shocking images.[1]

The initial idea for the present essay came from perceiving remarkable resemblances between two sets of images. The first is a series of photographs of María Teresa Hincapié's 1990 performance *'una cosa es una cosa'* ('a thing is a thing'). In this piece, the artist brought into a museum several bags containing all her household items, except for the furniture. Then, she took everything out and placed every item on the ground, creating a rectangle enclosing her. Next, the items were feverishly organized and re-organized by colour, by their function, or any other criterion over eight hours per day, for two weeks. A short text written by the artist serves to accompany the piece and reinforces its underlying notions of domesticity, ritual, and repetition:

> movement here. then. in the corner. in the centre. on one side. near him. very far. further. very far. very, very far. here are the handbags. here, the pocket. here the bag. here, the box and over it, the pocket. at one side, the box. in the corner, the pocket and the bag; in the centre the paper bags and very near, the box. leakage. dispersion. everything getting empty. everything disappears. everything scatters. disseminates. blends. stops. organise themselves in a cue in a random way. they mark a space. they separate in groups, one beside the other. common groups. where they are similar. because they are white. because they are made up of fabric [...] because they need one another as the toothbrush and toothpaste, but also because the paste is by itself and the toothbrush is with other toothbrushes, or by itself. [...] I, alone. she, alone. we, alone. they, alone. a space alone. a place alone. a line alone [...] everything is alone. all of us are alone. a heap of rice. a heap of sugar. a heap of salt. a heap of wheat. a heap of coffee. a heap of different things. (Hincapié 2000: 155)

In this piece, the repetitious everyday world of women's domestic labour is taken from the private sphere and is inserted into the public sphere of the museum, making the spectator bear witness to domestic experience and legitimising its presence within the public sphere.

Another irruption of the private into the public is present in the other set of images that gave birth to this essay. In this case, however, repetitious domestic daily life has been disrupted by terror and has, therefore, to be replicated in other spaces. The people in these images, having been forcibly displaced from their homes, occupied the headquarters of the International Committee of the Red Cross in Bogotá in 1998 to demand solutions from the national government. Twelve occupations of government offices or public places (with durations of between one day and three months) took place in Bogotá during 1998 (Osorio 2000: 197, note 12). During these occupations, they recreated the domestic space and the rituals of daily life: cooking, washing, sleeping.

Photo: Garry Leach

Hincapié's first performance of *'una cosa es una cosa'*, which took place eight years before these events, was, incidentally, repeated in 1998, suggesting connections between these images that go well beyond mere visual resemblance.

Hincapié's aesthetics of the ordinary, her repetitive action of organising, of making and unmaking a home, restores the sense of order of the world, and conveys the idea of daily ritual, of the sacredness of the everyday, of the sacredness of life, as well as the impossibility of permanently reclaiming a space.[2] Daily ritual continues even if both daily life and daily space have been disrupted by violence, as in the case of displaced communities. As Gaston Bachelard noted in his *Poetics of Space*: 'the house is one of the greatest powers of integration for the thoughts, memories, and dreams of humans, thus a being without a house would be a dispersed body' (Bachelard 1994: 5). For this reason, forceful displacement, along with massacre and disappearance,[3] is an extreme form of violence that fuses at once the fracture of identity, the destruction of the sense of place, marginality, and vulnerability:

> Living on the boundaries of civil society and along the margins of the law, the displaced also endure the consequences of the unequal relations of gender and class to which they are also subject. This is a world pitched between legality and illegality, visibility and invisibility, the public and the private. In a sense, the inhabitants of this world have abandoned their right to difference. They live on the threshold of dispersal and dissolution. It is difficult to give voice even to a residual sense of identity here; but if we can find one at all it might be [the] notion of a 'community of absence' or disavowal, one that is always positioned as an aporia, one that is always already marginalized. (Merewether 1996: 104)

By contrast with Hincapié, video artist José Alejandro Restrepo employs strong images of violence in a well-researched work entwining ethnography, myth, and history in an effort to analyse continuities and discontinuities between different forms of violence. His *Musa Paradisiaca* ('Heavenly Muse', 1994-97) looks at accounts of travel by Europeans in the nineteenth century, at the banana growing process and the violence associated with it, as well as at contemporary economic diplomacy (Herkenhoff 2001: 46). In *Musa Paradisiaca* (the scientific name of the common banana) bunches of bananas, which are deliberately left to rot in the exhibition space, have small television screens attached to the lower end of them playing fragments of news bulletins from Urabá (a banana growing region notorious since 1985 for the massacres of banana plantation workers),[4]

as well as images of a nude couple in a luxuriant natural scene. This
not only suggests links between violence and the idea of an exuberant
and exotic America, both sexually and in nature (Roca 2001: 7), but
also displaces the focus of history to other topics: to desire, to myth, to
war, and, finally, to the senses of the viewer (Gutiérrez 2002).

Indeed, banana plantations have strong connotations, in
Colombian collective memory, of violence and corruption. Gabriel
García Márquez's *A Hundred Years of Solitude* (1967), for instance,
retells the story of the 1928 massacre at the hands of the Colombian
army of a group of striking United Fruit Company workers. More
recently, the banana-growing region has been reinscribed in memory
as a site of violence, via television news which highlights the
involvement of large landowners, banana companies, unions and
workers, and guerrillas and paramilitaries, all set against the backdrop
of tensions imposed by globalization (Roca 2001: 7). These coalescing
elements have made this region the setting for a number of more
recent massacres and a location from which many people have been
displaced, a fact Restrepo relates to issues of space:

> [V]iolence as an instrument of conflict obeys certain norms of the
> senses. Terror, through spectacle […], goes much deeper: to a total
> rupturing of the senses […]. We are watching […] a confusing story
> which really, above all else, is a problem of geographies, geopolitics,
> and the strategic partitioning of territories, of passages and corridors.
> The best lands are areas of conflict, and there too are found the
> greatest number of large landowners. Thus, displacement in order to
> occupy and displacement in order to usurp are the strategies of the
> anachronistic feudal lords and their private armies. (Restrepo 2001:
> 63)

Sculptor Doris Salcedo agrees with Restrepo in pointing to
space as an underlying source of violence: 'I don't believe that space
can be neutral. The history of wars, and perhaps history in general, is
but an endless struggle to conquer space. Space is not simply a setting,
it is what makes life possible. It is space that makes encounters
possible. It is the site of proximity, where everything crosses over'
(2000: 12). In fact, Salcedo also makes reference to the banana-
growing region in an untitled piece known as 'White Shirts' (1989-
90), in which long metal rods impale neat stacks of white shirts. The
work alludes to the 1988 massacres at La Negra and La Hondura
banana plantations, where male workers were dragged out of their
beds and shot in front of their families.

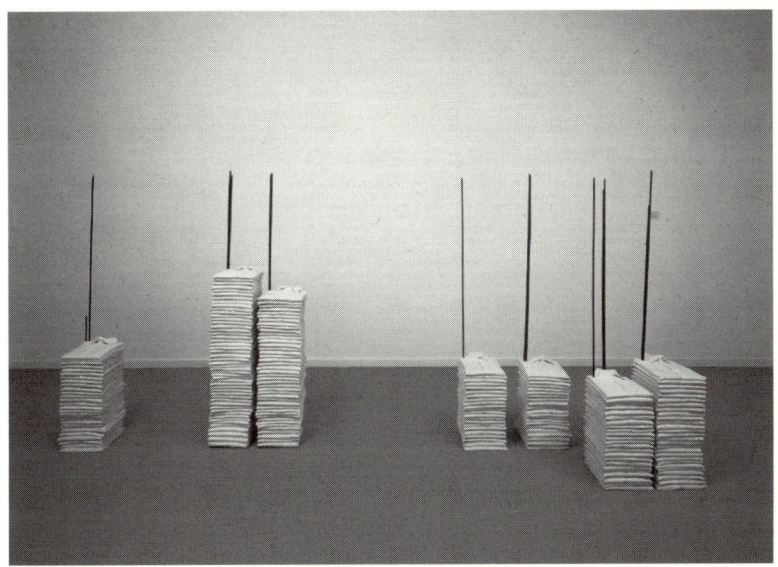

Doris Salcedo: Installation of Untitled Sculptures: 'The Spine', De Appel Foundation, Amsterdam, January-March 1994. Photo courtesy of Alexander & Bonin, New York.

While this work refers tangentially to forced displacement, in *La Casa Viuda* ('the widowed house') (1993-95), Salcedo refers to it more directly by 'implicitly represent[ing] the house as the place of refuge, shelter, a sanctuary now exposed, uncovered, and violated' (Merewether 1998: 20). The destruction of the dwelling place, of 'home', brings to mind the words of Elaine Scarry in *The Body in Pain*: 'The unmaking of civilisation inevitably requires a return to and mutilation of the domestic, the ground of all making' (Scarry 1985: 45). The pieces in *La Casa Viuda*, placed in in-between or decentred spaces in museums and galleries, are a conjunction of materials, furniture, clothing, bones, and cutlery forced or compressed into the surface of the furniture and often perceived only after a careful look:

'Bearing traces of violence, the objects are mute witnesses and testimony to the past. The house that had been a shelter, that concealed and protected, is violently altered into the tomb and burial site of its inhabitants' (Merewether 1998: 21). As Salcedo asserted, this piece 'makes use of [the notion of] non-place, that is a place of passage, where it is impossible to live' (Gutiérrez 1996: 49).

Doris Salcedo, 'La Casa Viuda', 1992-4. Photo courtesy of Alexander & Bonin, New York.

While *La Casa Viuda* evokes parts of a house which literally cling to the persons who have disappeared from its protection, in *Unland* (1995-98) an inanimate object duplicates the organic growth processes of the deceased as a way of keeping their presence alive (Cameron 1998, 14). *Unland* is composed of three pieces (*The Orphan's Tunic*, *Audible in the Mouth* and *Irreversible Witness*) meant to be seen together and each referring to a specific incident of violence, although the information is not provided to the audience. 'I do not illustrate testimonies', stated the artist in an interview (Merewether 1999: 82). In the case of *The Orphan's Tunic* (1996-97), it is known that the piece was inspired by the artist's encounter with a six-year old girl, witness to her mother's murder, who could not remember anything before this event but who refused to change the dress she wore daily because it had been sewn by her mother. The work consists of two wooden tables clashing into each other. One of them bears a white shroud of raw silk with an intermediate zone which the viewer only gradually recognizes is covered with human hair. Thousands of minuscule holes, as follicles, allow the table to breathe, to acquire the appearance of a living being (Peña 2003: 18).

Doris Salcedo, 'Unland: The Orpahan's Tunic', 1997. Photo: David Heald.
Courtesy of Alexander and Bonin, New York.

Unland, a poetic neologism inspired by the work of Paul
Celan, suggests that its subject matter is no longer that of an
abandoned site, but rather focuses on the place of homelessness,
for there is no place in officialdom for this repressed archive,
nor adequate social rituals to address the depth of collective
tragedy. As Salcedo comments:

> To place the invisible experience of marginal people in space is to find
> a place for them in our mind. I think of space in terms of place, a place
> to eat or a place to write, a place to develop life. So there's no way of
> isolating living experience from spatial experience: it's exactly the
> same thing. Certain types of contemporary work underscore this
> aspect of sculpture as a topography of life. (2000: 17)

Hence, Salcedo's work expresses an 'ethical commitment to combat
the anaesthesia present in dominant representations of violence in
Colombia' (Merewether 1998: 23), by salvaging fragments that, as the
artist asserts, are 'individual cases that are of little interest to
historians and to the Colombian justice system' (Salcedo 2003: 29).[5]

While Salcedo's work focuses on the recognition of individual
victims of violence, the work of Oscar Muñoz emphasises rather the
transitory and vulnerable condition of individual and collective
identity, as experienced under conditions of violence. His process-
intensive works can be considered to some extent as performances, as
they require the intervention of the viewer in order to be completed.
One such work is *Aliento* ('breath') (1996-97), which features a dozen
polished metal disks, each with a photo-screened image of a victim of
violence. With the use of a greasy medium (grease being a material
evocative of the Holocaust), the images are made imperceptible, while
the metal disk acts as a mirror reflecting the viewer's face. When the
viewer breathes on them, the faces of the victims briefly come into
view, only to quickly fade away. This work entails a double
movement between historical recovery and its simultaneous vanishing,
as the expired breath gives only an ephemeral glimpse of the subject
matter, leaving the viewers with only their own reflection, implicated
both in bringing these images to light and allowing them to be
forgotten.[6] Taken a step further, *Aliento* can be related to
disappearance and torture, which are also connected to displacement,
as individuals and communities flee from these threats.

The topic of fragility and the ephemeral explored in *Aliento* is
also present in the *Narcisos* series ('narcissuses') featuring Muñoz's
face posing in a way reminiscent of obituary photographs.

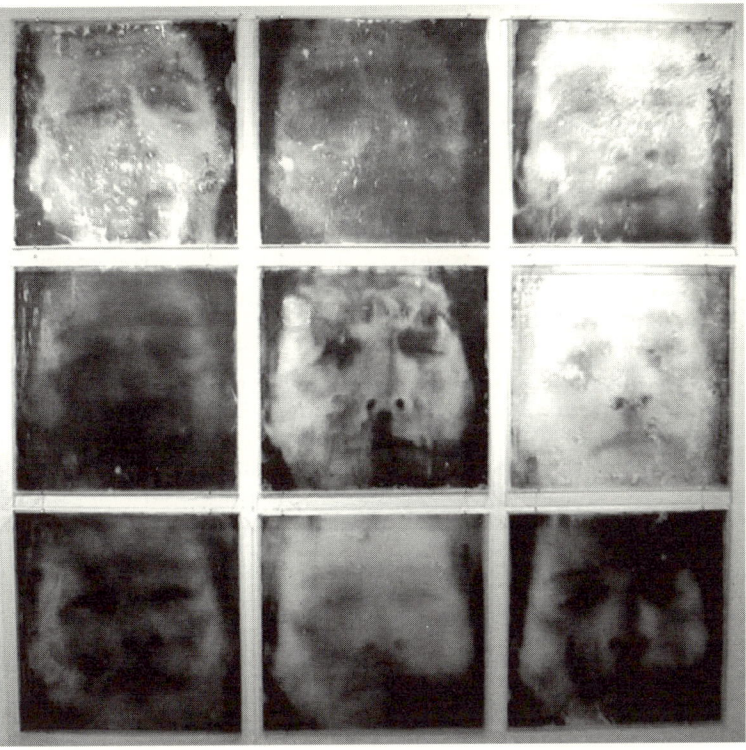

Oscar Muñoz, 'Narcisos'. Courtesy of Sicardi Gallery and the artist.

The image is obtained by sifting charcoal powder through a photo-silkscreen on to a tray of water. The precarious and unstable image floats on the water's surface and as the days pass, the water evaporates and viewers have a sense of interacting with the works, becoming active in the conformation of the image. On other occasions, the artist has floated pages from newspapers on the water, further complicating the process of translating his photographic image to the surface of the water. Despite the variations introduced by the artist, the series has in common that it not only reacts to the involvement of the viewer, but actually demands it for the work to be completed, which in turn can be seen as a comment on passivity and compliance in the face of acts of violence.

The notion of the dissolution of identity, fuelled by the loss of place (both spatially and socially) and the fearful desire for anonymity, is one of the traumas that displaced persons frequently suffer. This is symbolised in another aspect of the series, also called

Narcisos. Here, a self-portrait printed with charcoal powder, and floating on the surface of moving water, is contained in a draining sink. The image undergoes a slow deformation and depends upon a video camera to record the process of destruction of the image. The video *Narciso* (2001) registers the process from the beginning, from the moment the powder enters into contact with the surface of the water and creates the image, passing through its gradual deformation and ending in its imminent destruction by the emptying of the sink.

The dissolution of the self is, in the end, a mirror image of the dissolution of the community as a whole, which is the ultimate effect of wars on society, such as the one Colombia experiences

> [under repressive violence] the idea of community or collectivity [...] is continually threatened and always at stake. This history reveals a pervasive vested interest in removing from consciousness the death of people in order to effect the displacement of popular memory as an active element of hope and key impulse of collectivity. Terror is anonymous. Mutilation and disappearance are strategies by which identification is erased. Human identity and death are desacralized [...]. In this context, there can be no martyrs, no historical memory, no family shrines; nothing but anonymity. (Merewether 1996: 114)

Although the situation in Colombia continues to be extremely delicate, a positive feature is the active cultural and intellectual effort involved in grasping the issue from different perspectives, in contradiction to the idea that Colombia is victim to a self-destructive craze, destined to burn indefinitely in what international analysts consider a 'low intensity conflict'. In this sense, displacement is not the consequence of a senseless fratricidal war, but rather a strategy of war aimed at the control of territories and the exploitation of natural resources by both local and international interests.

The visual arts, working through their very powerlessness,[7] are part of this effort, opening spaces for reflection: by aesthetically undertaking transdisciplinary investigations into the sources of the ongoing violence, as in the case of Restrepo; or by establishing connections between the themes of identity and violence and involving the public in dialogue, as Muñoz does; and even functioning as witness to tragedies and victims which would otherwise be forgotten or exploited by the media (itself another way of forgetting), as does Salcedo.

Notes

[1] In *Real Pictures*, an installation about the massacres in Rwanda, Chilean artist Alfredo Jaar enclosed 550 photographs in individual black archival photographic boxes. None of the images were visible, but there was a text on the top of each box describing the photograph it contained. The work, described by the artist as a 'graveyard of images', also featured a phrase from Catalan writer Vincenç Altaió: 'Images have an advanced religion: they bury history' (Gallo online).

[2] Hincapié's work has shifted since the 1990s from the notion of the quotidian, evident in pieces such as *Punto de fuga* ('vanishing point') (1989) and *Vitrina* ('showcase') (1989) to that of the holy, suggested by works such as *Caminar es sagrado* ('walking is holy') (1994-1995) (Pini 2000).

[3] Disappearance is a strategy that adds symbolic violence, based on making the body invisible and the process of ignorance that accompanies it, to the physical violence of imprisonment, torture or death.

[4] For a recent history of violence in Urabá, see García (1996).

[5] Charlotte Delbo, in discussing the aesthetic rendering of traumatic memory, has suggested that what makes sense memory valuable is the fact it can resist historicisation by preserving in memory the affective experience itself (1995).

[6] A work comparable to that of Chilean artist Eugenio Dittborn, whose 'airmail paintings' present the faces and bodies of victims in an attempt to force the audience to bear witness to loss, and to confront the reality of political violence (Bennett 2002, p. 345).

[7] Which Salcedo explicitly acknowledges: 'I look for individuals as faces, as real presence, but in most cases unfortunately I encounter just the impossibility of finding the person because the person is gone and all that is left is a trace and all that is felt is his silence. All that remains is beyond my possibilities, beyond my reach. There is nothing or very little I can grasp of that life that is gone long ago. *This is what my work is about: Impotence, a sum of impotence, not being able to solve anything, or to fix a problem, not knowing, not seeing, not being able to grasp a presence, for me art is a lack of power*' (2003: 29, my emphasis). This suggests, as Jean-François Lyotard has argued, that art might function as a space of resistance to metahistories (1999: 73-74).

Bibliography

Bachelard, Gaston. 1994. *The Poetics of Space*. Boston: Beacon Press.

Bennett, Jill. 2002. 'Art, Affect, and the "Bad Death": Strategies for Communicating the Sense Memory of Loss' in *Signs: Journal of Women in Culture and Society* 28(1): 333-351.

Cameron, Dan. 1998 'Inconsolable' in *Doris Salcedo*. New Museum of Contemporary Art, Santa Fe: SITE.

Delbo, Charlotte. 1995. *Auschwitz and After*. New Haven: Yale University Press.

Gallo, R. 'The Limits of Representation' *TRANS* No 3/4. On line at: www.echonyc. com/~trans/Telesymposia3/Jaar/Telesymposia3eJaar.html (consulted 05.05.2004).

García, Clara Inez. 1996. *Urabá: región, actores y conflicto, 1960-1990*. Medellín: Universidad de Antioquia.

Gutiérrez, N. 2000. 'José Alejandro Restrepo *TransHistories*, Biblioteca Luis Angel Arango' in *ArtNexus* 43, March: Bogotá.

- - - . 1996. 'Conversación con Doris Salcedo' in *ArtNexus* 19, January-March: Bogotá: 48-50.

Herkenhoff, Paulo. 2001. 'El hambre polisémica de José Alejandro Restrepo' in *Transhistorias. Historia y mito en la obra de José Alejandro Restrepo*. Bogotá: Banco de la República.

Hincapié, Maria Teresa. 2000. 'una cosa en una cosa', in Fusco, Coco (ed.) *Corpus Delecti. Performance Art of the Americas*. New York and London: Routledge.

Lyotard, Jean-Francois. 1999. *The Postmodern Condition: A Report on Knowledge*. Minneapolis: University of Minnesota Press.

Merewether, Charles. 1998. 'To Bear Witness' in *Doris Salcedo*. New Museum of Contemporary Art, Santa Fe: SITE.

- - - . 1996. 'Zones of Marked Instability: Women and the Space of Emergence' in Welchman, John (ed.) *Rethinking Borders*. Minneapolis: University of Minnesota Press.

Osorio, F. E. 2000. 'Territorios, identidades y acción colectiva. Pistas en la comprensión del desplazamiento' in *Desplazamiento forzado interno en Colombia: conflicto, paz y desarrollo*. ACNUR: CODHES.

Peña, M.E. 2003. 'Object and Body Recalling Memory', unpublished paper.

Pini, Ivonne. 2002. 'María Teresa Hincapié Between the Quotidian and the Holy' in *ArtNexus* 45, September: Bogotá.

Restrepo, Jose Alessandro. 2001. 'Psicogeografías y transhistorias' in *TransHistorias. Historia y mito en la obra de José Alejandro Restrepo*. Bogotá: Banco de la República.

Roca, J. (ed.). 2001. *TransHistorias. Historia y mito en la obra de José Alejandro Restrepo*. Bogotá: Banco de la República.

Salcedo, Doris. 2003. 'Traces of Memory. Art and Remembrance in Colombia' in *Harvard Review of Latin America* 2 (3): 28-30.

Scarry, Elaine. 1985. *The Body in Pain. The Making and the Unmaking of the World*. Oxford and New York: Oxford University Press.

Taussig, Michael. 1992. 'Terror as Usual: Walter Benjamin's Theory of History as a State of Siege' in *The Nervous System*. London and New York: Routledge.

30

Fading into Metaphor: Globalization and the Disappearance of Exile

Rudolphus Teeuwen

Rudolphus Teeuwen (born 1955) studied Dutch and Comparative Literature at the University of Utrecht in his native Netherlands. After studies in the Comparative Literature Department at the University of Pennsylvania, he moved, in 1995, to Taiwan to become Associate Professor of English at National Sun Yat-sen University in Kaohsiung. He writes, among other things, on eighteenth-century literature, philosophy, and aesthetics. His own experiences of foreignness and faded nationality have also come to inform his thought and writing. This aspect of his work began in 1994 with the publication of an article on Edward Gibbon and (as Gibbon himself called it) his 'quality of foreignness'. In the book Teeuwen edited in 2001, *Crossings: Travel, Art, Literature, Politics*, he first expressed his unhappiness with postmodern and postcolonial treatments of exile, a theme he further develops in the article published here.

In this paper, he comments on how, in the age of globalization, public attention has been drawn to local differences: the differences between war zones and havens of peace; between pockets of poverty and enclaves of wealth; between regimes of repression and regions of tolerance. These differences generate movements of peoples across borders on a scale never seen before. So-called asylum-seekers, refugees, and illegal aliens are treated as crowds to be processed for admission, to be controlled, to be discouraged from settling, and to be ready for return at the slightest sign of improvement in the conditions (economic, political, racial etc) that they fled. They are not generally referred to as 'exiles', a term with a long history, which, in the mid-twentieth century, came to be used as a mark of prestige when applied to Europeans fleeing Nazism and the Communist regimes of Eastern Europe. Nevertheless, the term 'exile' has not entirely disappeared, being in constant use, according to Teeuwen, in the work of postcolonial scholars such as Edward Said and Homi Bhabha, who use it of intellectuals like themselves, who have made careers for themselves away from their personal (or family) homeland by reflecting on questions of 'home' and 'away'. He asks to what extent this is a nostalgic and self-serving use of the notion of exile, and whether 'exile' has become a metaphorical name for those who identify with a plight – that of the refugee and the asylum-seeker – they do not really share.

"The exile is a universal figure", writes George Lamming in his *The Pleasures of Exile*. He goes on to explain that the exile is someone who lives, politically, "without the right kind of information to make argument effective."

> We are made to feel a sense of exile by our inadequacy and our irrelevance of function in a society whose past we can't alter, and whose future is always beyond us. Idleness can easily guide us into accepting this as a condition. (Lamming 1960: 24)

Lamming writes this in 1960, as a "man of colonial orientation" (Lamming 1960: 24), and as a thirty-two year old writer. He had already been in self-imposed exile in England for ten years, in order to become that writer, and felt "that I have had it (as a writer) where the British Caribbean is concerned. I have lost my place, or my place has deserted me" (1960: 50).

It doesn't take much reading in *The Pleasures of Exile* to understand that Lamming, by declaring that "the exile is a universal figure" (1960: 24), is not claiming that everyone is an exile. Exiles, rather, are universal because they lack specificity and are inept in dealing within the precise contexts of their lives, whether Barbados or England. Or, to put it more positively (George Lamming's is not a gloomy personality): "The pleasure and paradox of my own exile is that I belong wherever I am" (1960: 50). Thus, the exile stands apart from the multitude of people who have more precise ways of attributing their happiness and unhappiness to a "geography of circumstances" (1960: 50). The pleasure of exile that Lamming describes is that of transcending both one's original and assumed environments.

Times have changed since the days of colonialism from which Lamming speaks. Postcolonialism and postmodernism followed and are now shading into the age of globalization, and the idea that would have appeared absurd to Lamming—that everyone is an exile—has gained currency. I regret this development and would prefer to resist it. I believe that the word and concept of 'exile' have undergone an unhelpful metaphorical extension, and that postcolonial critics such as Edward Said and Homi Bhabha have forged that extension.

To see what exile was like before its current metaphysical extension, and also before Lamming's mid-twentieth-century philosophical resignation, a look at the opening pages of Daniel Defoe's *Roxana* (1724) is instructive. Defoe's heroine doesn't actually use the word 'exile', but that very new word of the late seventeenth century designed to denote a specific kind of exile: 'refugee'. Roxana, when still a girl, came over with her parents to England from France. She is at pains, in the early pages of her story, to distinguish her family's coming over from that of other refugees, "[m]y Father and Mother being People of better Fashion, than ordinarily the People call'd REFUGEES at that Time were" (Defoe 1996: 5). Those refugees were the French Protestants or 'Huguenots' who fled their country after 1685 when, with the Revocation of the Edict of Nantes, France no longer tolerated Protestants on its soil. What Roxana vividly remembers from these early scenes of her English life, a life as a foreigner still, is how her father complained of being pestered for help by poorer and later arrivals:

> a great-many of those, who, *for any Religion they had*, might e'en have stay'd where they were, but who flock'd over hither in Droves, for what they call in *English*, a Livelihood [. . .]. My Father, *I say, told me*, That he was more pester'd with the Clamours of these People, than of those who were truly REFUGEES, and fled in Distress, *merely* [i.e., purely] *for Conscience.* (Defoe 1996: 5-6; italics in original)

Everything about Roxana's very short account of her early English years bears witness to her horror at being regarded as a refugee. Roxana's fear is that she will be permitted neither to transcend her French origins nor to assume her English destination. So she hurries into Englishness in barely a page, learning to speak the new language without keeping "any Remains of the *French* language tagg'ed to my Way of Speaking, *as most Foreigners do*" (Defoe 1996: 6; italics in original). The term 'refugee', John Mullan reminds us in a note in his edition of *Roxana* (and the OED backs him up), "seems to have been coined in 1685 specifically to describe the French Huguenots who fled to England" (Defoe 1996: 341). The newly-coined word derives from the French language (a Frenchness probably still palpable in the word's English newness) and intends a group of Frenchmen in England: the Huguenots, as it were, came over with a bridle of their own linguistic making, a *cordon sanitaire*. This linguistic containment is reflected in the small capitals, rare in Defoe's novel, with which the word is set off from other words on his page. And because the novel's Preface encourages us to understand this novel as Roxana's own verbal account of her life only slightly edited by a 'Relator,' the contempt for the French refugees is Roxana's own. She, taking her cue from her father, applies the word "refugee" to others to prove her own Englishness, and it is the word's offensive newness (rather than its French familiarity) that she throws in the face of the economic opportunists and the virtuously poor among her countrymen.

To those of us who, voluntarily or not, live the phenomenon of globalization, Roxana's invidious distinctions and anxious glosses will seem quaint: they have a remembered familiarity buried in deep irrelevance. The familiarity lies in the terms, the irrelevance in their application. We still know of refugees, but they are no longer French Huguenots or any other single and homogenous group. Being French or being English has become much more a matter of accidental difference than the essential and permanent divide it was to Roxana. Globalization doesn't do away with the notion of essentiality, but it does with that of permanence. Essentiality becomes the temporary quality of the flash points, civil wars, economic imbalances, floods, and famines of the moment (captured on tape for an international audience), and the havoc they create in people's lives. The very idea of globalization as well as its manifestations in economics, politics, and culture are all very much related to the experience and conviction that existing categories and distinctions fail to organize the world of human activities and feelings in a useful, desirable, truthful, or sensible way. Distinctions become temporary, transitory, or vague, scaffolding put up to be removed when a service provided by them is no longer required.

The speed with which bureaucratic categories for displaced people now spring up and replace each other attests to the relative powerlessness of those categories in the age of globalization. But categorical decomposition also has an impact on accounts of exile that people can give of themselves. These accounts, in any age, are usually intensely personal autobiographies, but as the notion of exile loses definition, the possibility of achieving the authority of authenticity for one's story of exile also diminishes. There is no questioning the authenticity of Roxana's voice fighting the category of 'refugee' that is looming over her beginnings, even though it is the authenticity of clamouring for an assumed identity. As Roxana begins the story of her life she knows that her story will be one of adultery, prostitution, child murder, avarice, vanity, deception, and endless cycles of guilt and imperfect penitence that will take her for long, un-English stretches to France and Holland. She therefore begins her account with a presentation of her credentials as a true Englishwoman so that her confessions and the lessons that they contain cannot be dismissed as those of a mere foreign floozy.

Roxana clearly does protest too much. It is different with Lamming, although there is no questioning his authenticity as a voice of exile either. Whereas Roxana realizes that any categorical equivocalness in her national identity would weaken the relevance of her case, George Lamming embraces that equivocalness. With Barbados still stuck in the posture of colonial backwater and England still in that of benevolent civilizer, Lamming has freed himself from belonging in either camp and wryly pays the exile's price of double irrelevance. But Lamming is too prickly-sensitive an author to be taken at his word. His professed irrelevance is not truly a form of disengagement but rather of heightened awareness of his incomplete submersion in the cultures of either his origin or his destination. Not fully sheltered by the forms of either culture, Lamming exposes Barbados and England to each other, and it is up to his readers to see how this mutual aloofness in Lamming gives form to cultural insights. Roxana's authenticity was that of a forceful desire to merge with her context of destination and to erase that of origin. Lamming's authenticity is that of insisting on Barbados when in England, and (in a more veiled manner: there is the matter of colonialism to redress) to insist on England when still in Barbados. This stance allows him to unravel some of the workings of racism by telling stories of working at the BBC Colonial Service, of black poets' poetry readings to over-appreciative English audiences, or by explaining black 'laziness' in the eyes of white governors. Most importantly, it allows him to see Prospero's island as Caliban's, and to tell of this insight to Prospero's face.

I call Roxana and Lamming 'authentic' exiles because they understand their lives as in active oscillation between two determinate places. But I realize that the concept of authenticity, for all its suggested stability, is an unstable one, especially when used in conjunction with the notion of dispersal that is so definitive of exile. The very word 'authenticity' assumed an aura of suspect fashionableness at its very heyday, in the existentialism of the 1950s and 1960s. Theodor Adorno castigates the authenticity craze that swept intellectual Germany in the wake of Heidegger's *Being and Time* in his caustic 1964 book *The Jargon of Authenticity*. The concept of 'authenticity,' Adorno feels, smuggles into the severity of philosophy all sorts of "slack and self-surfeited thought" (Adorno 2003: 49) that tells that nothingness is Being, and that "suffering, evil and death are to be accepted, not to be changed" (2003: 53). Heidegger, Adorno argues, is the ultimate philosopher of rootedness as a form of "*petit-bourgeois* kitsch" (2003: 45), and thus the one who turned the notion of authenticity into a jargon. Heidegger depicts the authentic state in contrast to the dispersed one and celebrates as authentic "the unending mumble of the liturgy of inwardness" (2003: 57). But the danger of an inwardness that doesn't want to know of dispersion is the "thinking oneself superior which marks people who elect themselves: the claim of people who consider themselves blessed simply by virtue of being what they are" (2003: 61). In Heidegger, authenticity is a "mythically imposed fate" of full self-possession, and not the answer to "the relatively innocent question about what is authentic in something" (Adorno 2003: 104).

Adorno's plea to regard authenticity as the simple but precise question of "what is authentic in something" (2003: 104) has largely fallen on deaf ears. In postmodernism and postcolonialism, precision is a form of *petit-bourgeois* ungenerosity, and in the age of globalization it hampers the expansion of whatever fate it is that globalization has in store for us all. Globalization entails the giving up of some of the linguistic, historical, and moral precision that is the triumph of earlier and more place-bound thinking and acting. Historical awareness is probably the biggest impediment for the various manifestations of globalization, and the replacement of the historical by temporal globalization's greatest project. One sees this attempted replacement of history already in much postcolonialist thought, and postcolonialism, no matter how justly critical of many of the manifestation of globalization, certainly is one of its earliest outposts.

Homi K. Bhabha, in 'DissemiNation' (1990), begins the celebration of temporal, metaphorical, transcendent existence as opposed to historical and autochthonous being. Bhabha contemplates the uncomfortable condition of living in between countries, allegiances, and senses of home, and he begins his essay beautifully. The first paragraph is a powerful evocation of the fate of the scattered people who gather at the edge of cultures not their own and are 'gathered' in the foreign nation's statistics banks. He goes on to explain:

> Gatherings of exiles and emigrés and refugees, gathering on the edge of 'foreign' cultures; gathering at the frontiers; gatherings in the ghettos or cafés of city centres; gathering in the half-life, half-light of foreign tongues, or in the uncanny fluency of another's language; gathering the signs of approval and acceptance, degrees, discourses, disciplines; [. . .]. Also the gathering of [. . .] incriminatory statistics, educational performance, legal statuses [. . .]. (Bhabha 1990: 291)

To these gathering individuals, 'nation' becomes a metaphorical concept as something they have carried with them across the distances "that span the imagined community of the nation-people" (Bhabha 1990: 291). Bhabha's use of the notion of metaphor determines his emphasis on culture and nationhood as something that is brought along rather than left behind. The scattering of people, to him, is less a destruction of a culture abandoned (perhaps through force) than the constitution of a culture that one enters by bringing along cultural fragments to a new accumulation of cultural fragments. Culture becomes a temporal construction of diverse disjunctive fragments and thus an agent against the pretensions of solid naturalness and immanence, backed up by a centuries-long history that dictates inclusions and exclusions. As such an agent against history, culture becomes 'performative,' a counter-creation of a certain weightlessness and impermanence that scattered people make through the behaviour and actions of their gathering. There is a sense of triumph in this achievement, a denial of the exile's irrelevance that Roxana fought through narrative sleight of hand and that Lamming embraced.

But there is also a bit of wilful depth in this play with the etymological roots of the words 'metaphor' and, elsewhere, 'translation' as applied to rootless people protesting by virtue of their metaphorical mode of being the nation state's pretensions of literal truth. Bhabha, in a voice that, to my ear, exchanges authenticity for the solemn, self-dramatizing jargon of authenticity, claims personal experience with this metaphorical way of living ("I have lived that moment of the scattering of the people that in other times and in other places [. . .] becomes a time of gathering" [Bhabha 1990: 291]), but his personal testimony begs the question of how he imagines a metaphorical experience to register on the sensorium. One wonders if Bhabha's notion of metaphorical being isn't itself a metaphor for the sort of truce that occurs when gathering cultures, all intending to carry on, are forced to settle for what can be cobbled together of elements that are carried over.

Bhabha's choice of the perspective of the communities that result from the scattering and gathering over of the communities that were left and entered is a legitimate one. It is also true that there is no thought imaginable without recourse to metaphor. Metaphor is endemic to thought because "[a] metaphor is a compromise struck between the old and the new, between the overwhelming authority of language and the irrepressible anarchy of wit" (Weiskel 1976: 4). As such a compromise, metaphor enables us "to grasp experience in terms sanctioned by the past" (Weiskel 1976: 4). Thomas Weiskel writes here of the sublime, and adds: "We cannot conceive of a literal sublime" (1976: 4). We also cannot conceive of literal exiles, of exiles who comprehend their condition without reference to earlier beings who lived a life of exile. But only someone who thinks of travel, of being scattered and gathered, as a metaphorical transaction of cultural fragments could imagine the question of the capacity in which one set out on one's travel to be unimportant. It matters to the scattered whether they are exiles, or refugees, or migrants, or expatriates, or émigrés: these are different states of being, not forms of a single metaphor. Bhabha's celebrated erasure of prior presence of the nation-people comes at the price of a self-erasure: one cannot destroy the claims of singular culture by insisting on one's own singularity. Bhabha takes the notion of metaphor too literally by omitting its inherent appeal to a sanctioning past. Thus, travellers who are literally metaphorical by carrying all they amount to with them fade into a general metaphor and are robbed of the distress, courage, triumph, and despair of a personal history.

Bhabha indicts national history as a confining-excluding concept that must be counteracted by the temporal gathering of metaphorical, translated beings on a nation's edges. In this process, the very history of terms such as exile and refugee is threatened with forgetfulness. But some who reflect on their lives as shaped by globalization are more linguistically responsible. Pico Iyer, for instance, in an attempt at defining people like himself, comes up with terms like "off-shore beings" (Iyer 2001: 22) and "global souls", persons who have "grown up in many cultures all at once" and who live "in the cracks between them" (2001: 18). He writes:

> [a] person like myself can't really call himself an exile (who traditionally looked back to a home now lost), or an expatriate (who's generally posted abroad for a living); I'm not really a nomad (whose patterns are guided by seasons and traditions); and I've never been subject to the refugee's violent disruptions: the Global Soul is best categorized by the fact of falling between all categories [. . .]. (Iyer 2001: 23)

We see Iyer here rejecting metaphors for himself that are readily at hand. Instead, he gropes for an accurate metaphor. In those of "global soul" as well as "off-shore beings" there is a spiritual capitalism at work, with reverberations of transcendence ("soul," "beings") joined with words that conjure cable networks, business ventures, and extra-territorial waters. The struggle with (self-) definitions of people caught up, willingly or not, in the swirls of globalization is, to me, globalization's rare but most worthwhile enterprise. It is here, in the search for a particular, precise metaphor, that the images of global modernity are forged, and this enterprise of giving or withholding names involves our taste and temperament, our politics and civilization, our contentment or our discontent with the world and our figure in it. There is much at stake in the contestation of the words that whirl around so frequently in discussions of postcolonialism and globalization: immigrant, refugee, migrant, expatriate, asylum seeker, exile. Naming truly shapes reality here: all these words refer to having or lacking a legal status, and legality is the way language enforces reality. This brings up—as a matter of taste, or purpose, or tact, or ethical niceness—the question of how reluctant one should be in applying these words in an extended or metaphorical way to oneself.

The term 'exile' is probably the one that has suffered most in this respect from the historical, linguistic, and moral latitudinarianism of postcolonialism, and it is the one most in need of new attention. Once the designation of a horrible fate, 'exile' today is a term so eagerly embraced that a deep forgetting of what it means to be an exile must be at the root of it.

In his "The Romance of Exile," Ian Buruma, irritated by the appropriation of exile as a fashionable image, writes:

> Now it is exile [rather than consumption, i.e., tuberculosis] that evokes the sensitive intellectual, the critical spirit operating alone on the margins of society, a traveller, rootless and yet at home in every metropolis, a tireless wanderer from academic conference to academic conference, a thinker in several languages, an eloquent advocate for ethnic and sexual minorities—in short, a romantic outsider living on the edge of the bourgeois world. (Buruma 2001: 33)

"Margins," "rootless," "metropolis": Buruma conjures the lofty sadness of exile, but then pierces the nobility and grinds his axe: the mention of academic conferences and the championing of ethnic and sexual minorities bring the exile into an interested modernity of posturing and posing. Buruma wants to register his protest against the eagerness with which quite a few intellectuals – postcolonial intellectuals who are perfectly at home in their adopted North America or Western Europe – glory in seeing themselves as exiles. Without ever having had to experience the sadness of banishment, they aren't shy to take the authority that comes with it. Buruma is thinking in particular of the five contributors to a lecture series at the New York Public Library whose papers are collected in the book *Letters of Transit: Reflections on Exile, Identity, Language and Loss.* The five are "Edward Said [who] is introduced as a Palestinian in exile, Eva

Hoffman as Pole in exile, Bharati Mukherjee as Bengali in exile, Charles Simic as Yugoslav in exile, and Andre Aciman, the editor of the book, as an exile from Alexandria" (Buruma 2001: 33).

Buruma taunts those who are merely metaphorical exiles with their simulation of 'real' exile. This simulation is deeply nostalgic for an authentic state of being, one that requires courage and the overcoming of hardships. Buruma distanced himself from the simulation, but he shares the nostalgia. It is this nostalgia that motivates his criticism of metaphorical exiles as cheapeners of that valued figure of the exile. And there is some scope indeed for considering these scholars as abusers of category: they can quite accurately be regarded as émigrés, or residers abroad or, for that matter, as more or less ordinary immigrant Americans or Canadians. As Buruma points out, "Of the five witnesses to exile, only two were forced to leave their country of origin: Aciman, whose family was kicked out of Egypt, and Simic, whose parents could not live under communism" (2001: 33). These two, presumably, can legitimately claim their status as exiles (or, actually, *dependents* of exiles), but the other three live in a more metaphorical and literary state of exile. And whereas actual exile is a prohibition of travelling back rather than an allowance to travel, metaphorical exile brings no travel restrictions at all.

Buruma's nostalgia for absolute authenticity is a form of what Adorno dismissed as the "jargon of authenticity". It affords him the advantage of legislating exile and leads him into the unfairness of absolute rhetorical power. To be exiled has never conferred a precise and literally circumscribed residency or legal status on anyone, but taken such a status away from one. It is this very negativity that makes exile such a hard fate to countenance for human beings, and that sets them the task of self-definition. In the essential subjectivity of self-definition, the term 'exile' becomes available for metaphorical, connotative, and literary uses. New states of actually being of questionable residency status in our present age – new forms of negative being – are those of the *sans papiers*: asylum seekers, illegal aliens, refugees, and migrants.[1]

The shift from 'exile' to 'refugee' to 'migrant' represents a shift in perspective away from individual distress and escape toward international crowd control and the movement of peoples; from being pushed out to being processed for admittance; from the importance of spies and informers to that of customs and immigration officials. The exile's envelopment in the jargon of bureaucratic classification is an assault on his or her authenticity. Exile too has finally entered the age of mechanical reproduction, to borrow Walter Benjamin's phrase, and with this, exile has lost its aura. The loss of individuality and authenticity marks the exile for consumption and disappearance. The refugee or asylum seeker now has to contest his status rather than quietly embrace an exile's homeless peace upon stepping into a host country. Interviews with lawyers and counsellors precede interviews with immigration officials, and refugees are wise to exaggerate their plight so as to create an impression of authenticity. Part of the current facelessness of exile is that the problem of identity, as it figures in the refugee debate, now centres on the identity of receiving nations, that is to be kept intact, rather than that of displaced persons. Modern legislation with respect to refugees does not even use or recognize the term 'exile,' for instance for individual intellectuals or academics fleeing political persecution, but lumps them together with all other asylum seekers. The United Nations Convention on Refugees, first drafted in 1951, speaks of refugees and of refugees only, but intends the term for the individual victims of Communism and "[u]ntil the end of the 1980s, refugees continued to be propaganda tools in the proxy Cold Wars across the globe" (O'Toole 2001: 12). 'Refugee' is a legal status, conferring the right of protection, but this status is under pressure as the term 'refugee' is threatened by dissolution into the term 'migrant,' a term without recognized legal status. As O'Toole shows, since the 1980s the term 'refugee' has slipped away from designating individually persecuted individuals, partly because the term 'persecution' itself has experienced slippage, and come to include a suffering of hardships that are not directly life-threatening, such as economic depression or social environments intolerant of, for instance, non-heterosexual orientations. The word 'refugee,' increasingly pressed into the service of designating a logistical, economic, legal, moral, and identity problem of receiving nations, starts to refuse to do this hatchet job. 'Migrant' (a word that prays that those who come will go again) is, for now, the current denotative term in the bureaucracy of immigration policies, although the two terms haven't yet clearly divided the field of distress between them. Erika Feller, director of UNHCR's International Protection Department, worries about the waning powers of the word 'refugee.' Pam O'Toole quotes her as saying, "'[w]hat is required from our perspective is the disentangling of asylum from the migration debate, the decriminalization of asylum seekers who are increasingly seen as backdoor migrants'" (2001: 13).

With exile largely abolished as a legal and literal state of being, and with terms such as refugee and migrant newly established as categories of unmediated misery, the interesting question now is where the attraction of the term lies, and where the desire comes from to be counted among the metaphorical exiles. Why this desire to be metaphorically dispossessed on the part of those who possess so much cultural and, often, material capital?

One part of the answer is that in and of itself the status of exile confers cultural capital, precisely because of its pedigree in literature and revolution. Being an exile – calling oneself one – is entering (metaphorically) the tradition of Heine and Adorno, Marx and Joyce, all living away from a home that hadn't always expelled them. This is a tradition of knowing more, of seeing more acutely because one sees with foreign eyes, because one knows as a foreigner knows, in isolation.

Another part of the answer to the attractiveness of exile is that the painful negativity that the word 'exile' connotes truly corresponds to an experience, a psychological state into which many nowadays can enter. The word 'exile' answers the desire for a label that fits a state of being. To describe this state, this experience, I'd like to enlist the help of Susan Stewart and apply, more or less, the way she uses the terms 'authenticity' and 'transcendence' throughout her book *On Longing* to my problem of defining the exile's experience. The two terms are opposites for Stewart, rather as 'authenticity' and 'dispersal' are for Heidegger but without the mutual exclusiveness of Heidegger's terms, and also without the 'Blubo' (the Nazi *'Blut und Boden'*) overtones that Adorno detected in them. The exilic experience, then, is partially one of a lack of authenticity, of living outside of one's original context and feeling nostalgic for a return to an (imaginary) situation of living in full and immediate experience of a personally known world. But the experience of exile is for another reason the opposite of this. The experience is, then, the exhilarating one of transcendence, of knowing the world many times over through the mediated experiences of others, of knowing the world as a structure of patterns and repetitions rather than as a unique and singular event. For transcendence one needs to turn to outsiders and their experiences. What is specific to exiles is that they repeat the world in themselves, and become their own outsiders by living their lives more than once, in more than one situation. In the trade-off between the felt lack of authenticity and the pleasure of transcendence, prospers and festers that peculiar mixture of sadness, self-dramatization, cultural insight, and condescension that marks the exile.

In 'Intellectual Exile: Expatriates and Marginals,' the third of his 1993 Reith Lectures (presented for BBC radio, broadcast worldwide, and collected as *Representations of the Intellectual*), Said is aware of the pleasure to be found in the state of exile, as long as the exile is metaphorical: "the intellectual as exile tends to be happy with the idea of unhappiness, so that dissatisfaction bordering on dyspepsia [. . .] can become not only a style of thought, but also a new, if temporary, habitation" (1994: 39). Said goes on to reflect on the intellectual career of one of his main heroes, Theodor Adorno, a true refugee from Nazi Germany. Adorno inspires metaphorical exile Said with the knowledge that, even in metaphor, the exile is not condemned to spineless accommodation. The metaphorical exile is held to the task of carrying over Adorno's severity: that of not giving in, of not becoming comfortable in a new life, but of remaining marginal and alienated to the environment one finds oneself in. The "rewards and, yes, even privileges" (Said 1994: 44) of such exile are advantages of perspective: of seeing with the eyes of both insider and outsider.

But Said ends his lecture in spinelessness, even though, in mitigation, he must be assumed to do so out of politeness to his audience. The end of the lecture reveals that Said considers an "intellectual exile" a sort of metaphorical exile stretched beyond even the need of physical travel. "Even if one is not an actual immigrant or expatriate," Said tells his audience, "it is still possible to think as one, to imagine and investigate in spite of barriers, and always to move away from the centralizing authorities toward the margins, where you see things that are usually lost on minds that have never travelled beyond the conventional and the comfortable" (1994: 46-47). Mental travelling can, indeed, be a movement of exile, as evidenced in situations such as that of the former Soviet Union where mental self-exile was a means for many intellectuals of moving away "from the centralizing authorities toward the margins." But to the extent that Said's listeners and readers are inhabitants of relatively free and democratic countries all over the globe, his sanctioning them to stay quietly at home while nonetheless enjoying all the privileges of an exile's distressed kind of travelling is nothing but a polite extension of a culturally enviable marker to whoever wants to don it. Said too, no matter how passionately he identifies with Adorno, speaks in the jargon of authenticity. As any metaphor, 'exile' too strikes a compromise between the past and the present, a present that is widely felt as a lack or a loss of authenticity such as an exile experiences this. The term 'exile' dignifies that modern experience by association with a less modern form of it, in which the distress is not an existential human condition, but the consequence of an exceptional turn of fate: to be proscribed residence in one's place of birth. In the metaphorical exile, longing – the desire for what is irretrievably lost – is itself metaphorical: it is the longing of one suffering an existential fate for an exceptional fate. So what Said confers on his listeners and readers is an unearned distinction. The proportional dissymmetry between the existential and the exceptional fate has here given rise to rhetorical abuse.

But why insist on actual travel for the metaphorical and (even more metaphorical) intellectual exile? The travel that matters here is, after all, the metaphorical travel of alienation. The task of the intellectual exile is to stick to this real, actual alienation, this unassimilated foreignness, and to use it as a form of transcendence against the centre. This is the heroism of exile that, in various forms, both Bhabha and Said celebrate. My answer would be that alienation and transcendence are not unique to the exile: an interaction between the two is, indeed, the defining condition of the age of globalization. But the alienation of a 'global soul,' such as Pico Iyer, walking around in Los Angeles International Airport or at the Atlanta Olympic Games leads to a radically different stance in life compared to that of the exile. Iyer sees the airport as "the spiritual centre of the double life: you get on [a plane] as one person and get off as another" (2001: 42), and elaborates this by bringing together alienation and transcendence in his account of spending a few weeks at LAX. Iyer is remarkable for his mood of abstracted, non-judgmental, unfazed, and kind comfortableness with the way the world presents itself to him. Always in transit, he is always at home. In some respects, Iyer's way of finding authenticity (rather than alienation) in transcendence and multiplicity is akin to George Lamming's. But to Iyer's 'global soul' there is, beyond the nuisances of jetlag, very little agonizing and not a beginning of bitterness in reflections upon one's life in transit. There is blandness in Iyer where there is fierceness in Lamming. The exile's pining for a return is a mood simply cancelled for Iyer, but cancelled in the manner in which a flight may be cancelled: without ultimate finality.

A final consideration of Said's rush into metaphorical exile may show it to be masking a form of actual exile, after all. Not in all aspects, and not under all conditions, is an actual exile heroic.

Whereas a metaphorical exile may choose his alliance with the heroic exile, the actual exile is often less than a hero. In his willingness to please his audience, Said perhaps betrays an exile's not-quite-being-at-home. An exile (one who actually lives away from home) is someone who is in the position of a guest, and one who must try not to overstay his welcome. Said pays no conscious attention to the exile as guest, but his polite balancing of the exile's freedom of not "having always to proceed with caution, afraid to overturn the applecart" (1994: 47) with the solicitous and cautious assurance that everyone can be an exile shows up an unacknowledged tension in an exile's mode of being. A good part of the misery of the exile is this prolonged sense of being around other people's lives, and depending on those others, without being one of them. The rebellious independence and *saeve indignatio* of the exile must be matched with the suave politeness of the cultured beggar.[2] If we view Said as an actual but unheroic exile (rather than a metaphorically heroic one), his authenticity as an exile is enhanced by a very touching weakness that he is at pains to screen from view.

If I am right in saying that to call oneself, metaphorically, an exile betrays a desire to be a hero at a discount, and opens one up to the risk of becoming a guest who is no longer welcome, then I think we should abandon that tired metaphor with all its pretensions of transcendence and risks of ridicule. Heroism, it seems to me, is globalization's first victim because globalization is this condition in which affiliations become vague. For the exile, globalization is the cruel denial of his suffering as it erases the divisions (ideological, geographical, polemical) that underwrite his exile. If exile indeed becomes a historical category of distress, we should respect the history, retire the term, and not dilute the suffering it denotes by metaphorical continuation. Those of us who are not exiles should learn to be unassuming, should learn to live without borrowed sorrow, and, most of all, should rejoice not to have been handed the fate that is made more bitter by anachronism.

Notes

[1] In my discussion here of Buruma, Edward Said and the notion of metaphorical exile, I borrow from earlier ideas and formulations I developed in 'The Ends of Travel – The Argument from Satire,' my introduction to *Crossings: Travel, Art, Literature, Politics* (2001).

[2] I develop this point of the exile's susceptibility to being seen as a sponger (for instance in Diderot's *Le neveu de Rameau*) a bit further in 'The Ends of Travel – The Argument from Satire' (2001).

Bibliography

Adorno, Theodor. 2003. *The Jargon of Authenticity*. (tr. Knut Tarnowski and Frederic Will). First published 1973. London: Routledge Classics. Trans. of *Jargon der Eigentlichkeit: Zur Deutschen Ideologie.* Frankfurt: Suhrkamp, 1964.

Bhahba, Homi K. 1990. 'DissemiNation: Time, Narrative, and the Margins of the Modern Nation' in Bhabha, Homi K. (ed.) *Nation and Narration.* London: Routledge: 291-322.

Buruma, Ian. 2001. 'The Romance of Exile' in *New Republic* (12 Feb. 2001) 33-38.

Defoe, Daniel. 1996. *Roxana or The Fortunate Mistress.* 1724. (ed. and introd. John Mullan) (World's Classics). Oxford: Oxford University Press.

Iyer, Pico. 2001. *The Global Soul: Jet Lag, Shopping Malls, and the Search for Home.* New York: Vintage Departures-Random.

Lamming, George. 1991. *The Pleasures of Exile*. 1960. (Foreword Sandra Pouchet Paquet). Ann Arbor: University of Michigan Press.

O'Toole, Pam. 2001. 'The Road to Refuge' in *BBC On Air* (June 2001) 11-14.

Said, Edward W. 1994. 'Intellectual Exile: Expatriates and Marginal' in Said, Edward *Representations of the Intellectual: The 1993 Reith Lectures.* London: Vintage-Random: 35-47.

Stewart, Susan. 1993. *On Longing: Narratives of the Miniature, the Gigantic, the Souvenir, the Collection.* 1984. Durham: Duke University Press.

Teeuwen, Rudolphus. 2001. 'Introduction: The Ends of Travel – The Argument from Satire' in Teeuwen, Rudolphus (ed.) *Crossings: Travel, Art, Literature, Politics.* Taipei: Bookman: 1-28.

Weiskel, Thomas. 1976. *The Romantic Sublime: Studies in the Structure and Psychology of Transcendence.* Baltimore: Johns Hopkins University Press.